THE NAVY WIFE

THE NAVY WIFE

THIRD REVISED EDITION

By

Anne Briscoe Pye

and

Nancy Shea

NEW YORK

HARPER & BROTHERS

PUBLISHERS

In loving memory of
LIEUTENANT WILLIAM SATTERLEE PYE, JUNIOR
a naval aviator who lost his life in
war maneuvers September 30, 1938, off
the coast of Coronado, California
and
LIEUTENANT COMMANDER JOHN BRISCOE PYE
lost in submarine *Swordfish* in
enemy action off Okinawa, 1945

CONTENTS

	INTRODUCTION	ix
	ACKNOWLEDGMENTS	xiii
I.	THE UNITED STATES NAVY TODAY	1
II.	TRADITIONS AND CUSTOMS OF THE NAVY	16
III.	THE COMMISSIONED PERSONNEL	31
IV.	THE NONCOMMISSIONED PERSONNEL	42
V.	NAVAL AVIATION	51
VI.	THE SUBMARINE SERVICE	63
VII.	THE MARINE CORPS	76
VIII.	THE COAST GUARD	86
IX.	ENGAGEMENTS AND WEDDINGS	96
X.	BUSINESS OF THE NAVAL HOUSEHOLD	122
XI.	CHANGE OF DUTY	145
XII.	ENTERTAINING IN THE NAVY	169
XIII.	NAVY JUNIORS	199
XIV.	NAVY LIFE IN WASHINGTON	214
XV.	ILLNESS, HOSPITALIZATION, AND EMERGENCIES	227
XVI.	BEYOND THE CONTINENTAL LIMITS	249
XVII.	SERVICE IN EUROPE AND SOUTH AMERICA	283
	GLOSSARY OF NAVAL TERMS	309
	BIBLIOGRAPHY	325
	INDEX	327

INTRODUCTION

THE United States Navy is a dynamic organization constantly adapting itself to changing world conditions. Political, economic, and social forces at home and abroad are influencing its character and modifying the life of its personnel.

World War II and the continuing threat to world peace that has followed have completely changed the relationship between the civilian and the military personnel of our nation from that which previously existed. Before World War II, our peacetime armed forces were small, and consequently the portion of our population that had any direct contact with military personnel was almost negligible. More than ten million men and women were inducted into the armed forces during World War II, and today the United States is maintaining military forces far in excess of those previously maintained during peacetime. Because of these facts, there is scarcely a family in the land that has not become closely connected with some men or women of our armed forces.

The recent past, present, and future size of our armed forces has created a situation that never before has existed in the United States: Every girl who marries during the next few years probably will wed a man who has served, is serving, or still must serve at least two years in some branch of the Service.

Since you selected this book to read, I presume that you are a Navy wife, or at least a potential one, and that you are seeking information on the kind of life you may expect to live as a Navy wife, and on the ways in which you can aid your husband to make a success of his naval career.

Perhaps one of the conditions of Navy life most difficult for civilians to understand is the relations between officers and enlisted men. In the interest of discipline and leadership, a definite line of demarcation between commissioned and noncommissioned personnel must be maintained. Certainly, fraternizing between officers and enlisted men is never encouraged, as the Navy demands certain formalities in officer-enlisted man relationship.

To some people this line of demarcation seems an outmoded carryover from the Middle Ages, when an officer was appointed from the aristocracy or landowning squirearchy to lead his "commoners" into battle. At that time there was a real distinction between the lord of the manor and the worker.

American democracy today is a far cry from this medieval military concept based upon heredity and economic power. Abrogating the privileges of landed aristocracy, we adhere to the basic principle of a free society which encourages every man to attain a place of distinction by means of hard work and merit alone. Education is a help, but a combination of effort, initiative, and experience is more important; and it must not be forgotten that the spirit of public service, involving certain extra obligations as an American, is the fundamental requirement for a Navy commission.

The Navy wife can point with pride to the fact that her husband is a member of the most democratic navy the world has ever known. At the same time, she must recognize that a navy is built on discipline, and that true discipline demands a definite line of demarcation between officers and enlisted men. It is for this reason that the Department of the Navy requires officers to wear distinctive insignia, to live apart from the enlisted personnel, and to confine their social contacts in the Navy to other officers.

Everything a commander does is potentially related to some future moment of crisis, when his decision, and his men's readiness to act upon it, will mean success or failure for the whole team. This decision may well mean ordering his men to risk their lives in the service of their country. Common sense, therefore, requires that between the commander who must make the decision and the men who risk their lives to carry it out a certain distance must be maintained to insure fair and impartial treatment. The basis for this separation is the same in peace or war, for the commander's responsibility is continuing and all embracing.

This does not mean that the commander-leader is not close to his men. On the contrary, he makes a continuous effort to be on warm and friendly terms with them all; he is their parent, brother, and father-confessor. This relationship is personal, frank, and cordial, but it is based on sympathetic understanding rather than on social familiarity. Most enlisted men understand and appreciate this line of reasoning. In fact they have little respect for the officer who attempts to curry favor by undue familiarity.

There is no rank among Navy wives; however, custom requires every Navy wife to show deference to wives of persons senior in rank to her husband. There is nothing snobbish or antisocial in this custom; it prevails among the wives of all professional and business men in civil life. Enlisted men's wives should never have an inferiority complex when dealing with officers' wives; if they will simply be natural, they will be well received. Frequently, officers' wives and enlisted men's wives work together on some charitable or benevolent project. Such work can be interesting and profitable if all so engaged will be co-operative, polite, and gracious.

Before World War II, most men who became officers expected to make the Navy a permanent career. The tremendous expansion of the Navy during that war brought into the Service many Reserve officers who previously had planned their lives as civilians and who contemplated leaving the Service as soon as the war was over. Similarly, the continuation of the draft since the war has caused many young men to become Reserve officers most of whom contemplate a future civilian career.

Also, previous to World War II the enlisted personnel were all volunteers, most of them considering the Service as a permanent career. They soon learned that to support a family on the pay of a seaman, or even of a petty officer, was almost impossible. Consequently, they generally postponed marriage, at least until they had become petty officers first class.

The continuation of the draft law, making every qualified young man subject to being drafted for two years' military service, has caused many men to seek commissions in the Naval Reserve, or to volunteer as enlisted men, with a view to completing such service before trying to establish themselves in civilian jobs.

But today, with the feeling that at the end of their two to four years' service they can obtain a more remunerative position on shore, many of these young men get married during or even before they have begun their two years' obligated service. The fact that so many of them have married undoubtedly has raised the average intelligence, education, aptitude, and social qualifications of enlisted men's wives. But it has also greatly complicated the housing and transportation situations, and dissatisfaction in this regard together with the feeling of impermanency, or "doing time," to some extent has lowered morale of both husbands and wives.

Professional morale can be seriously affected by unsatisfactory family relations, even to the extent of seriously decreasing a husband's efficiency. In fact, it is generally recognized that a principal element contributing to high morale is a happy home life; and for a married man an essential to a happy home life, especially in the Navy, is a loving, loyal, and competent wife. There is not a shadow of a doubt but that such a wife is one of the greatest assets to a man in the naval service.

Navy life has many compensations. Though you can never become rich in the Navy, the pay and allowances and the perquisites of naval personnel and dependents, such as medical care and hospitalization, will keep the wolf from the door. As you follow your husband in his various changes of duty, you will see many parts of our beautiful country, and probably some foreign ports. And wherever you go you will find friends. In the United States, civilians respect naval personnel and their wives and show them many courtesies. Abroad, our naval personnel are considered representatives of the United States and receive attentions accorded few civilians in any walk of life.

So do not look upon your future with alarm. You will have a colorful, cosmopolitan career. You will live in many interesting places, and hold dearly as friends not only your comrades in the Services but many civilians as well. You and your husband will have separations, but an equal number of happy reunions. When he retires or ends his naval career, together you will relive in memory the glamorous years and know that Navy life, in spite of all its handicaps and heartaches, has been a glorious adventure.

ANNE BRISCOE PYE

ACKNOWLEDGMENTS

MANY Navy wives and officers have been gracious and interested enough since this book was first written in 1941 to contribute current information over the years in order to keep each edition up to date. For this present edition, acknowledgments are particularly extended to:

Admiral Henry Crommelin, USN
Rear Admiral C. G. De Kay, USN
Rear Admiral R. J. Arnold, USN
Colonel R. F. Crist, Jr., USMC
Captain F. B. Selby, USN
Captain B. E. Moore, USN
Captain Robert Wheeler, USN
Captain R. S. Smith, USN
Captain J. P. Monroe, USN
Captain B. F. McCaffery, USN
Captain J. C. Myers, USN, and Mrs. Myers
Commander W. H. Lytle, USN
Commander J. P. Conway, USN, and Mrs. Conway
Lieutenant Commander A. E. Carlson, USCG
Lieutenant Commander E. E. Bracken, USNR
Lieutenant Commander Merlin Ditmer, USN, and Mrs. Ditmer
Lieutenant R. P. Lewis, USN
Lieutenant Ray Robinson, USN

Lieutenant Dean Fritchen, USN
Lieutenant Robert Smoak, USAF, and Mrs. Smoak
Lieutenant Frank Copeland, USMC
Miss Katharine Briscoe Knox
Mrs. Howard R. Prince
Mrs. G. H. Mills
Mrs. Ralph Skylstead
Mrs. Stuart Jones
Mrs. Darryl Bailey
Mrs. M. A. Batey
Mrs. M. Paolozzi
Mrs. Clyde Stone
Mrs. C. R. Rank
Mrs. J. M. Wilson
Mrs. W. J. Brooks
Mrs. J. V. Sportelli
Joyce Betcher Roberts
Mrs. Wayne Hunter
Mrs. Gordon Barclay
Mrs. C. Deibler
Midshipman J. L. DeGroff

THE NAVY WIFE

Chapter I

THE UNITED STATES NAVY TODAY

THE United States Navy is the most powerful navy in the world. The power of a navy comprises, first, an effective control organization, such as the Navy Department; second, an adequate, effective shore establishment; and last but by no means least, a suitable number of fighting ships and service forces, properly adapted to modern use in types and characteristics, manned by highly trained personnel, and so disposed as to be immediately ready to perform their assigned missions in the event of war.

During World War II, the need for joint command—that is, a common commander over all units engaged in one operation or in one war area—was proved and adopted as a policy. Also, the tremendous expansion of the Air Force, then a part of the Army, was such that it was entitled to a control organization of its own. In 1946, therefore, Congress passed a law creating a Department of Defense, which, under the President as Commander-in-Chief, was to control and co-ordinate the activities of the Army, Navy, and Air Force. The head of the Department of Defense was made a cabinet member. Under his control, there were established three subordinate departments: the Department of the Army, the Department of the Navy, and the Department of the Air Force. Each of these sub-departments is headed by a Secretary, but these Secretaries do not have cabinet rank.

To advise the Secretary of Defense in regard to the co-ordinated needs of the armed forces and to develop strategic plans for combined operations of the three Services, Congress established the Joint Chiefs of Staff. The Chairman of the Joint Chiefs of Staff, appointed by the President for a four-year period, conducts the meetings of that body but has no vote. The chairmanship is held in rotation by officers of the three Services. The Commandant of the Marine Corps becomes a temporary member of the Joint Chiefs whenever matters affecting the Marine Corps are under consideration. The

Joint Chiefs are assisted by a staff of officers limited to 210 in number, approximately one-third from each Service.

The continental United States is divided into naval districts, and two small areas in the vicinity of Washington called the Potomac River Command and the Severn River Command. The Hawaiian Islands and the Panama Canal Zone are also organized as naval districts. Within each naval district are naval operating bases, naval air stations, naval shipyards, naval hospitals, minor naval operating forces for local defense, and frequently, special activities which operate under the direct control of a Navy Department bureau.

For more effective co-ordination of naval forces operating in defense of our coast or of sea lanes in the vicinity of the coast there have been established sea frontier commands on the Atlantic and Pacific coasts and in the Hawaiian Islands.

Now, Nancy Lee and Sue, as Navy brides, the foregoing remarks about shore activities of the Navy will permit you to visualize what Bill and Jack have in mind when they speak about shore duty. But for the present you may be more interested in the operating forces of the Navy in which most Navy men spend much more than half of their naval career.

TYPES OF SHIPS

One of the most confusing things about Navy ships is the designation of types by letters, such as BB for battleship. In many cases the type of ship may be told by its name. The following information will help you in identifying types of U.S. Navy ships.

Battleships are designated by the letters BB followed by a number, the number of the ship of that class in order of construction. They are named for states of the Union.

Aircraft carriers are designated by the letters CV followed by a third letter denoting class, and by a number—as CVA 10, Heavy Aircraft Carrier No. 10; CVL, small aircraft carrier; CVE, escort carrier. They are named for famous battles, famous old ships, bays, and sounds. The only exceptions to date are the *Franklin D. Roosevelt* and the *James V. Forrestal.*

Cruisers are designated by the letter C followed by one or more letters denoting the class and a number: heavy cruiser, CA; large cruiser, CB; light cruiser, CL; antiaircraft cruiser, CLAA. Cruisers are named for cities.

Destroyers are designated by DD, and for special types an additional letter: DDL, destroyer leader; DDE, escort destroyer; DDK, destroyer specially designed as a submarine killer; and DDR, destroyer radar picket. Destroyers are named for individuals connected with the Navy who have rendered distinguished service to their country.

Submarines have SS followed by a letter indicating type and a number: SS, normal submarine type; SSK, submarine killer type; SSG, one carrying guided missiles; SSP, submarine transport; and others. Submarines are named for fish.

Ships of the amphibious forces are too numerous to record, but in general the designator for large ships begins with A standing for an auxiliary type—as AK, cargo ship; AP, transport. Landing craft have LS followed by one or more letters showing type, as LST, landing ship capable of carrying tanks. Ships having an A designator are named for mountains, counties, or astronomical bodies, or for distinguished men. Heretofore, landing craft have not been named, only numbered; but the Navy Department, in the belief that a ship's name aids morale, is contemplating giving all landing craft names.

Minecraft all have the letter M, as DM, high-speed mine layers; and mine sweepers all have the letters MS, as AMS, auxiliary mine sweeper.

Patrol vessels all have the letter P, as PT, motor torpedo boats; PF, patrol frigates. Most patrol vessels have no name, simply the class designator and a number; but the frigates are named for smaller cities.

THE NAVY AND THE SERVICEMAN

The Navy Department does its sincere best to make the life of servicemen on board our ships more comfortable and agreeable. In new ship designs, and in our present ships as they come up for overhaul, the crew's quarters are being arranged to provide locker space for each man; flourescent lighting is being provided in living spaces; and colored paint is being used to make such spaces more attractive.

The Chief of Naval Operations and the Chief of Naval Personnel are fully aware of the necessity of improving conditions for naval personnel to insure retention in the Service of an adequate number of top-grade officers and enlisted men. They are striving to raise the caliber of officers and men by selecting out officers whose capabilities do not justify promotion; arranging to offer to the best Naval Reserve officers of the grade of Lieutenant and below commissions in the Regular Navy; permitting resignation of officers after four years' active service, except those who have voluntarily accepted longer periods of service; permitting the retirement of Regular Navy officers after twenty years' service; refusing to re-enlist persons who are unsuitable, or whose performance of duty is inferior; and improving sea and shore duty rotation for all career personnel.

They are reducing the hardships on naval personnel due to our heavy world-wide commitments by reducing our naval forces in distant waters as much as possible; considering more carefully the effect of operating schedules and training procedures on individuals; extending command tours and reducing turnover in order to avoid unnecessary uprooting of families; keeping foreign-duty tours short in order to prevent long separations for personnel whose dependents are unable to follow, and providing more opportunities for foreign-shore duty for personnel whose families desire to live abroad; and making Navy shipyard overhauls at greater intervals and scheduling them well in advance to aid in family planning.

They are attempting to add to the dignity and satisfaction of a Service career by keeping officers and men more fully informed as to the operations of the forces to which they are attached in order that they may recognize the important part they are playing; insuring, so far as possible, concurrent travel so that the officer or man can travel with his family in changing station; permitting Petty Officers to wear rating badges upon dungaree uniforms; possibly returning to the practice of allowing the enlisted man's blue hat to carry the name of his ship; and providing facilities to Navy Wives' Clubs for luncheons, meetings, and recreational gatherings.

To increase the material rewards and security of a naval career, the bonus payments for re-enlistment have been increased, as has the weight allowance for transportation of household effects; and a new law known as the Contingency Options Act makes it possible on retirement to elect to receive a somewhat smaller retirement pay with such pay to continue during the lifetime of the man's wife and until his children are eighteen years of age. The Navy Department has recommended an increase in pay for Service personnel; the extension of medical care for dependents, to include the payment for civilian doctors and hospitalization when no armed forces doctors or hospital facilities are available; and the availability of veterans' benefits to men who would be entitled to them while such men are still on active duty.

During the long period of World War II, and to a less extent during the Korean War, it was impossible for many Navy dependents to follow the ship as they often had in prewar days. Most Navy wives settled down in one place, usually the home port. Even since the Korean War this practice seems to be general. Thus the life of a Navy wife today is more normal, less nerve-racking, and the separations often are no longer; there are just more real homes awaiting the Serviceman's return.

But, Nancy Lee and Sue, the fascinating features of Navy life remain: the cosmopolitan life; the vast number of old, true friends; the knowledge that your husbands are serving in an honorable profession, dedicated to the preservation of our country and to the peace of the free world. You, as Navy wives, can do much to maintain their high morale.

SOURCES OF OFFICER MATERIAL

As a bride and newcomer into naval circles, perhaps you wonder about the officers, their backgrounds, and how they obtained their commissions in the Navy.

In our democracy any ambitious and military-minded citizen who is qualified and can meet the prerequisites may compete to win a commission in the armed forces.

Commissioned officers for the Regular Navy are obtained from:

1. USNA   The United States Naval Academy
2. NROTC Reserve Officers' Training Corps
3. OCS   Officers' Candidate School

Others who may become commissioned officers in the Regular Navy:

Enlisted men and Warrant Officers of the Navy and Marine Corps
Officers on extended active duty
Distinguished graduates of OCS courses
Distinguished graduates of Senior NROTC
Civilians qualified for appointment in Navy Medical Service (doctors, dentists)
Individuals qualified for appointment in Judge Advocate General Department (lawyers)
Individuals qualified for appointment as chaplains
Individuals possessing essential technological background

Navy Reserve Officers' Training Corps
and
the Importance of NROTC

By far the majority of naval officers today are commissioned from the NROTC, and the Navy, Army, and Air Force also depend on ROTC for the vast bulk of their officer corps. In the past, as you probably know, when the Navy was a comparatively small organization, it depended almost entirely on the Naval Academy for its officer corps, a group it was admirably able to supply. Today over fifty colleges and universities offer Navy-operated ROTC courses.

How it works: College students are enrolled in the basic course upon meeting prescribed mental and physical standards. After completing a basic course, students may apply for enrollment in the advanced course, which is selective. Those who complete the advanced course of two years are obliged to accept a Reserve commission. Resignation is possible at any time before graduation but the student who resigns must return all monies received up to that date. Students receive uniforms and textbooks. Those in the advanced course receive a stipulated per diem pay, and they also receive pay at the six-week summer camp.

The Reserve Officer

The end product of the NROTC program is the Reserve officer, that ubiquitous young man who receives a bachelor's degree and a Reserve Ensign's commission at the same time. After laying aside cap and gown, he goes out to remote regions of the world, returning to civilian life after two years, considerably matured and often still wearing his gold bars. Reserve officers did a splendid job in World War II, and many were recalled to active duty the second time for Korean service. They have reflected admirably our oldest military tradition of the citizen-soldier or "territorial officer," who is prepared to leave his hearth and office at a moment's notice in order to fulfill the obligation of his commission.

To the Naval Reserve officer and his wife go some of the benefits of Regular Navy status and all of the responsibilities. Promotion is generally slower because his inactive period is lost time as far as "date of rank" is concerned. Added expense for uniforms, moving, the insecurity of his reserve status, and the necessity for readjustment to civil life can cause some tension and anxiety to the wife who is not used to quick changes and who prefers domestic security to travel. Usually a young college girl, she is loyal to the American naval tradition by performing her mission as an officer's wife, wherever her husband goes.

THE UNITED STATES NAVAL ACADEMY

The site of the present Naval Academy was once an old Coast Artillery post on the banks of the Severn. In 1845, during the term of George Bancroft as Secretary of the Navy, the Naval Academy was established. Bancroft was a scholar, historian, statesman, and an experienced school administrator and organizer. At first the course was five years, of which the first and last years were spent at the Naval School, the other three being passed at sea. In 1850 the name was changed to the U.S. Naval Academy. Colonial Annapolis is one of the most picturesque, colorful, and interesting state capitals in the United States. Its names have been Providence, Town of Proctors, Town at the Severn, Anne Arundel's Town, and finally, in 1694, Annapolis, in honor of Princess Anne, at that time heir to the British throne.

Today Annapolis stands, still proud of its mansions of the Golden Age, but prouder still of the old families who built their homes here on the Severn. These old homes are gems of architecture with their beautiful doorways, fanlights, and palatial interiors. The drawing rooms, ballrooms, and dining rooms are interesting with their imported marble mantels and fine hand-carved mahogany doors ornamented with sterling silver doorknobs and latchstrings.

"As Long as There Is an Annapolis" Midshipmen will always look forward to week ends when the "One and Only" girl visits the Naval Academy. Youth will be youth, and romance will be served. Uncle Sam's "embryo naval officers," known as Midshipmen, are the cream of American manhood; they are the finest cross section of young men, drawn from every state in the Union. Annapolis is the cradle of scores of fighting Admirals such as Halsey, Carney, and Stump.

There is a lure about the sea, a glamour about men who go down to the sea in ships; and the names of far-off ports like Saipan, Rio,

Guantánamo, and Manila take on added charm when "Bill's and Jack's ship has been there." From the days of the old sailing vessels' return to New England harbors until yesterday, when the sleek, stream-lined carriers, cruisers, and stolid battle-wagons proudly sailed into port, the scene has been a stirring one.

When the ships are in port everyone is happy. There is something about a Navy blue uniform, starched whites, and gleaming gold buttons that appeals to all members of the feminine sex, young or old. Everybody loves a sailor.

Meet Nancy Lee and Suzanne

Nancy Lee Patterson is what we might call a landlocked citizen or a landlubber; that is, she claims a little inland town in South Carolina by the name of Pinecrest as her home, and what she doesn't know about the Navy will fill this book and probably more. Nancy Lee is a smart girl, however, and she learned much in the short week that she knew Midshipman William Satterlee Tyler while he was on leave, visiting her southern home town.

Suzanne Todd, better known as Sue, has grown up in a Navy at-mosphere. She remembers the long anxious years of World War II when her father was serving in a destroyer in the Pacific and she is a true Navy junior. She speaks the Navy lingo, thinks Navy-wise, and is having the most exciting romance with Jack Ford, who has recently returned from Korea. Sue does Red Cross work at Bethesda Naval Hospital and met Jack when he came in as an air evacuee with a shrapnel wound and a broken leg from Seoul. He is a Boatswain's Mate First Class; they are already engaged and you can take up their romance and wedding later in Chapter IX.

Nancy Lee is now beginning her first year at a Washington prepara-tory college, and to date she has been a bit homesick. But the follow-ing invitation in the morning's mail alters all that.

> U.S. Naval Academy
> 2002 Bancroft Hall
> Saturday

Dear Nancy Lee:
  Next week end closes exam week at the "Navy Tech," and a good show is being put on by the Masqueraders. I have been planning to ask you down for the week end since we met during my last leave. I've decided to

be generous and give the Midshipmen here a break in letting them meet you.

How about bringing along your two roommates in the snapshot? Think possibly I could dig up two dates for them out of the 4,000 men in the Brigade! Be sure to bring something to wear sailing. We may go for a round-the-world cruise down the Severn.

Answer pronto.

Love,

Bill

To Bill, Nancy Lee wrote:

Dear Bill:

The week end sounds like fun. Barbara, Fran, and I are already making plans and expect to arrive Saturday on the one o'clock bus. We are all looking forward to seeing the Academy, and interested to see if what Hollywood says about Annapolis is true.

Fran is taller than I am (that is why she is sitting in the picture), Barby is shorter, so be sure to select Midshipmen accordingly. Can hardly wait for the big cruise!

Till Saturday . . . be sweet.

Nancy Lee

(From now on, Nancy Lee, we shall talk directly to you.)

You are beset with several very important questions. What to take and what not to take? Where will you stay? How much will the week end cost? How does one reach this more or less inaccessible state capital of Maryland that shelters the Naval Academy?

So it is your first visit to Annapolis! For a successful visit plans are laid well in advance, and letters are exchanged. Saturday finally arrives, and the week end of all week ends is under way.

There are two ways of reaching Annapolis. Believe it or not, neither of these is by bona fide railroad. The easiest approach from Washington, forty miles distant, or Baltimore, about thirty-five miles, is by hourly bus or private motorcar. There is no train from Washington or Baltimore.

You are wise in planning to arrive on the one o'clock bus, because Midshipmen are not allowed to leave the Yard until after the noon meal formation on Saturday. By that time Bill will be able to meet you at the bus stop at Carvel Hall. Upon your first visit you will appreciate this attention. No doubt he will have suggested that you put up at Carvel Hall, and probably he already will have made a reservation for you. If you want to make a hit with Bill, don't arrive hungry. Just before you take the bus in Washington fortify yourself with a good substantial lunch, enough food to keep you happy until you dine with him in the evening. There are two reasons for this tip. In the first place, Bill may have already lunched when he meets you. Secondly, Saturday minutes are precious at Annapolis. There may be a football game scheduled and you won't want to be late for the kick-off. He will begrudge even the amount of time that it takes you to register and settle in your room.

Very likely you will strike up an acquaintance on the bus, or you may know some of your fellow passengers. It will be a special bus marked Annapolis and will be filled with young, attractive, well-dressed girls who are going to the Naval Academy for the week end and a good time. There will be young careerists, college girls, débutantes, and a host of the youthful government employees. The entire group will radiate happiness, good cheer, and the spirit of youth.

The first and most important thing in any woman's life is *clothes*. They can make or mar the most exciting of week ends. Reduce your clothes and your luggage to a minimum. For the bus or motor trip down, you will probably wear a tailored suit or sports dress and carry a topcoat or fur coat. Spotless gloves, a crisp blouse, and a nosegay in the lapel of your jacket are fresh little extra touches. Look your best and remember that first impressions are most important. By all means wear comfortable walking shoes, because if Bill meets you there will be the walk over the uneven brick sidewalks to the Academy grounds. Also, choose the lightest piece of luggage you possess, and confine your choice to one piece.

Your wardrobe need not be extensive, as the week-end activities usually consist of the following: Saturday afternoon, a sail, a hike, or a football game; Saturday night, a formal hop (formal dress) at Dahlgren Hall, or a formal battalion hop in Memorial Hall. On Sunday afternoon there may be an informal hop at Smoke Hall or you may be invited by an officer and his wife for Sunday dinner, but such good fortune is not likely on your fist visit.

You should take:

For a sail: Slacks, of fairly warm material; the most becoming color and the best-tailored ones that you can afford. A cardigan or topcoat, rubber-soled shoes. A scarf for your hair.

For a football game and a hike: Tailored suit or the spectator sports dress you wore down, with a warm topcoat or fur coat. Walking shoes.

For dinner concert, or dance: Your very best evening dress, evening wrap, or fur coat, lined galoshes to protect those gold or silver slippers on a wettish night. A foldable pliofilm raincoat is an added protection.

For Sunday morning: A daytime dress, or suit.

This wardrobe should see you through your first week end, and after that you may wish to add to or subtract from your clothes budget. If you must go nautical, then take your own seafaring togs.

Custom has it that whenever a Midshipman sees a girl wearing his cap he plants a kiss right where it should be. Since Midshipmen are not allowed to uncover in public, this popular custom tempered by discretion shouldn't cause public embarrassment. Obviously, a Midshipman never fails to meet the crisis. Remember, the penalty for putting on a Midshipman's cap is a kiss—so forewarned is forearmed. Remember too that a Midshipman's buttons, belts, and insignia are expensive items, and parts of his uniform which he must replace immediately. Don't make off with them or ask to wear any part of your host's uniform. Many a budding romance has been blighted by a filched buckle, and girls have been wished into "the brig" for less.

A recent innovation might be termed the "Pajama Game" at Annapolis. Midshipmen go to great lengths to purchase a pair of pajamas at the Exchange, then stencil them in naval phraseology with clever art work in the form of ships, subs, and airplanes. The drags enjoy wearing these back at college as a proof of their popularity.

CARVEL HALL AND MARYLAND INN

Rates at Carvel Hall are subject to change without notice. During June Week the hotel rates are advanced about 40 per cent. At Carvel Hall single rooms are $3.00 per day without bath to $5.50 with bath. Double rooms are $6.75 to $8.50. Meals cost from 75 cents to $1.00 for breakfast, $1.25 to $1.75 for luncheon, and $1.75 to $3.00 for dinner.

Upon your second visit (if you are invited down again), you can find out about the private homes in Annapolis that take paying guests. A list of these is kept by the official hostess, and it is wise to make a reservation. The cost is as low as $3.00 per night, but these homes should be regarded as exactly what they are: the private homes of old Annapolis families. In most cases the hosts are FFM's and are entitled to the respect of their guests. It is a nice touch to show them some courtesy, and at least express your appreciation.

The homes on the approved list measure up to the highest moral standards. At Carvel Hall or in any of the private houses your escort carries your luggage only to the parlor. And, my dear, I mean parlor; so does the hotel staff, so does the Commandant, and so does the whole Naval Academy faculty. Going upstairs or into a guest's bedroom is definitely not to be considered by a Midshipman, and the hostesses of private homes on the list to take paying guests are most particular on this point. A Mrs. Grundy seems to be tactfully in evidence at every turn. Of course, the case of a Midshipman's mother, grandmother, father, or visiting Congressman is something else; but you are not interested in his family connections on this particular week end.

Upon your second or succeeding visits you may choose to take an earlier bus to Annapolis in order to avoid the rush.

BEING AN ANNAPOLIS DRAG!

Since you received a special invitation from Bill, you are his "drag" for the week end. It may not sound particularly flattering at first, but "drag" is Academy lingo. If you spend frequent week ends at the Academy with Bill as your host, you will be known as his OAO. It means "One and Only," or as some cynic has said, "One Among Others"!

Remember, it sometimes requires even more effort to be an agreeable guest than it does to be the perfect host. Midshipmen are universally famous for their gallantry, their good manners, and the wonderful hospitality they extend to their feminine guests. Your host will spend his all, if need be, to show you a good time, and he will strain his wallet as far as Uncle Sam will let him. A Midshipman may take his drag to dinner (outside the Yard). If your host is very careful about movies and magazines during the month he may even save out enough for a modest corsage, but don't expect this extravagance. A *Plebe* draws three dollars spending money a month. It is referred to as the "monthly insult"; however, since a Plebe is not allowed to attend hops he hasn't much use for playboy money.

A *Youngster,* or second-year man, draws seven dollars a month, which allows him possibly one riotous week end. But remember that out of this princely sum he must also buy magazines, postage stamps, and a holiday ice-cream soda or malted milk. A *Second Classman* draws nine dollars a month, while a *First Classman* advances to thirteen dollars.

A drag is expected to pay her own transportation both ways, her hotel bill, and all of her meal checks except those for Saturday night dinner and Sunday luncheon. If there is a football game, your host will have tickets. You will be his guest at dinner and for the hop, also for any informal hops and refreshments that may be sandwiched in on Saturday afternoon and Sunday.

Midshipmen enjoy being invited out for a meal when visited by their mothers, relatives, or Congressmen.

After the football game in Tompson Stadium there may be time for a coke at the Steerage or one or two dances, before your host must fall in to muster. By this time you must hurry away to dress for dinner and the evening hop.

You may dine amid the splendors of Carvel Hall, in gleaming candlelight, or within short walking distance of the Yard. There are many quaint little tearooms, such as the Hitching Post, the Port Lounge, and the Little Campus. The prices are modest to suit the wallets of the Midshipmen.

FORMAL HOPS

The regular Saturday evening hops are always formal and are presided over by a hostess, who receives the guests. She is selected from among the wives of officers on duty at the Academy. The First Lady, the wife of the Superintendent, or the wife of the Commandant always receives at the opening ball in the fall and at the Graduation Hop. On these occasions, the chairman of the Hop Committee receives with the selected lady, standing first in line and presenting the Midshipmen and their guests by name to her.

Be very gracious when you are being introduced. There is no need to say anything except "How do you do," but be natural and *smile*. Not one of those revealing toothpaste smiles, for remember, "the eyes of the Navy are upon you."

And how many pairs of eyes! The stag line is probably the longest in the world—something to make any girl's heart skip a beat. All three classes attend, and encircling the balcony above are the cherubic faces of the Plebes, who are allowed only to gaze enviously upon their betters from afar and dream of the time next year when they will take their places in line. Everything comes to him who waits, they hope, and Plebes are painfully chronic waiters.

The hops begin at nine o'clock. By ten o'clock all the guests have passed through the receiving line and the dance is in full swing. Your very best evening dress is appropriate, but do not go in for exotic, extreme styles. The girl in the simple dress of good material and youthful, becoming design is often the belle of the ball.

There are several special dances throughout the year. The Victory Ball takes place whenever Navy defeats the Army in football. The "N" Dance during June Week is quite a gala affair, given in honor of the athletes who have won the coveted "N" during the current academic year. There are also dances on Halloween, St. Valentine's Day, and St. Patrick's Day, and the Graduation Ball, but the biggest evening of a Midshipman's life at the Naval Academy is the Ring Dance, when he receives his class ring.

June Week and Graduation

June Week at Annapolis is a glorious six days of happiness during peacetime! Every Midshipman who had looked forward to June Week with its attendant colorful festivities and traditions must have felt a bit cheated when his class was graduated early, as was the case during the war. However, that is life.

One of the high spots of June Week is the Presentation of the Colors parade, when the colors are formally presented to the Color Company. The points in competition are awarded for aptitude, class standing, athletics, and drill. The Commander of the winning company selects a girl, who is invited by the Superintendent to present the colors to his company. "After the regiment is formed with the company which is to receive the Colors immediately in front of the reviewing stand, the Color Girl is escorted by the Superintendent, and she steps forward onto the Field carrying a huge bouquet and followed by a Midshipman chosen from the winning company." The Color Girl makes a few congratulatory remarks to the winning company, then with the aid of the Midshipman Brigade Commander transfers the national and regimental flags from the old to the new color guard.

The new Color Company salutes the Color Girl with three cheers, then resumes its place in line. The Superintendent, with the Color

Girl on his arm, takes a position in front of the reviewing stand. The Color Girl is really Miss America for the day!

Thousands of visitors attend the graduation exercises. The address is always given by some public figure, such as the Secretary of Defense, the Secretary of the Navy, or the Chief of Naval Operations. The graduating class is seated early in their shining white uniforms without shoulder marks, with their Midshipman caps beside them. The honor or star men of the class are seated in the first row, and behind the graduating class is placed the rest of the regiment. Proud parents, interested relatives, and friends in gala attire comprise the large audience. The Chaplain of the Academy opens the exercises. Then the Superintendent introduces the speaker, who delivers the graduating address, and later the diplomas are presented by a high-ranking officer (usually the Chief of Naval Operations), who swears the class in for their commissions in a body.

After the honor men receive their Bachelor of Science degrees, the other members of the graduating class receive similar degrees in alphabetical order. No one knows, until the official list is published later, just who will be the "anchor man" or the "goat" of the class. The anchor man is not only recognized; he carries a cardboard anchor and is tossed in the air by his classmates and cheered.

When the last graduate has resumed his seat, the cheerleaders conduct the class in singing "Navy Blue and Gold." Three cheers are given "for those about to leave us" by the undergraduates, which are returned by the graduating class "for those we leave behind." At the end of the third cheer, the graduates toss their Midshipman caps high into the air, whereupon ensues a vigorous scramble by relatives and girl friends trying to secure a cap for a souvenir. Often Navy juniors get the coveted caps.

The Plebes have now become Youngsters. They make a wild rush into the Academy ground, racing madly for the up to now forbidden Lover's Lane and diving for the Youngsters' Benches. They snakedance around Herndon monument, one of them climbs to the top of it, and the fourth class becomes the new third class. This signifies their joyous freedom and abandon at being released from the restrictions, trials, and tribulations which have to be smilingly endured by Plebes. It is often said that of all the promotions throughout a naval career none is received more ecstatically than that of Plebe to Youngster, and none constitutes so real an advancement.

Chapter II

TRADITIONS AND CUSTOMS
OF THE NAVY

NAVAL traditions are unwritten rules pertaining to the character and conduct of naval personnel and accepted by them for their guidance. They are based on historical precedent, and their value is incontestable. Although most such traditions are founded upon the action of some officer, it is largely because at the time the action was taken the officer was in a position of authority and responsible for making a decision. Enlisted men have performed innumerable equally heroic deeds.

Many of our naval traditions are hoary with age, dating back to the early days when "iron men went down to the sea in wooden ships" (some facetious young Ensigns like to reverse this quotation when speaking of the modern Navy).

A THUMBNAIL NAVAL HISTORY

The early history of the American Colonies is largely the story of a maritime people. All the original settlers faced the perils of the deep to reach their new homes, and in those days transatlantic passage certainly was most uncomfortable and perilous. From over the sea came all the crude necessities of life except the plainest food and the logs with which to build and heat their simple dwellings; back over the sea in trade when the products of their skill and toil.

Even between the different Colonies the sea was the quickest and safest means of transportation. With the early development of a shipbuilding industry fostered by the excellent timber from the forests of New England, by the rapidly expanding fishing industry, and by the gradual increase in trade, the people of the Colonies early became sea-minded. By 1775 more than one-third of Great Britain's seaborne commerce was carried in vessels built in the Colonies.

George Washington was among the first to recognize the important part that sea power might play in gaining the independence of the Colonies. Soon after he took command of the Army near Boston in July, 1775, he arranged with some Massachusetts shipowners to arm and man their ships and to send them to sea in hopes of capturing some British ship from which might possibly be obtained powder and other supplies badly needed by his army. These vessels have sometimes been called "Washington's Fleet." They captured one or two small ships, but on the whole their operations were of little importance.

From the Colonial merchant ships came most of the officers and men who manned the fleet later built for the Continental Navy.

Among those who came into the Navy from merchant ships, most of which were operating as privateers or under letters of marque, were many men who later became naval heroes: Hopkins, Barry, Truxton, Decatur, Porter, Biddle, Preble, and Perry.

During the Revolution there took place one of the American Navy's greatest exploits, a foundation stone of its traditions. This was the defeat of the British frigate *Serapis* by the *Bon Homme Richard*, the latter an old converted merchant ship in the command of Captain John Paul Jones. It was in this battle—with the ships foul of each other and lashed together, the *Bon Homme Richard* torn by shells, on fire, and leaking badly—that John Paul Jones, upon being hailed by the British Captain and asked if he had surrendered, made the never-to-be-forgotten reply, "I have not yet begun to fight!" and proved it by winning the battle. What a glorious example!

As soon as the War for Independence ended, the Navy was allowed to disintegrate, and in 1785 the last of the ships of the Continental Navy was sold. Upon the inauguration of President Washington in 1789, the administration of the Navy was placed in the War Department, but by act of Congress of April 20, 1798, the Navy Department was created as a separate administrative branch of the government. Benjamin Stoddert was appointed the first Secretary of the Navy.

During the years 1798–1800 France conducted an undeclared quasi war against United States shipping. The Navy had been abolished, and at the beginning of this period the only vessels available for counter-action were those of the Revenue Marine. Several years earlier the construction of six frigates had been authorized, but work on them had been slow, and even though Congress provided additional funds to expedite their completion, only two, the *Constellation* and the *Constitution*, were commissioned in time to participate in operations against the French.

Early in the War of 1812 against England, the United States frigate *Chesapeake*, newly recommissioned and with an untrained crew, was defeated off Boston by the English frigate *Shannon*. But though this defeat was a serious blow, the words of her mortally wounded Captain, "Don't give up the ship," made him a hero and provided our Navy with an undying tradition. Later in the War of 1812 Captain O. H. Perry at the Battle of Lake Erie as an inspiration to his officers and men carried at the masthead of his flagship a long white flag bearing in blue letters Captain Lawrence's last words. And after winning the battle Captain Perry sent the famous message, "We have met the enemy, and they are ours."

In the Mexican War and in the Civil War the operations of the Navy were largely confined to bombardment and blockade.

The War with Spain was primarily naval. The actual state of war was precipitated by the blowing up by a mine of the U.S.S. *Maine,* at anchor in Havana Harbor. The war was brought to a successful conclusion by the destruction of the Spanish fleets by Commodore Dewey at Manila and by Admiral Sampson off Santiago, Cuba. As incidents of this war, the Navy cherishes the calm order of Commodore Dewey in opening the Battle of Manila Bay, "You may fire when ready, Gridley," and Admiral Sampson's message presenting the Spanish fleet destroyed off Santiago as a Fourth of July present to the American people.

In World War I the activities of our Navy, because of the inferiority in the number of surface ships of the German Navy compared to its opponents, were restricted chiefly to antisubmarine and escort operations. However, there was ample evidence that the officers and men of the modern Navy are of the same material as those in the days of "wooden ships and iron men." Commander Joseph K. Taussig commanded the first division of United States destroyers to be assigned to duty with the British Navy. Upon arrival at Queenstown, Ireland, Commander Taussig, in person, immediately reported the arrival of his destroyer division to Vice Admiral Lewis Bayly, Royal Navy, commander of the naval forces based there. This old British sea dog inquired in a gruff and haughty voice, "Commander Taussig, how soon can your division be ready for active duty?" As such a long trip for destroyers usually entailed an overhaul period of several days, the Admiral was quite surprised to receive the reply, "I shall be ready when fueled," a process requiring only a few hours. From that time on, the Admiral was very partial to American naval personnel.

The attack on Pearl Harbor on December 7, 1941, was the scene of the start of the Pacific conflagration. For history students of the future there is a new and glorious page in the records of the United States Navy. Pearl Harbor always will be remembered as a story of the daring bravery, coolheadedness, strength, and skill of the Navy. An American Admiral gave his life in giving help to brother officers; four young Reserve Ensigns manned a destroyer and fought like veterans in the thickest of the fight; a dying Captain, disemboweled by flying shrapnel, continued to give orders and refused to be moved, but ordered his junior officers to leave the burning deck.

No records of heroism in our Navy are brighter than those of the pilots of torpedo-plane Squadron Eight, who, knowing that unless they turned back they would have insufficient fuel to return to their carrier, continued on and and pushed home an attack upon the Japanese fleet in the Battle of Midway. This attack won the battle, but only one of the pilots, who later was rescued from the water, lived to know that their daring attack was the turning point of the war against Japan.

Nor are any brighter than that of the Commanding Officer of a submarine who, lying severely wounded on the upper deck, directed his executive officer, "Take her down!" knowing full well that such order would mean death by drowning for him but might save his ship and crew. Other events of World War II which are still vivid in everyone's memory prove without a doubt that the Navy of today is establishing traditions for the American Navy of the future.

In such a short review it is impossible to mention more than a few incidents upon which its traditions are founded. Use some of your time, Nancy and Sue, to read a detailed naval history. It will make you proud to be a Navy wife!

NAVAL CUSTOMS

Some naval customs have come down to seafaring men of today from the seamen of Greece, Phoenicia, Carthage, and Rome; others are of more recent origin. Naval customs are so numerous that it will be necessary to consider them by classes if one is to appreciate their full significance. The most important customs are designed to inculcate

1. Respect for God
2. Respect for the nation
3. Respect for authority
4. Respect for the individual.

RESPECT FOR GOD

The Commanding Officer of each ship to which a chaplain is attached, by Regulations is required to hold divine service every Sunday unless conditions make it impracticable to do so.

During divine service on board a ship of the Navy, a pennant called the church pennant, a white triangular field with a blue cross, is hoisted on the same halliard with, and above the national ensign. This is the only occasion on which it is ever permissible to hoist any flag or pennant on the same halliard or at the same staff, above the national ensign.

For centuries, since flags were first used to indicate nationality, the hoisting of one nation's flag below another's has indicated a capture by the force of the nation whose flag is flown above. The hoisting of the church pennant over the national ensign during divine service is the Navy's way of indicating its recognition of the supremacy of God.

Divine service is held, weather permitting, on the quarter-deck under an awning. The portable altar is draped with the national ensign. At the beginning of the service the bugler sounds "Church Call"; the ship's bell is tolled; and the Boatswain's Mate passes the word, "Out smoking lamp! Quiet about the decks!"

No smoking, card playing, or other games are allowed on deck or in officers' messrooms, no loud talking or boisterous behavior. But the rights of the individual are recognized, and no person except the members of the band, who supply the music as part of their duty, is forced to attend the service.

The only times it is permissible to half-mast the national ensign are: during funeral services of naval personnel; during the transfer of the body of a deceased officer or man from ship to shore; while the body of a deceased Captain of a ship, or that of a Flag Officer, is on board the ship in which he died, except when at sea; and when so ordered by higher authority during periods of mourning, or as a memorial for the dead. In the case of the death of the Captain or of a Flag Officer, such Captain's pennant or Flag Officer's flag is half-masted until sunset on the day of the transfer of the body to shore or burial at sea. All Navy ships at anchor within sight of the ship which half-masts her colors follow her movements in half-masting and hoisting colors. The custom of half-masting colors is in recognition of the power of God over life.

RESPECT FOR THE NATION

To all seafaring men the national ensign is symbolic of the nation. The colors constitute the only mark which distinguishes the nationality of a ship. Hence when at sea another ship is in sight during daylight (except another ship of the U.S. Navy of the same fleet), or when within sight of inhabited land, the colors are hoisted so long as there is light enough for them to be seen.

A merchant vessel, upon passing a warship, dips its colors (lowers them to half-staff) and hoists them only after the dip has been answered by the dipping of the warship's colors. The custom is in recognition of the status of the warship as a representative of the power and dignity of the nation.

During battle, ships always hoist their colors, and the striking or hauling down, of a ship's colors is a recognized token of surrender. When the colors are hoisted upside down, it is a signal of distress indicating that the ship is in immediate need of assistance.

When the ship is not under way, the colors are hoisted at a staff at the stern at 8:00 A.M. and hauled down at sunset. The ceremonies at these times are designed to bring to the minds of officers and men the respect due the colors as the symbol of the nation, and a mental renewal of their oath of allegiance. The jack, similar to the blue field of the national ensign, is hoisted simultaneously with the colors at a staff at the stem of the ship.

Morning colors: At morning colors the guard of the day (usually Marines) and the band are paraded on the quarter-deck facing the flagstaff. As the ship's bell strikes eight, the bugler sounds "Attention," all officers and men on deck face aft and stand at attention. The Marine Guard presents arms. The band plays the national anthem, at the first note of which all officers and men raise their right hands to their caps in salute. The colors are run smartly to full staff, meaning to the top of the staff. Upon completion of the national anthem officers and men drop their hands to their sides; the bugler sounds "Carry On" and the ceremony is completed. When no band is available a bugler will sound "Colors" in lieu of the playing of the national anthem.

Evening colors: The ceremonies at evening colors (at sunset) are the same as for morning colors except that the colors are started down at the first note and lowered slowly so as to be completely down with the last note. Great care is observed that the colors do not touch the deck.

You may be interested to know that a national ensign when unfit for further use *must be burned* in order to prevent its desecration by use in any other form.

When an officer or man reaches the upper platform of the gangway ladder in boarding a ship, or steps onto such platform in leaving a ship, he faces aft and salutes the quarter-deck. Also during daylight a similar salute will be given upon reaching the quarter-deck by way of a hatch or from any other part of the ship.

The origin of this custom is uncertain. It is known to have existed before nations had flags. In the earliest periods of seagoing, Chinese junks carried idols on the upper deck near the stern, and later early Christians similarly placed a shrine, presumably in each case to insure the protection of their respective divinities against the dangers of the sea. Today, however, the salute is considered a salute to the flag, which usually can be seen from the quarter-deck, and is rendered when boarding or leaving a ship.

RESPECT FOR AUTHORITY

In the conduct of war unquestioning obedience is essential. Such obedience can be obtained only by inculcating respect for authority. Authority means responsibility. It is for this reason that throughout the ages a Captain of a sinking ship has been the last to leave the ship. He accepts the responsibility for the condition of the ship and before he leaves must insure that all other persons precede him in seeking to save their lives.

In order to establish an order of precedence in succession to command it was necessary to establish ranks, and seniority within each rank. To inculcate respect for authority as indicated by rank, its honors must be rendered not to the holders of the rank as individuals but in recognition of the authority and responsibility conferred upon them. Hence there is a table of honors, indicating from President to Ensign the honors to which each is entitled by virtue of his election, appointment, or commission.

MANNING THE RAIL

Manning the rail consists of stationing men along the rail of all weather decks, facing outboard, at arm's length. In most navies, at a given signal all men extend their arms reaching to the shoulders of the men adjacent on either side. In the days of sailing ships the men instead of manning the rail manned the yards—the large booms extending horizontally across the mast from which sails are suspended. Presumably such practice came from a desire to show off the proficiency of the crew and to indicate to the sovereign that his men were willing to take risks in his honor.

GUN SALUTES

Gun salutes are fired only by ships equipped with a saluting battery of small guns carried solely for the purpose—battleships, aircraft carriers, cruisers, and a few others. The internationally accepted national salute is twenty-one guns.

National salutes are fired by ships of the United States Navy at noon on February 22 and July 4. At noon on May 30, Memorial Day, a salute of twenty-one guns is fired at the rate of one gun per minute. Minute guns are a customary form of salute to the dead.

Upon entering a foreign port where there is a saluting station, a saluting ship fires a national salute in honor of the nation of the port, the national ensign of such foreign nation being flown at the mainmast head during the salute.

The President, rulers of other nations, and members of royal families are saluted with the national salute. There is an established scale of salutes, less than twenty-one guns for various public officials, members of the diplomatic corps, "Flag" Officers of the Navy and Coast Guard, and the "General" Officers of the Army, Air Force, and Marine Corps. All salutes are given in an odd number of guns. Why, no one knows, but in early times it was considered that an even number of guns fired meant that the Captain or Master was dead. Not so today in our Navy. Should an even number of guns be fired, it would merely mean that the gunner couldn't count or that some error had been made.

Piping the Side

The term "piping" is derived from the use of the boatswain's pipe during the rendering of honors. A boatswain's pipe is a special type of whistle—a metal tube about six inches long, at one end of which there is a hollow metal ball without a top, an opening for the escape of air when the other end of the tube is blown into. The escape of the air produces a sharp, piercing sound whose tone, within limits, can be varied by changing the pressure of the fingers over the escape hole.

The present ceremonial custom of piping the side evolved from a practical custom of sailing-ship days, when ships carried no gangway ladders. The means of reaching the deck in those days was by rope ladder hung over the side of the ship or by a sea ladder consisting of metal strips attached to the ship's side as steps. Such a climb was difficult at times, especially if the ship was rolling. Frequently it was necessary to provide a boatswain's chair. This was merely a flat seat of plank with lines from each end meeting overhead, at which point they were attached to a line which passed through a pulley block overhead and then to the deck. By this means a person sitting in the seat, pushing against the side of the ship with his feet, could be hoisted to the ship's rail with little danger to him.

When the boatswain's chair was used, men were stationed to haul on the line to hoist the chair. The boatswain, watching over the side to note a favorable moment for hoisting, gave the signal by a blast on his pipe. The chair was used more often by elderly officers who had grown stout with the years, so as a rule the higher the rank of the officer to be hoisted on board the larger the number of men required. Hence today we have the Boatswain or Boatswain's Mate piping the side and the number of side boys increasing with the officer's rank—two for an officer up to and including Lieutenant Commander, four for Commanders and Captains, six for Commodores and Rear Admirals, and eight for officers and officials of higher rank.

Hand Salute

Hand salutes are exchanged between officers and between officers and enlisted men, except when under arms or in formation, on every occasion of their meeting, passing near, or being addressed, except:

1. Men at work, except when addressed, do not salute.
2. Men seated at work, at games, or at mess are not required to rise or to salute except in the case of a Flag Officer or Captain.
3. Officers seated in boats shall salute without rising except when a senior enters or leaves the boat, or when acknowledging a gun salute.
4. Officers of one's own ship other than the Captain, except during inspections, are to be saluted only on their first daily meeting and upon addressing or being addressed by their seniors.

The hand salute is a friendly greeting and acknowledgment of membership in a military service. It is a dignified and military gesture. It is just as incumbent on officers to salute their seniors as it is for enlisted men to salute officers; it is equally incumbent on the senior to return the salute. In the Navy the hand salute is not made when the head is uncovered.

Official Calls

Official calls are visits of ceremony or courtesy. Flag Officers, upon assuming command, at the first opportunity pay official calls upon seniors in the chain of command. Commanding Officers and unit Commanders call only on seniors in the type of ship to which assigned.

Officers junior to Commanding Officers are required to call upon their Commanding Officer in his cabin on board ship within forty-eight hours after reporting for duty.

RESPECT FOR THE INDIVIDUAL

Respect for the individual can be demonstrated no better than by the attitude of seniors to juniors and by the manner in which correction and punishment are administered.

Discipline is that characteristic of military forces which insures immediate and effective execution of orders given by a superior in rank. It is acquired by training which corrects, molds, strengthens, and perfects.

Wives Visiting the Ship

In normal peacetime when the ship is in the home port, officers' wives frequently go on board after 4:00 P.M. to see their husbands, and stay for dinner and the movies, returning to shore about 10:00 P.M. Except by special invitation a wife should never go on board ship during working hours, nor should she go on board or remain on board while her husband is on watch as Officer of the Deck. So, Nancy Lee, when Bill's section has the duty you will be welcome on board between 4:00 P.M. and 10:00 P.M., except during the periods in which Bill is actually on watch as Officer of the Deck.

But do not forget that ships' boats run on an exact schedule. Be sure that you are at the boat landing well in advance of the scheduled departure of the boat you have been told to take. Watch the boats as they approach the landing, and when you see a motorboat (a type of boat having a canopy, which is provided for the use of officers and their guests) having on its bow the name (or the abbreviation of the name) of the ship in which your husband is serving, go to the coxswain of the motorboat, tell him your name, and show him your Armed Forces Dependents Identification Card or, if one has been given you, the card showing your permission to use the ship's boats, and tell him that you have been invited on board. Be sure not to mistake the Captain's gig (marked with an arrow on the bow) or the Admiral's barge (marked with stars) for the motorboat.

At the movies when the Captain, or Admiral, appears on deck, "Attention" will be called, at which all officers, enlisted personnel, and male guests rise and remain standing until the order "Carry on."

Normally, the wives and friends of enlisted personnel are welcome on board ship between 1:00 P.M. and 5:00 P.M. on Saturdays and Sundays, and often for longer periods on holidays.

Boat Etiquette—Embarking

A lack of understanding of boat etiquette frequently results in confusion when a group of people are about to embark in a ship's boat. There are two general rules: (1) Passengers embark in inverse order of precedence; except that (2) ladies embark ahead of gentlemen. In this as in all other cases where precedence will be mentioned, the precedence of a Navy wife corresponds to that of her husband; civilians holding diplomatic rank or political office are given the precedence to which such office entitles them, and their wives are given similar precedence; civilians holding no office are given precedence in accordance with age or, when known, in accordance with national or local prominence. The procedure of seniors embarking last being at variance with the usual custom of seniors going first does cause confusion. Young Navy wives can assist in reducing such confusion by hurrying into the boat. Naturally one does not stop to inquire dates of commissions before getting into the boat, but knowledge of the general rule will make things easier.

Upon embarking, juniors take the seats nearest the bow of the boat. Ladies in taking seats should leave room between them for a gentleman embarking later to be seated.

DISEMBARKING

In disembarking the passengers leave the boat in order of precedence, ladies disembarking first. An exception may be made to this extent: When at a landing or alongside a ship ladies require assistance in disembarking and there is no officer on deck or gangway ladder platform to offer it, then one or two officers may precede the senior lady on to the landing or gangway platform in order to provide such assistance.

There may be times when because of wind or sea conditions a lady should be assisted all the way up or down the gangway ladder. In such case a gentleman should precede a lady and help her on the ladder.

NAVY TIME—THE ENIGMA

Perhaps we have misled you a little by our use of P.M. above. In the Navy there is no A.M. or P.M. Time is reckoned in twenty-four-hour periods beginning at midnight, and is expressed in four figures. The first two figures represent hours and the last two, minutes; thus one minute past midnight is 0001, noon is 1200, and your 4:00 P.M. is the Navy's 1600. When Bill tells you to take the boat that leaves the landing at 1610, you must remember that such hour is 4:10 in the afternoon, by your watch.

CEREMONIES PERTAINING TO THE SHIP

Before a ship is ready for operations there are three ceremonies to be performed: the laying of the keel, the launching and christening, and the commissioning.

By "laying the keel" is meant the securing on the building ways of the first strips of metal to form a portion of the ship's keel.

The next ceremony is the launching and christening. Ships are normally constructed on building ways on land, and when adequate hull work is completed to insure her being watertight, the ship is permitted to slide down the inclined ways into her natural element. This day is a gala day at the building yard. The Secretary of the Navy invites a lady to sponsor the ship. She selects a maid or matron of honor. On this day, only less than on her wedding day, the sponsor is the center of all eyes and attention. Her duty is to christen the ship— to give it a name just as it starts sliding down the ways.

The christening, or naming, of ships dates back long before the Christian Era. Launching ceremonies have not always been happy occasions with flowers, flags, and pretty speeches. In olden days it was customary to offer up human sacrifices when the new ship first entered the water. The Vikings and early Norsemen attached human victims to the rollers over which the ship glided into the water.

A much nicer but rather extravagant custom was to drink prosperity to the ship out of a silver cup which was then thrown overboard. This practice seemed too expensive, and in 1690 the British decided to break a bottle on the bow instead.

The first record of a christening of a United States ship of war is that of the *Constitution*, October 20, 1797, on which occasion, following the British practice, the ship was christened by Captain James Sever, U.S. Navy, who "broke a bottle of wine over the bow of the frigate."

The first record of the christening of a United States Navy ship by a woman is found in Preble's, *History of the Portsmouth Navy Yard,* which quotes a press item: "The 'Concord' glided beautifully into her destined element and was christened by a lady of Portsmouth." Unfortunately, this lady's name has been lost to posterity as at that date, 1828, it was considered indelicate for a lady to permit her name to appear in a newspaper.

The commissioning ceremony begins the life of the ship as an operating unit of the Navy. During construction and trial runs, and until accepted by and delivered to the Navy, a ship is under the control of the builders. After such delivery, until placed in commission, she is under the jurisdiction of the Commanding Officer of the Navy shipyard at which delivered.

The "crossing the line" ceremony, a custom still observed, began as an act of worship of a deity. The present ceremony of a fictitious Neptune on board is a relic of the Middle Ages when it was performed not at the equator but upon arriving in the tropics, passing certain landmarks, entering the Arctic Circle, and so on.

During the early part of the seventeenth century the custom arose, and is carried out to this day on board ships crossing the equator, of dressing a member of the crew in the garb of Neptune, complete with crown, trident, seaweed hair (made of rope-yarns), and having a large retinue of mermaids, mermen, and other mythical inhabitants of the deep. Appropriate ceremonies are held when the vessel crosses the equator, and all the novitiates, or polliwogs, pay a forfeit or find themselves lathered with salt-water soap, shaved with a wooden razor, and tumbled backward into a tank of salt water.

ARMED FORCES DAY

Prior to the unification of the armed forces under the Department of Defense, each Service had its day: Navy Day, October 27; Army Day, April 6; and Air Force Day, September 18. These separate days have been abolished, and all of the Services now unite in celebrating Armed Forces Day, the third Saturday in May. On this day, Navy ships are full-dressed, and all ships and shore establishments hold open house to the public. Likewise, the Army and Air Force open their establishments. All Services hold drills, demonstrate their weapons, and provide an opportunity for the people of the nation to learn at first hand something about the men and material of their armed forces. There is a move afoot to abolish Armed Forces Day and revert to former original Service days.

MEMORIAL DAY

On Memorial Day, May 30, detachments of sailors and Marines frequently march in parades and take part in memorial services. In many ports a Navy ship is detailed to carry to a near-by area of the open sea relatives of officers and enlisted personnel who have been lost at sea, in order that such relatives may cast flowers upon the sea in memory of those they have lost. At noon, a salute of twenty-one minute guns is fired in honor of those who gave their lives for their country.

VETERANS' DAY

For many years we have celebrated Armistice Day, November 11. This was the date of the signing of the armistice which ended World War I. The 83rd Congress, apparently believing that the designation of November 11 as Armistice Day belittled the days upon which the several armistices that ended World War II were signed, passed Public Law No. 380, signed by the President on June 1, 1954, designating November 11 as Veterans' Day, in place of its prior designation as Armistice Day. Parades and ceremonies to honor the veterans of all wars will be held on Veterans' Day hereafter.

Chapter III

THE COMMISSIONED PERSONNEL

BEFORE an officer of the armed forces can receive his commission, his name must be submitted by the President of the United States to the Senate, where it must be confirmed by a majority vote. The honor conferred by such a commission is shown by its wording:

To all who shall see these presents, greeting: Know Ye, that reposing special trust and confidence in the patriotism, valor, fidelity and ability of [the officer's name in full], I do appoint him [or her] a [grade] in the UNITED STATES NAVY to rank as such the [number] day of [month], nineteen hundred and [year].

This officer will therefore carefully and diligently discharge the duties of the office to which appointed by doing and performing all manner of things thereunto belonging. And I do strictly charge and require those officers and other personnel of lesser rank to render such obedience as is due an officer of his rank and position. And this officer is to observe and follow such orders and directions, from time to time, as may be given by me, or the future President of the United States of America, or other Superior Officers acting in accordance with the laws of the United States of America. This commission is to continue in force during the pleasure of the President of the United States of America, for the time being under the provisions of those Public Laws relating to Officers of the ARMED FORCES of the UNITED STATES of AMERICA and the component thereof in which this appointment is made.

GRADES IN THE ARMED FORCES

In all branches of the armed forces, officers are distributed in grades. Authority and responsibility increase with each advance in grade. Beginning at the bottom (with the exception of the grade of Chief Warrant Officer, which will be described later) and progressing upward, the corresponding grades are:

31

Navy and Coast Guard	Army, Air Force, and Marine Corps
Ensign	Second Lieutenat
Lieutenant (junior grade)	First Lieutenant
Lieutenant	Captain
Lieutenant Commander	Major
Commander	Lieutenant Colonel
Captain	Colonel
Commodore (retired list only)	Brigadier General
Rear Admiral	Major General
Vice Admiral (temporary)	Lieutenant General (temporary)
Admiral (temporary)	General (temporary)

Chief Warrant Officers are Warrant Officers who have served as such for a period of not less than three years, and whose efficiency is recognized by their promotion to a commissioned status, ranking with but after Ensigns. Commissioned Warrant Officers are of three grades, W-2, W-3, and W-4. With each advance in Warrant Officer grade there is an increase in pay and allowances.

The temporary grades of Vice Admiral and Admiral on the active list are assigned to officers holding specifically designated positions of great responsibility, such as the Chief of Naval Operations, Commanders of Fleets, and the Chief of Naval Personnel.

During World War II, in recognition of their high efficiency in the performance of war duties of great responsibility, by special act of Congress the grades of Fleet Admiral and General of the Army, next above the grades of Admiral and General respectively, were created and conferred upon four naval officers and four Army officers. The naval officers so honored were Fleet Admirals William D. Leahy, Ernest J. King, Chester W. Nimitz, and William F. Halsey, Jr. The Army officers were: Generals of the Army George C. Marshall, Henry H. Arnold, Dwight D. Eisenhower, and Douglas MacArthur. These grades, with full pay and allowances, are to be retained for life.

In the Navy and Coast Guard the general term used to designate officers of and above the grade of Commodore is "Flag Officers." This term is used because officers of these grades when embarked in ships or in command on shore are authorized to fly a flag indicative of their grade and command status. In the Army, Air Force, and Marine Corps, officers of the grade of Brigadier General and above are called "General Officers." They too are authorized to fly flags to indicate grade and command status.

CLASSIFICATIONS OF NAVAL OFFICERS

Naval officers are of two general classifications, line officers and Staff Corps officers. Line officers constitute the executive branch; they exercise military command of naval ships, aircraft, and most naval shore establishments and perform general administrative duties pertaining to command responsibilities. They supervise the design and construction of naval ships and aircraft and are responsible for their effective operation and maintenance. They are responsible for the design, construction, operation, and maintenance of propulsive machinery, equipment, and weapons.

Staff Corps officers perform specific duties pertaining to the health and spiritual welfare of naval personnel, to the conduct of financial matters and the procurement and storage of essential naval supplies, and to the construction and maintenance of all buildings, roads, docks, and airfields under the Navy's jurisdiction. Staff Corps officers do not exercise command except over certain shore activities specifically assigned to their control. The grades held by Staff Corps officers are identical with those of line officers up to and including Rear Admiral.

Officers specifically ordered to assist a Flag Officer in the performance of his duties are said to be serving on such Flag Officer's staff and are for the most part line officers; but officers of the Medical Corps and Supply Corps frequently serve on the staff of a Fleet Commander. Please make sure that you understand the difference between Staff Corps officers and officers serving on a Flag Officer's staff.

INDICATORS OF GRADE AND CATEGORY

On blue uniforms naval officers of all categories wear gold stripes on their sleeves to indicate their respective grades, and insignia above such stripes to indicate their respective categories. Near the lower end of each sleeve an Ensign wears one one-half-inch stripe; Lieutenant (junior grade), two stripes, the lower one-half inch wide and the upper one-quarter inch wide; Lieutenant, two half-inch stripes; Lieutenant Commander, three stripes, two one-half inch wide and between these a quarter-inch stripe; Commander, three half-inch stripes; Captain, four half-inch stripes; Commodore, one broad stripe, two inches wide; Rear Admiral, one broad stripe and above this one narrow (half-inch) stripe; Vice Admiral, one broad and two narrow stripes; Admiral, one broad and three narrow; Fleet Admiral, one broad and four narrow.

On white uniforms and on khaki uniform blouses, shoulder boards are worn on both shoulders. For grades from Ensign to Captain the background of such boards is blue, with the grade indicated by gold stripes as stated for blue uniforms. For Flag Officers the background is gold, the grade being indicated by embroidered half-inch silver stars, one for Commodore, two for Rear Admiral, three for Vice Admiral, and four for Admiral. For Fleet Admiral there are five smaller silver stars arranged in a circle.

On blue uniforms, above the stripes line officers wear a gold emboidered one-inch star; Staff Corps officers wear the embroidered particular insignia of their respective corps: Supply Corps, an oak-leaf cluster with three acorns; Medical Corps, an oak leaf with one acorn; Dental Corps, an oak leaf with two acorns; Medical Service Corps, an oak leaf without acorns but having an extended stem; Nurse Corps, an oak leaf without stem or acorns; Civil Engineer Corps, four interlaced oak branches; and Chaplain Corps, for a Christian Chaplain a cross and for a Jewish chaplain a representation of the Torah (the Mosaic Law) over which is embroidered a six-pointed star (the Star of David).

On the shoulder boards, an officer's category is shown by the above-named insignia embroidered above the stripes, except that in the case of line Flag Officers an embroidered silver anchor is substituted for the gold star.

On the khaki uniform shirt, grade and category are indicated by devices worn on the tabs of the collar. Line officers wear the device indicating their grade on both tabs; Staff Corps officers wear the device indicating their grade on the right tab, and their corps device on the left tab.

The collar devices to indicate grade are as follows: Ensign, a gold bar; Lieutenant (junior grade), a silver bar; Lieutenant, two silver bars; Lieutenant Commander, a gold leaf; Commander, a silver leaf; Captain, a silver eagle; Commodore, one silver star; Rear Admiral, two such stars; Vice Admiral, three stars; Admiral, four stars; and

Fleet Admiral, five stars arranged in a circle. The collar devices to indicate category are the same as explained above.

Naval officers' caps are similar in all respects except the visors. For officers from the grade of Ensign to Lieutenant Commander the visors are plain black leather; for Commanders and Captains the visor has one row of gold embroidery and for Flag Officers, two such rows.

Chief Warrant Officers on blue uniforms wear a one-half-inch stripe similar to that of an Ensign except that the gold stripe is not continuous, being broken at intervals with sections of blue. On shoulder boards and collars their specialty is indicated by a specific device: for one specialized in ordnance, a bursting bomb; in electricity, a streak of lightning; and for the hospital corps, a caduceus (the staff of Mercury with two serpents twined about it), the familiar insignia for the medical profession.

Line officers qualified as aviators wear on the left breast above their service ribbons a pair of gold wings between which is a shield resting on an anchor. The design for an aviation observer is a similar pair of wings, but between them an anchor within a circle. For a flight surgeon the center device is that of the Medical Corps; and for a flight nurse, that of the Nurse Corps.

A line officer qualified in submarine duty wears in the same position a device representing two dolphins flanking the bow of a submarine. The submarine medical insigne is the same except the center device is the Medical Corps insigne. For those qualified in submarine engineering the dolphins flank a circle within which is a three-blade propeller.

The sword, which has been long absent from the naval uniform equipment, has now been re-established as part of the full-dress uniform.

Officers' Pay and Allowances

The officers of the Navy receive a fixed base pay to which is added a certain amount for longevity (length of total naval service). The longevity pay increases slightly for every two years of total service up to twenty-two years, after which it increases every four years up to thirty years. Because of this longevity pay, the total pay received upon entering any grade except that of Ensign is more than the base pay for that grade. In the table below is given the base pay for each grade

and in the next column the total pay which normally will be received
by an officer upon entering the grade. In the third column is shown
the extra-hazardous-duty pay received in each grade by those officers
qualified to receive it. The figures represent dollars per month.

		Base Pay	Total Pay	Extra-Hazardous-Duty Pay
Rear Admiral (upper half) and above	O–8	$963.30	$992.94	$150.00
Rear Admiral (lower half) and Commodore	O–7	800.28	829.92	150.00
Captain	O–6	592.80	607.62	210.00
Commander	O–5	474.24	489.06	180.00
Lieutenant Commander	O–4	400.14	414.96	150.00
Lieutenant	O–3	326.04	355.68	120.00
Lieutenant (j.g.)	O–2	259.36	289.00	110.00
Ensign	O–1	222.30 3rd yr.	237.12	100.00
Chief Warrant	W–4	332.90	348.04	100.00
Chief Warrant	W–3	302.64	310.21	100.00
Chief Warrant	W–2	264.82	272.38	100.00

A naval officer is paid an allowance of $47.88 for subsistence; and
when no government quarters are assigned to him, he gets an allowance for quarters, the amount of which varies with grade and number
of dependents. The amount of such quarters allowance per month is
as follows:

Pay Grade	Without Dependents	With One or More Dependents
O–8	$136.80	$171.00
O–7	136.80	171.00
O–6	119.70	136.80
O–5	102.60	136.80
O–4	94.20	119.70
O–3	85.50	102.60
O–2	77.10	94.20
O–1	68.40	85.50
W–4	94.20	119.70
W–3	85.50	102.60
W–2	77.10	94.20

Officers of the Regular Navy do not receive any allowance for uniforms. Under certain conditions Reserve officers do receive such an allowance, but such conditions are too involved to be discussed here.

Officers holding temporary grades of Vice Admiral and Admiral are paid a personal allowance, $500.00 per year for a Vice Admiral and $1,000.00 per year for an Admiral. Usually such officers are provided with an automobile to be used only for official business.

WAVE OFFICERS

As originally organized, the Waves were a portion of the Naval Reserve. The officers were college graduates who upon being accepted as candidates were enrolled in the Naval Reserve Corps and given a special course of indoctrination and naval training. The work assigned to Wave officers was mostly in the line of communications and clerical work; it was later extended to many types which could be performed by women as well as by men.

The Army, the Coast Guard, and eventually the Marine Corps followed the Navy's example in enrolling officers and enlisted women Reservists. The members of the Navy's women's Reserve were called Waves; the Coast Guard Reserves, Spars; the Army Reserves, Wacs; and the Marine Corps Reserves, Women Marines. The Nurse Corps of the Navy and of the Army were similarly enrolled in the Reserve, but each of these organizations retained its original name.

The official name or the abbreviated title of Waves was derived from the title of the Congressional bill authorizing the organization, "Women Accepted for Voluntary Emergency Service." Miss Mildred McAfee, president of Wellesley College, was appointed head of the Waves with the rank of Lieutenant Commander, later raised to Captain. The organization was a success from the beginning, partly because of the high standards Waves had to meet to be accepted, partly because the Navy spared no effort to see that they were properly looked out for, and most important of all because the women had an overpowering desire to make good.

During its first two years the Waves alone freed enough officers and men to man a fleet of ten battleships, ten aircraft carriers, twenty-eight cruisers, and fifty destroyers. These women performed a vital service to their country. Each one may feel that she had a share in the victory, and that she is fully entitled to the veterans' benefits which Congress has provided.

At the end of the war the Waves were rapidly demobilized, but a shortage of personnel made it expedient to retain on active duty some who were specialized in certain types of work. In 1948, Congress passed a bill permitting the transfer of a limited number of Waves from the Naval Reserve to the rolls of the Regular Navy. This act states that the number of enlisted women on the active list of the Regular Navy shall not exceed 2 per cent of the authorized enlisted strength of the Regular Navy; and that the number of commissioned and warrant women officers shall not exceed 10 per cent of the authorized enlisted women personnel. The number of Wave officers in the grades of Commander and Lieutenant Commander shall not exceed 10 per cent and 20 per cent, respectively, of the actual number of women officers. One Wave officer, while serving as assistant to the Chief of Naval Personnel, has the grade of Captain.

Navy Nurse Corps

The Navy Nurse Corps was established by law May 13, 1908, as a part of the Regular Navy. Navy nurses held equivalent rank with officers of the Navy and enjoyed many of the privileges of officers. However, on February 26, 1944, Congress provided that the Navy Nurse Corps, during the war and for a period of six months thereafter, should hold actual commissioned rank. Thus they had the honor and dignity of actual military rank and increased authority consistent with the degree of responsibility which they carry. A more recent law removed the time limit on the holding of actual rank.

In World War II the duties of Navy nurses were many and varied, both within and without the continental limits of the United States. They followed the fleet in hospital ships and were assigned to transports for the evacuation of casualties. Navy nurses in hospitals at Pearl Harbor, Kaneohe Bay, and on the U.S.S. *Solace*, as well as those in the Philippines, Guam, and Midway, felt the first impact of the war. Five were made prisoners of war when Guam was captured. Eleven were taken as prisoners in the Philippines. One nurse, who was part of an operating unit serving with the Army on Bataan, escaped to Australia in a submarine. She was the first person to receive the

Legion of Merit, an award given for outstanding performance of duty.

The Regular Navy nurse chooses the Navy as a career and begins with a three-year appointment. The Reserve Nurse Corps is available for duty with the Navy in time of war or national emergency. The Reserve nurse may transfer to the Regular corps if she meets the requirements. When war broke out in 1941, there were 822 nurses on active duty; on October 19, 1944, there were 8,720, with approximately 1,500 on overseas duty in advanced bases and in hospital ships.

The Navy nurse may assist our Navy doctors in the most modernly equipped naval hospital and dispensary, or she may be called upon to set up a field hospital in a remote, primitive war zone. In continental hospitals, her duties are of two types: supervising the nursing being done by hospital corpsmen and teaching and training of these corpsmen. The tremendous advances in the sciences of caring for the ill and wounded call for highly trained, skillful nurses, with a well-developed capacity for imparting their skill and art to untrained corpsmen. In the last war, wounded men recovered three to one over those in World War I. This fact is proof of the importance and of the excellence of the nurses' work.

The Director of the Nurse Corps has the rank of Captain while serving in that office. The number of Commanders and Lieutenant Commanders shall not exceed 1.75 per cent and 7.75 per cent, respectively, of the number of officers of the Corps serving on active duty.

PROMOTION

Until 1916, promotion in the Navy was by seniority. This system proved entirely unsatisfactory; junior officers spent long periods in each grade, and those who lived long enough reached the Rear Admiral grade usually with but a year or two to serve before retirement.

Although promotion by selection had been in effect for many years, it was not until the passage of the Officer Grade Limitation Act of 1954 that there was established a definite method of insuring the necessary flow of promotion. In each grade above Lieutenant (junior grade) there was established a maximum permissible years' service. The same law established a minimum years' service in each grade before an officer became eligible for promotion. The minimum and maximum years' service in grade are:

	Minimum	*Maximum*
Ensign	0	3
Lieutenant (j.g.)	2	3
Lieutenant	4	6
Lieutenant Commander	4	6
Commander	5	7
Captain	3	5

The maximum period of service in grade may be extended one year in the case of an officer who has failed of selection in order to permit his name to be considered by another selection board.

FORCED SEPARATION FROM THE SERVICE

Lieutenants (junior grade) or Lieutenants who twice fail of selection are honorably discharged with a separation pay of two months' active duty pay for each year of commissioned service, but not to exceed two years' pay.

FORCED RETIREMENT

Lieutenant Commanders, Commanders, and Captains who twice fail of selection are placed on the retired list on June 30 of the fiscal year in which they complete a prescribed period of service: For officers of the unrestricted line, these periods are as follows: Lieutenant Commanders, twenty years; Commanders, twenty-six years; Captains, thirty years. There are some slight variations in the cases of certain Restricted Duty line officers and Staff Corps officers. Officers so retired receive retired pay at the rate of $2\frac{1}{2}$ per cent of their active duty pay (plus longevity but without allowances) at the time of their retirement, multiplied by the number of years of service, but not to exceed 75 per cent of active duty pay.

No officer is permitted to remain on the active list beyond the first of the month succeeding his sixty-second birthday. Officers thus retired for age, or those who may be forced to retire because of physical disability incident to their service, receive $2\frac{1}{2}$ per cent of their active duty pay for each year of active service performed.

NAVAL OFFICERS' POSTGRADUATE EDUCATION

In addition to many short courses of indoctrination and training in specialized activities, the Navy conducts the Navy Postgraduate

School and the Naval War College. Selected naval officers also attend the postgraduate schools of the Army, Air Force, and Marine Corps, and the National War College in Washington.

The Postgraduate School, located at Monterey, California, has two educational components: the General Line School and the Engineering School.

The Naval War College at Newport, Rhode Island, conducts a course designed to improve the student's ability to exercise command in war operations. It teaches the latest ideas in naval tactics, strategy, and logistics. In posing hypothetical situations to be solved, the course provides opportunity for students to demonstrate their knowledge of such subjects.

Most of the students are of the grades of Commander and Captain in the Navy. There also are in attendance a smaller number of officers of the Army, Air Force, and Marine Corps, of corresponding grades, and several representatives of the Department of State.

OFFICERS' FITNESS REPORTS

In the Navy Department is a file of "Fitness Reports" on each officer, covering his entire career from appointment as an Ensign until he retires or leaves the Service. A report is submitted by the officer's immediate superior each six months, with an additional one upon each change of station. Though on these reports there are no remarks concerning the officer's wife, her efficiency is reflected thereon because an unhappy home life inevitably reduces the husband's efficiency. The wife, therefore, gradually acquires a reputation, favorable or unfavorable. It is often a deciding factor in the selection or rejection of the husband for a desirable assignment, possibly a stepping stone in his career. Her responsibility is great.

Chapter IV

THE NONCOMMISSIONED PERSONNEL

THERE is an old Navy saying that the Warrant Officers and Chief Petty Officers constitute the backbone of the Navy. By their energy and efficiency they have advanced through the various ratings from recruit up. They are the leading men of the crew and by their ability and character set a standard for the ship's company. No ship can be efficient and happy without a high percentage of competent, patriotic, and loyal Warrant and Chief Petty Officers.

The Navy discourages enlistment until the applicant has graduated from high school. It recognizes that education pays off in dollars and cents, both to the government and to the individual. The Navy's need for high-quality, continuous-service men (those having served more than one enlistment) has been so well expressed by Admiral Carney, Chief of Naval Operations, that we quote an excerpt from one of his speeches recently printed in *All Hands*, the Bureau of Naval Personnel monthly information bulletin.

There will always be need for keen resolute men, skilled in the business of controlling the sea, the air above the sea, and the dark depths below the surface. Whatever the shape of their ships, planes and weapons, those men—Navy men—must do the job.

Our Navy needs to attract and hold A-1 people. Give us a good body and a good brain and we will endeavor to instill all those qualities—but (and this is important) we need both quality and an assured tenure of service.

The normal course of promotion of enlisted personnel is from recruit to rated man through Petty Officer Third Class, Petty Officer Second Class, Petty Officer First Class, and Chief Petty Officer. The Warrant Officer is next above the Chief Petty Officer but by no means all Chief Petty Officers care to, or have the specialized training to, become Warrant Officers.

A man desiring to serve in the Navy must meet stiff physical requirements and must prove his educational fitness by making an acceptable mark in the Navy Qualification Test. If a minor and not less than seventeen years of age, he may enlist only with the consent of his parents or guardian. A minor may enlist for the period of his minority or, as is the case with those of age, for a period of four or six years, whichever he chooses. In any case, enlistment entails an obligation to be subject to call for active service for a total period of eight years, that portion in excess of his period of enlistment being spent in the Active Reserve, explained later.

Upon being accepted and sworn in, the recruit begins drawing pay and is sent for indoctrination and training to one of the three main naval training centers, located at San Diego, California; Great Lakes, Illinois; and Bainbridge, Maryland—usually the one nearest to his place of enlistment. There he is furnished uniforms and a full outfit of Navy regulation clothing.

The period of training at the naval training center is about eleven weeks. In the Service this is known as "boot training." It is devoted to instructing the recruit in naval traditions and customs; physical culture, personal hygiene, and sanitation; the use of firearms and the elements of close-order drill. Also, during this period the recruit's capacity for immediate advanced training is carefully ascertained and his preference for a particular line of work determined.

As in every walk of life, the young man who has a definite idea of the line of work he desires to pursue has a tremendous advantage. The Navy provides training in sixty-two modern trade skills. Proficiency in any of these leads to rapid advancement in the Navy and a more remunerative job in industry or business when one's naval service is completed.

As soon as possible, therefore, the recruit should determine at least the general character of the work he would prefer. Ratings and Petty Officers are classified by groups such as Deck Group, Ordnance Group, Electronics Group, Aviation Group, Engineering and Hull Group, Administrative and Clerical Group, and Medical and Dental Group. The recruit should decide to which of these groups he prefers to be assigned.

During the period of boot training, each recruit will have an opportunity to qualify, by his ability and initiative, for training in the trade in which he desires to specialize. If he qualifies, he may be sent direct to one of the Navy's trade schools. Those recruits not so qualified are sent to ships in active service. Being sent to a ship does not mean that the recruit has lost his chance for assignment to such a school. If he shows ability, he may later be returned to shore duty for schooling.

Upon reporting to a ship, the recruit is assigned to a definite division of the ship's company, but not until he has been interviewed and his record examined to determine for which of the stations available in the ship his ability and desires will best fit him. The attainment of specialized ratings which increase his pay, or of Petty Officer ratings, is primarily dependent upon two factors: first, the need of the Navy for men of that particular rating; and second, the man's behavior and his energy, initiative, and ability in preparing himself for advancement.

In its tabulated Rating Structure, the Bureau of Naval personnel has established approximately 200 General Service Ratings. To assist enlisted personnel in preparing themselves for advancement, the Navy conducts "on the job" training and, in addition, provides more than 200 correspondence courses, each designed to prepare the student for a particular rating. In large ships, and at most naval stations and bases, an officer is detailed as "Education Officer" to assist the men in selecting and completing such correspondence courses.

CHIEF PETTY OFFICERS

The goal of most enlisted men is to become a Chief Petty Officer. The Navy recognizes the importance of this rating by prescribing a uniform of similar cut to that of the commissioned officer and on board ship and at naval stations, where practicable, providing separate living quarters and mess for CPO's.

WARRANT OFFICERS

Warrant Officers are so called because they receive a warrant instead of a commission. A warrant, like a commission, continues in force until the holder is promoted, retires, or resigns, or until it is rescinded. During the late war, many temporary warrants were issued; most of the men holding such have permanent appointments as Chief or First-Class Petty Officers, and should the temporary warrant be revoked they will revert to their permanent status.

Warrant Officers are specialists, each in a particular line of work, such as deck duties, ordnance, electricity, engineering, or hospital duties. They are appointed from among Chief Petty Officers or, rarely, from First-Class Petty Officers who have excellent proficiency and conduct records. A Warrant Officer does not become eligible for promotion to Chief Warrant Officer until he has served three years in his appointment.

On board ship and at many stations, the Warrant Officers have a mess of their own, with specially assigned cook and mess boys. They are provided with staterooms on board ship.

Their uniforms are the same as for Chief Petty Officers except that on the sleeves of blue uniforms and on shoulder boards they wear one one-quarter-inch stripe. The cap device is slightly different, and the chin band is only one-quarter inch wide.

THE NONCOMMISSIONED WAVES

In July, 1945, the Waves attained a numerical strength of approximately 90,000 officers and enlisted women on active duty. Enlisted Waves performed nearly every type of shore duty, including duties of gunnery instructor, ballistic expert, and navigation instructor as well as those of skilled technical worker, yeoman, storekeeper, and hospital corpsman.

In recognition of their excellent work during the war, in 1948 Congress passed the "Women's Armed Services Integration Act" which made the Waves a part of the Regular Navy, and gave women a chance to make the Navy a career. Today, enlisted Waves fill twenty-seven of the Navy's sixty-four General Service ratings and are serving in overseas billets in England, France, Norway, Germany, Italy, Japan, and Newfoundland, in addition to our outlying possessions of Hawaii, Alaska, Puerto Rico, and Guam.

The Navy maintains schools for training Waves along professional lines. Waves are encouraged to develop their talents, whether they expect to remain in the Navy or return to civil life. They may earn the same Petty Officer ratings and receive equal pay and occupational advantages to those enjoyed by Navy men.

A Wave recruit must be between the ages of eighteen and twenty-five (inclusive), a high-school graduate or equivalent, a citizen of the United States, of good character and background, able to meet Navy physical and mental standards, and unmarried and without dependents. Wave recruits receive $75.00 a month base pay. They are provided with an initial outfit of Navy uniforms and regulation clothing and are furnished quarters and food. The Navy attempts to provide suitable and comfortable living for its women personnel. On many bases there are beauty parlors, cleaning and pressing shops, a Navy Exchange store, and free movies. There are also many recreational facilities.

PAY AND ALLOWANCES

The rate of pay of our Service personnel is inadequate, but they have certain privileges, such as medical care and the use of Commissaries and Exchange stores, and certain money allowances, such as those for quarters, for extra-hazardous duty, and for special qualifications, which reduce the discrepancy between Service pay and that received by persons in industry engaged in similar types of work. The pay and quarters allowance is shown in the table below. The pay grades shown by letters and numbers, which have the following meanings when expressed in rates: W-1, Warrant Officer; E-7, Chief Petty Officer; E-6, Petty Officer First Class; E-5, Petty Officer Second Class; E-4, Petty Officer Third Class; E-3, seaman, airman, or equivalent rate; E-2, apprentice; E-1, recruit of over four months' service;

			Quarters Allowance			
Pay Grade	Base Pay	Extra-Hazard-ous-Duty Pay	No Dependents	One Dependent	Two Dependents	Three or more Dependents
W–1	$219.42	$100.00	$68.40	$85.50	$85.50	$85.50
E–7	206.39	75.00	51.30	77.10	77.10	96.90
E–6	175.81	67.00	51.30	77.10	77.10	96.90
E–5	145.24	60.00	51.30	77.10	77.10	96.90
E–4	122.30	52.50	51.30	77.10	77.10	96.90
E–3	99.37	45.00	51.30	51.30	77.10	96.90
E–2	85.80	37.50	51.30	51.30	77.10	96.90
E–1	83.20	30.00	51.30	51.30	77.10	96.90
* E–1	78.00					

* E-1, recruit of less than four months' service.

The base pay as shown in the table is increased by longevity pay, which in each grade amounts to between seven and eight dollars a month for each two years of accumulated total service up to a total of twenty-two years; and for Chief Petty Officers the pay is again increased after twenty-six years' service. The quarters allowance is not paid if the government provides quarters, or if such quarters are offered and declined.

In addition to the pay stated, enlisted personnel on sea duty or on shore duty overseas receive monthly:

E-7	$22.50	E-3	$9.00
E-6	20.00	E-2	8.00
E-5	16.00	E-1	8.00
E-4	13.00		

Extra-hazardous-duty pay is paid only to enlisted personnel assigned to submarine duty or as crew members of aircraft. The sum of $50.00 a month is paid to enlisted personnel assigned to aviation as non-crew members, or for duty involving parachute jumping; as members of demolition crews; or for duty in connection with the Navy Deep Sea Diving School, Experimental Diving Unit, or Submarine Escape Tank Training. Qualified Navy divers also receive from $10.00 to $20.00 additional per month, depending upon their classification.

THE NAVAL RESERVE

The Naval Reserve has two main subdivisions: the Active Reserve and the Stand-by Reserve. The Active Reserve is subject to call to active duty upon a proclamation of national emergency by the President of the United States. The Stand-by Reserve is subject to call to active duty only upon direct action by the Congress, such as a declaration of war.

Naval Reserve personnel on active duty or in the Active Reserve are eligible for selection for promotion at the same rate as personnel of the regular service, and if selected will be promoted if they meet certain prescribed conditions. The Navy provides many correspondence courses for Naval Reserve personnel to assist them in acquiring sufficient knowledge to pass the tests for promotion.

Uniforms of Noncommissioned Personnel

Except for rating badges and service stripes the uniforms of all enlisted personnel up to Chief Petty Officers are practically identical. The rating badge, worn on the left arm between the shoulder and elbow, indicates the individual's specialty and, if a Petty Officer, his class.

There are sixty-four specialty marks of enlisted personnel. The Deck Group, for example, have crossed anchors or a steering wheel; the Ordnance Group, crossed cannon, a range finder, or a torpedo; the Administrative and Clerical Group, symbols in which appear either a quill pen or a key; the Engineering and Hull Group, a tool; the Medical and Dental Group, a caduceus; and the Aviation Group a pair of wings.

Petty Officers are indicated by one or more chevrons with point down. The Third-Class Petty Officer wears one such chevron directly under his specialty mark; the Second-Class Petty Officer, two chevrons; the First-Class, three chevrons; and the Chief Petty Officer, three chevrons with a curved band extending between the upper points of the upper chevron, enclosing the specialty mark between the chevrons and the curved band. All enlisted personnel except Chief Petty Officers wear the same type of hat, blue or white. The Chief Petty Officer wears a cap, somewhat similar to the officers' cap, but with black leather visor and chin band and as a cap device a foul anchor with the initials USN.

On blue uniforms the specialty mark is embroidered in white, and the chevrons are red. On white uniforms both the specialty marks and the chevrons are blue.

All continuous-service men wear on the left arm below the elbow one diagonal service stripe for each enlistment period they have completed. After twelve years of continuous service, if the Serviceman has a good-conduct recommendation at the end of each enlistment, the service stripes and rating badge are of gold.

Shore Duty at Home and Abroad

Normally, enlisted personnel are not assigned to shore duty until after completion of six years of sea duty. The Bureau of Naval Personnel maintains an eligibility list for assignment to shore duty and is using every effort to assign men to the location of their choice. There are many more shore billets now than formerly, a large number of them abroad or at outlying naval bases. Most tours of shore duty are for a period of two years, but at stations outside the continental limits they may be extended to three years by request.

VETERANS' BENEFITS

Officer and enlisted personnel who served on active duty during the Korean fighting are allowed many benefits. Inquiries should be made to find out to which they are eligible.

Several states have authorized veterans' benefits, some in cash, some in land, and some in scholarships.

At least five states and many other organizations provide scholarships for dependents of Service personnel killed in action. The Society of Sponsors of the United States Navy, an organization composed of ladies who have christened combatant ships of the Navy, provides two or more scholarships a year to sons of deceased or retired naval and Marine Corps personnel to preparatory schools for the United States Naval Academy.

SERVICE MEDALS AND RIBBONS

The custom of decorating those who have distinguished themselves by deeds of valor goes back a number of centuries, but until recent years it was customary to bestow decorations only upon those of high rank. In our own country during the Revolutionary and Civil wars, medals were awarded by the government to commemorate victories on land and sea, but they usually were of great size and not intended to be worn. The Commanding Officers received gold ones, which were kept on display; the subordinate officers received replicas in silver.

On December 21, 1861, by act of Congress the United States Government established its first decoration. Since that time various medals and decorations have been awarded in recognition of an act of heroism or some especially noteworthy service rendered by an individual, regardless of rank:

Medal of Honor: for conspicuous gallantry involving risk of life above and beyond the call of duty
Navy Cross: for extraordinary heroism in action against the enemy

Distinguished Service Medal: for exceptionally meritorious service to the Government of the United States in a duty of great responsibility

Silver Star: for gallantry and intrepidity in action

Legion of Merit: for exceptionally meritorious conduct in the performance of outstanding service to the Government of the United States

Distinguished Flying Cross: for heroism or extraordinary achievement in aerial flight

Navy and Marine Corps Medal: for heroic conduct not involving actual combat with an enemy

Bronze Star: for heroic or meritorious achievement or service during military operations

Air Medal: for meritorious achievement in flight

Purple Heart: to persons killed or wounded in action

There are two other medals awarded to all members of a unit which performed exceptionally meritorious service: Presidential Unit Citation, and Navy Unit Commendation.

In addition to the medals mentioned above, campaign medals are awarded to Servicemen who served in various theaters of war. These are too numerous to mention.

In the Navy, with the exception of the Medal of Honor, which is worn suspended on a blue ribbon hung around the neck, all medals are worn on the left breast, and they are worn only with dress uniforms. They are worn in rows, in order of their importance as stated above, beginning with the right on the top row. Campaign medals follow those decorations, the places of honor being given in chronological order.

On service uniforms the ribbons of the various decorations and campaign medals are substituted for such medals.

Chapter V

NAVAL AVIATION

A Navy Flyer's Creed

I am a United States Navy flyer. My countrymen built the best airplane in the world and entrusted it to me. They trained me to fly it. I will use it to the absolute limit of my power. With my fellow pilots, air crews, and deck crews, my plane and I will do anything necessary to carry out our tremendous responsibilities. I will always remember that we are part of an unbeatable combat team—the United States Navy. When the going is fast and rough, I will not falter. I will be uncompromising in every blow I strike. I will be humble in victory. I am a United States Navy flyer. I have dedicated myself to my country, with its many millions of all races, colors and creeds. They and their way of life are worthy of my greatest protective effort. I ask the help of God in making that effort great enough.

T O BE the wife, mother, or fiancee of a flying officer has its thrill, but each has a special work cut out for her. High morale among flyers is important. Domestic troubles and worries have killed more aviators than engine failure, high-tension lines, and low ceilings. Yours is a big job!

Morale of Navy Wives

Navy wives today live full lives, and wisely. Regardless of whether social, intellectual, or athletic activities occupy the days, keeping busy serves as a defense against the tension that accompanies flying. At first you may regard the regimented, organized structure of life on an air station as unnecessary and trying, but it has its psychological worth in cushioning the tension in training, the long absences from a mate, the constant change of home situation, and the sudden shock of death.

Flying is a highly specialized career; it takes more than just ability to fly. The pilot's actions at the controls must be instinctive; his judgment in an emergency must be perfect. His mind cannot be disturbed by worry over unpaid bills, the determination to make it home for the party or "bust," or the news phoned him by an unthinking wife that Johnny fell out of a tree-house and broke his arm. The arm will heal, but a mistake in judgment on the part of a pilot may claim the lives of many.

To the unsophisticated eye, the wives of flyers do not stand out as being worriers, and Navy wives carry on despite the tension by keeping more than busy. This is as it should be. Aviators are often temperamental, so be prepared to adjust your social and home life to your husband's vocation. Such adjustments are vital and necessary to his flying; early in your marriage you will find that they pay off in making for contentment and real happiness.

The Navy is seeking the country's best young men, to mold them into members of a sea-air fleet capable of maintaining control of the sea and air, supporting overseas bases required for defense, and assisting in normal peacetime industrial interchanges between nations.

There is a magic word today for young men of vision and strength and an urge to fly who also want to have a hand in great events. It is NavCad—the Navy's abbreviation for Naval Aviation Cadet. The Naval Aviation Cadet Program rewards successful candidates with commissioned rank and the opportunity to fly with the world's greatest fleet. These proud young Americans will officer the air Navy of tomorrow.

There are no deadlines for flight training classes at the Naval Air Training Command. The course lasts from one year to eighteen months including finishing school at either Corpus Christi, Texas, or Hutchinson, Kansas, where students go for advanced training. Don't worry, darlings, if you stand by while Bill and Jack take their training at the "Cradle of Naval Aviation"; you will feel very definitely that you have earned *your* wings too. Many naval aviators upon graduation present their wives with shiny new "wings of gold," a miniature of their own. Most wives pin on their husband's first wings at his designation ceremony.

"Cradle of Naval Aviation"

Pensacola, over which five different flags have flown, is a city steeped in romance. It has been the home of the Navy since 1826, when a Navy yard was built on the site of the present air station.

In the forty years that naval aviation and Pensacola have intertwined, some forty thousand pilots have been trained. Today, this training is valued at more than $69,000 per man. It is a type of training which no amount of money in civilian life could purchase. Pensacola is known as the "Cradle of Naval Aviation."

Pensacola Naval Air Station, located three miles from the city limits of Pensacola, is the headquarters of the Naval Air Training Command. Also based here is the Naval Photographic School, Naval Hospital, a Naval Flight Instructors School, the Naval School of Aviation Medicine, and a large Overhaul and Repair Department. The United States Naval School, Pre-Flight, is located at the Pensacola Naval Air Station and all student aviators report to this school when entering flight training.

The Naval Air Basic Training Command at Pensacola is composed of the main Naval Air Station and six Naval Auxiliary Air Stations (NAAS). We mention four of the activated ones because before the course is over you will probably be well acquainted with them. They are NAAS Corry Field, NAAS Saufley Field, NAAS Whiting Field, and NAAS Barin Field. The fifth, Ellyson Field, trains only helicopter pilots. This training is not included in the regular course.

A good thing to do as soon as you are settled is to get your husband to take you on an orientation tour of the station. An informed wife is certainly a better wife and your husband will be pleased if you show an interest in his work and where he works.

PRE-FLIGHT SCHOOL

First, all men who undergo flight training at present are either "cadets" or "student officers." They begin flight training at the Naval School of Pre-Flight, a separate command which is based at the Naval Air Station at Pensacola.

The first week of training is devoted to indoctrination followed by fourteen weeks of intensive training for the cadet and five for the officer . . . and further indoctrination. The course is designed to introduce the student aviator to naval life, teach him naval history, customs, traditions, and etiquette, and provide him with a thorough background of aeronautical subjects to be used when actual flight training begins.

Pre-Flight training is divided into three departments—academic, athletic, and military—each comprising an important part of the curriculum.

The Academic Department gives each student classroom study in navigation, aerology, engines, basic aerodynamics, and naval orientation.

In the Athletic Department keen minds and bodies are developed. A spirit of teamwork is necessary in naval aviation. It is instilled by competition in basketball, football, boxing, tumbling, wrestling, swimming, and other sports.

In addition, each student receives intensive training in the latest techniques of survival under all climatic conditions. Swimming is stressed and each student must pass rugged tests of swimming ability. It is during this period that the student aviator is obliged to make a satisfactory escape from the "Dilbert Dunker," a synthetic device that simulates an aircraft being ditched in the ocean and turning over.

The "Dilbert Dunker" is a mock-up, or full-scale model, of the section of a fighter plane fuselage which contains the pilot's cockpit. It is mounted on tracks which run from the top of a tower down into the water of the swimming pool.

The student climbs the tower, crawls into the "cockpit," and is strapped in with shoulder harness and safety belt just like those in an actual fighter plane cockpit. The "dunker" is then released and shoots down the rails. As its nose strikes the water, the cockpit flips over upside-down and sinks several feet below the surface of the water, but not, of course, clear to the bottom, where it would pin the pilot to the bottom of the pool. This simulates the action that takes place many times when a fighter plane is "ditched" at sea. It gives the student a dress rehearsal of the predicament he might find himself in.

At the pool (which is indoors) students also are checked out in the proper procedure to be used in slipping out of their parachute harness when parachuting down at sea, so that they will not get themselves fouled up in the shroud lines or let the big nylon canopy come down on top of them and entangle them. They are also instructed in the use of other survival equipment, how to inflate their life rafts and crawl into them, etc. Before passing any of the above tests the student must pass a swimming test to insure that he can handle himself in the water.

The Military Department, staffed principally by Marine Corps personnel, gives the student a lasting indoctrination in military administration, courtesy, and bearing.

After successfully completing the Pre-Flight course, the student approaches his first flight and one of the greatest thrills of his life. This is the day he has lived for! Students receive their primary or basic flight instructions first at Corry Field or Whiting, then at Saufley Field and Barin Field.

For advanced training they go to Corpus Christi, Texas, or Hutchinson, Kansas. Advanced training in fighters, attack planes, and multi-engine seaplanes is conducted at Corpus; advanced training in multi-engine land planes, at Hutchinson. Men who are already naval aviators may undergo helicopter training at Ellyson Field, in the Pensacola area, and "lighter-than-air" or "blimp" training at NAS Glynco, Georgia.

Everybody in aviation dreams and talks about jets. Fighter-trained pilots reporting to Advanced Training Jet Unit at NAAS Kingsville, Texas, see that dream come true.

Following completion of advanced training, all students return to Pensacola and at this time they learn why they are called naval aviators instead of merely aviators: they learn to make aircraft carrier landings. Every student makes six successful carrier landings before completing this training period.

With 250 flight hours to his credit plus six carrier landings each student is checked out after receiving a seven-hour course in the Link Trainer. By now he is ready for his Navy wings and if a Cadet, his commission in the Navy or the Marine Corps.

LIFE IN PENSACOLA

Pensacola has a rich historical background, having been sighted by Ponce de Leon in 1513. The harbor is guarded by old Fort Pickens and Fort San Carlos.

The climate is that of north Florida, quite different from that of Palm Beach. There are mild winters and hot, hot summers, although in the afternoons a refreshing breeze usually blows. Also, just because you are going to Florida, don't expect to wear a bathing suit all winter. It does get cold, and a camel's-hair topcoat or even a light fur coat will be a welcome addition to your wardrobe.

Married student officers and their wives live in town. While conditions are crowded, as in all naval and military concentration points, an adequate number of houses are available for rent or for sale as considerable building has been done in this area since the war. Warrington is a near-by suburb, and many Navy people rent apartments there or live in the Bay Shore section near the Country Club. Several new residential areas have sprung up in the Warrington area, some of them right on the bay. The subdivisions are Navy Point, Aero Vista, Pen Haven, Lakewood, Forest Park, Pinehurst, and Edgewater. Rentals run from $75.00 to $125.00 per month up, with many permanent personnel buying homes to live in during their two-year tour of shore duty. Most students do not buy, as they are continually moved from field to field and live in a highly transient state.

The popular San Carlos Hotel is located on Palafox Street, the main thoroughfare. The San Carlos cocktail lounge is a rendezvous for the Navy crowd. Around its walls is a frieze cleverly decorated with naughty Navy cartoons. In every way the San Carlos features naval aviation. Even the cocktail napkins have small planes on them. The food is exceptionally good; especially famous is the deviled crab and the sea-food plate.

Among other popular Navy gathering spots are Carpenter's in Warrington, specializing in steaks; Martine's at Mobile Circle just west of Brownsville; Bartel's just off Garden Street in downtown Pensacola, specializing in homemade wines and fried chicken; Pirate's Cove on the road to Corry Field from NAS Pensacola, specializing in exotic Oriental dishes; and Patranzino's Italian Restaurant, specializing in many elaborate Italian dishes, on East Gregory Street just off Palafox. The beautiful Driftwood Restaurant serves excellent food at reasonable prices.

Food is plentiful and reasonable in Pensacola. The fish markets are wonderful, with a wealth of sea food, including the delicious Bon Secour oysters. Everyone lives well, and at a reasonable cost in comparison with eastern and western stations.

The station offers an excellent Officers' Club and almost every type of outdoor recreational facility: tennis courts, bowling alleys, hobby shops, picnic areas, etc. The finest beaches on the Gulf coast are here. There is also a good eighteen-hole golf course, membership fees are low, instruction from a professional may be had, and many wives learn to play golf here. A water-ski beach is operated, and boats and outboard motors are available at low rentals for skiing and fishing.

Sherman Cove, a fishing camp, offers boats and motors and deep-sea fishing gear. Fishing is excellent in Pensacola waters. People have beach parties, picnics, and outings continually, and often wind up eating their own catches of crab, mullet, grouper, scallops, and red snapper.

Mustin Beach, directly behind the Mustin Beach Officers' Club, is on Pensacola Bay and offers swimming and sunbathing at an extremely convenient location all during the warm months.

The Little Theatre Group in Pensacola and the Command Performers aboard the Pensacola Naval Air Station are very active drama clubs. They are eager to welcome Navy personnel, civilian employees of the Navy, and dependents into their ranks.

The American Red Cross is an active organization, and the junior DAR welcomes Navy affiliates, as does the Navy Officers' Wives Club. Any sorority connections may prove valuable.

There are about one hundred sets of officers' quarters on the station assigned to permanent officers of all ranks. Some of these beautiful old quarters date back to the pre-Civil War days of the Navy yard. Others are recently built houses and apartments of red brick.

Corpus Christi, "Playground of Texas"

Corpus Christi, the "Playground of Texas," has always been a tourist resort and is famous for its fine fishing in summer and good hunting in winter. The climate is mild, and spring and autumn are lovely seasons. The wild flowers in spring, with Texas bluebonnets covering the countryside, are a sight you well never forget. The summers are hot, but there is generally a cool breeze from the southeast.

The Naval Air Station at Corpus Christi is located on Corpus Christi Bay at Four Bluffs, a small settlement ten miles away. The population of Corpus Christi is over 100,000. The tiny town of Four Bluffs was formerly a land of brush and sand, of coyote and rattlesnakes and chaparral. Today, large hangars replace the sand dunes; the roar of jets and bombers drowns the lonely cry of the sea gull; the sleepy fishing village has been transformed into a great modern air training station. Lightweight clothing is worn most of the year with tropical dresses for summer use. Lightweight woolens are comfortable during the intermittent cold spells called "northers," and a good warm topcoat is necessary. Warm blankets are needed for midwinter.

The most desirable location for a home is between the air station and the city. Housing units are located at Rodd Field, Cuddihy Field, and Peary Place. The enlisted men's housing at the Naval Air Station is located in the vicinity of the South Gate. Additional housing is available at the Laguna Shores Housing Project. There is also a trailer park at Rodd Field for both officers and enlisted personnel. Since there are insufficient housing units to take care of all personnel, some married men find it necessary to live in Corpus Christi, where housing is plentiful.

THE NAVAL AIR STATION AT JACKSONVILLE

Living conditions in Jacksonville are above average, and the people of Jacksonville are very proud of the Naval Air Station, which was commissioned in 1940. Its 3,600 acres are located on the south bank of the beautiful St. John's River, about ten miles south of the city.

As one of the Navy's major air stations, NAS Jacksonville is designed and operated for the support of fleet aircraft. In addition, it is a major supply point, providing naval supplies to near-by Cecil Field; Glynco, Georgia; and Green Cove Springs, Florida; and aviation supplies to many activities within the Sixth Naval District. Integrated with the Naval Air Station is the Marine Barracks, a command charged with security of the entire establishment. Aside from the Marine Barracks, five separate commands are based aboard the Naval Air Station Jacksonville.

Jacksonville, one of the South's most rapidly growing metropolises, is an active seaport but also sustains many widely diversified industries. Recently it has become known as "The Insurance Center of the South" with the location here of the headquarters of many major insurance companies. Its tight metropolitan center has a population of about 240,000, only slightly less than that of Miami.

Jacksonville is a very friendly city, offering many opportunities to Navy families in almost every field. Among the popular clubs open to naval personnel are the Yacht Club; the Timuquana Country Club; the Jacksonville Woman's Club; and the Bath Club, part of the Ponte Vedra Country Club at Ponte Vedra Beach, twenty-five miles south of the city.

Jacksonville's public beaches—Atlantic, Jacksonville, and Neptune—extend for eighteen miles along the broad ocean front as far south as Ponte Vedra.

Cultural opportunities are open in Jacksonville to those who enjoy them. The city supports its own symphony orchestra, a Civic Music Club, an active Art Center in the Riverside area, an excellent Children's Museum, and the largest Garden Club in the United States.

Jacksonville is also the home of a junior college, a boys' military school (Bolles) which is a Naval Honor School, a girls' school (Bartram), and many private schools teaching art, dancing, music, photography, and similar subjects.

Climate

The climate in northeast Florida is mild and pleasant. Medium and lightweight suits with a light topper for occasional cold spells are good for fall and winter. In the summer, which comes early, much time is spent at the beaches where swim suits, shorts, and similar resort apparel is popular. For town wear in summer, simple cottons or nylons, frequently sunback in style, are good. The same materials are used for evening and dinner dresses.

Quarters

There are 100 officers' quarters located on the station and 1,025 enlisted housing units including those in Dewey Park—a naval housing establishment directly across Roosevelt Boulevard from the station —and in the Cumberland Road development on the south edge of Jacksonville.

Senior officers' quarters are of frame construction, Southern Colonial in style, located on or near the river. Surrounding oak trees, Spanish moss, and beautiful green lawns make them cool and attractive in appearance.

Jacksonville's real growth is apparent far beyond the city limits in the rapidly expanding residential and shopping subdivisions. Popular with Navy families because of their proximity to the Naval Air

Station are those of Lake Shore, Murray Hill, Riverside, Avondale, Ortega, and Venetia.

City Housing

Most houses and even apartments are equipped with kerosene-burning circulating heaters, sufficient for the mild climate. Apartments are not hard to find, with rentals ranging from about $40.00 to $100.00 or more, depending on size and location. Usually refrigerators, stoves, and hot-water heaters are provided.

Not many houses are for rent; but Navy families with children often buy homes, making small down payments and selling to other Navy families when they leave.

The leading hotels in Jacksonville are the Roosevelt, George Washington, Seminole, and Mayflower. In addition there are many fine motels, including the Air Base Motel just outside the gates of the Naval Air Station on Roosevelt Boulevard. Rates are average.

THE NAVAL AIR STATION CECIL FIELD

The meteoric rise of Cecil Field from an auxiliary air station to its commissioning in 1952 as a master jet field with full naval air station status was due to two factors: the Korean War and the introduction of jet aircraft.

Located seventeen miles southwest of Jacksonville, it occupies about 4,600 acres. Its mission is to provide operational facilities, logistic support, and training facilities to carrier air groups and utility squadrons. At present there are three 8,000-foot runways, required by the modern jet aircraft flown by squadrons based here, and corresponding required facilities.

Housing units are few, with only about 120 available, including both officers' and enlisted quarters. However, new construction is going on at a rapid rate, and additional housing units may be added in the future.

INFORMATION—PLEASE!

Here is some general information about naval aviation that may or may not interest you upon your first perusal. But it is good data to have in the back of your mind in order to be what every man appreciates most in a woman, an intelligent listener. About the only safe rule to follow is that of the wise old owl; listen if and when you must, but give the impression of profound intelligence by keeping your knowledge to yourself.

You will hear a lot about aircraft carriers—most frequently referred to as "flattops" and also known as "the fighting ladies" of the ocean. They are the mobile landing fields of the sea. Their flat decks give them a distinctive and odd appearance. The decks are as level as a tennis court, and there is no superstructure except a single island on the starboard side on which is the bridge. Stacks are set to one side. A carrier is always under way when planes take off and land, thereby creating a wind necessary for this operation.

Aircraft carriers are divided into the following classes: attack carriers (Midway, Forrestal, and Essex classes—CVA's), escort carriers (Commencement Bay Class—CVE's), light carriers, Independence Class—CVL's), and antisubmarine carriers (Essex Class—CVS's).

FLYING TERMS

Bail out: To parachute out of a plane, in flight. Also called "hitting the silk" or "going over the side."

Blackout: Condition of temporary unconsciousness which occurs when a pilot puts excessive strain on himself in an acrobatic maneuver.

Bounce-hop: Plane or planes at landing practice, where a full stop is not made. Planes merely "touch down," continue rolling down the runway, and take off again.

Break: Synonymous with Peel off.

Cut: The LSO's signal to a pilot to "Cut the gun" and land.

Ditch: Making a forced landing on water in a land plane.

ETA: Estimated time of arrival.

ETD: Estimated time of departure.

ETE: Estimated time en route.

ETP: Equi-time point; "point of no return."

G-suit: Skin-tight flying suit worn by pilots to protect them from "blackout" or excessive force of gravity on the body causing unconsciousness.

Grey out: A mild blackout.

Hard hat: Rigid, fiberglas crash helmets worn to protect pilots' heads in single-engine aircraft, in case of a mishap.

Into the drink: Into the sea.

Join-up: Synonymous with "rendezvous"—planes join up with each other into a formation of planes.

Klunker: An old, tired, worn-out airplane.

LSO: Landing Signal Officer, who stands at the ramp on a carrier and signals flight instructions to pilot "coming up the groove" on a carrier landing.

Mae West: Inflatable rubber life jacket worn by pilots flying over water, to be inflated in case pilot goes "into the drink."

Mushing: Flying barely above stalling speed. In this condition, the plane is also said to be "hanging on the prop."

Paddles: Nickname for LSO.

Peel off: Dive out of formation, one by one.

Poopy-suit: Immersion suit worn to protect pilots from exposure to cold water, in case of mishap.

RON: Remaining overnight.

Round Robin: Flight where plane flies to a certain destination and turns around and returns without landing.

Washout: A complete strike.

Wave-off: The LSO's signal to a pilot that he cannot land on that particular "pass" at the ship, and that he must go around the landing pattern and try again.

Whirlybird: A helicopter. Also known as "chopper" and "egg beater."

Chapter VI

THE SUBMARINE SERVICE

Swish, swish, swish, the craft is diving
  Straight for a case of native wine.
Let's get boosted to the skies,
  Then go down and never rise,
We're the cruisin', shootin' boys of Subdiv. Nine!

B ILL, having spent his first year in a surface ship with the Fleet, is eligible for the Submarine School. Jack may volunteer for submarine duty from the Fleet or he may attend Submarine School direct from boot camp.

An officer or enlisted man in the submarine Service is a sub-marine-er, with the accent on the second syllable of "marine," not a *sub*-mariner!

THE SUBMARINE SCHOOL

If an officer or enlisted man asks for submarine duty, his qualifications are carefully screened. If he is accepted, he will be sent to the Submarine School located at New London, Connecticut. The course of instruction for enlisted men is of eight weeks' duration, while for officers a six months' course of study is given.

Submarine officers and enlisted men are trained to know thoroughly all parts of a submarine's equipment. They must be able to perform efficiently the duties at many stations besides the one to which they are assigned on board. The course of study includes the tactical operation of submarines, with instruction on Diesel engines and lead-acid storage batteries, electricity, torpedoes, mines, fire control, electronics, and communications. Together with these theoretical and practical studies, the students receive practical training on board submarines.

Officers who graduate are eligible, after serving one year in submarines, to take examinations for the merit designation of "Qualified in Submarines." This carries with it the privilege of wearing the

"Dolphin," submarine insignia worn on the uniform in the same manner as an aviator wears his wings. A higher degree of excellence is reached when the submariner progresses to the stage where he is designated as "Qualified for Command."

SUBMARINE QUALIFICATIONS

Bill's first year aboard submarines will be a busy one, for, in addition to his regular ship's work he will be preparing for qualification. Each submarine officer is expected to be able to operate every piece of equipment on the ship, and to prepare a notebook describing operational procedures, design characteristics, and general descriptions of the entire ship and its equipment. At the end of the year he will be examined for qualification by his division commander and the skippers of two other submarines.

Enlisted men are required to serve on board a submarine for a period of nine months before they can become qualified to wear the silver dolphin. Qualification procedures are similar but less extensive in scope than those for officers.

The Combat Pin Award, worn by both officers and enlisted men, signifies the accomplishment of a successful war patrol, the sinking of one or more ships. An additional bronze star is added for each successful patrol.

There are two special schools, one at New London, the other at Pearl Harbor, known as the PCO Schools (Prospective Commanding Officers). Every eager young submarine officer wants to complete the PCO School.

LIVING CONDITIONS IN NEW LONDON

On the whole, living conditions are about the same as in other crowded Navy ports today. However, in some ways New London might be said to have the edge on some of the more expensive stations.

During the time Bill is a student at Submarine School he will be eligible for student housing—a pleasant furnished apartment on the Submarine Base a short walk from the Submarine School. The rent is about $85.00 per month.

If after graduation Bill is assigned to a New London submarine he will no longer be eligible for his undergraduate apartment but will be able to find very adequate housing in the New London area with rentals averaging $85.00 to $125.00 per month. There are three new civilian apartment projects in New London of such proportions that it is currently possible to report for duty and secure a new apartment the same day.

There are seventy-five sets of government quarters available for married officers. Sixty of these are normally reserved for use by Submarine School officer students and the other fifteen are used for transients. In addition there are thirty Quonset huts on the base available for occupancy for periods of thirty days or less by married enlisted men. Several government-sponsored housing projects in the New London area have rents varying between $75.00 and $90.00 a month. The usual furnished and unfurnished apartments ask similar rents. Rental housing for married personnel with large families is quite difficult to find and rents are usually high. The servant situation is the same here as anywhere else. Who has servants?

The social life is pleasant. New London society is conservative, but many agreeable contacts are open to Navy personnel. The U.S. Coast Guard and Navy groups are so large that these units are absolutely self-sustaining as to social recreation, yet relations are pleasant among all branches of the government service. The U.S. Coast Guard Academy and Connecticut College for Women offer many improving opportunities as to music, literary programs, and athletic events. New Haven, with all of Yale's resources and advantages, is only fifty miles away. Social activity is very lively Navy-wise, and among civilians in and about New London.

There is a splendid Officers' Club, and an unusually active and able Navy Wives' Club for enlisted personnel. The hotels are good, but there are only two of them—the Mohican and the Crocker House. The base publishes a snappy weekly newspaper called the *Dolphin,* in which are recorded important announcements, Marine Barracks' notes, and "everything that's fit to print" about the submariners at New London.

A VISIT TO A SUBMARINE BASE

For almost a year, on our frequent visits to the Pearl Harbor Navy Yard, we had been curious about that tall silo-looking building, as high as an eight-story skyscraper, that overlooked the harbor. We thought of it as a naval observation tower or lookout, but after much questioning we were finally informed that it was a submarine escape training tank.

There is another one of these unique structures at the submarine base at New London, and it is in these tanks that the training of a submariner begins. The early subs acquired the name "pig boats" because of their shape and because living conditions used to be very unsanitary. Vast improvements have been made and today the sub is the only completely air-conditioned craft in the Navy. Owing to a higher ration allowance, the finest food obtainable is served. The limited space makes it necessary to carry many fresh frozen foods; even the meats are trimmed and all bones removed before being taken on board. Vitamin tablets and sun lamps take the place of sun for the submerged crews when the submarines are in operation. We also learned that these death-dealing ships do not carry big guns or heavy armor. Their mission is to lurk beneath the waves with their deadly torpedoes and to fire when they are at periscope depth or even deeper. They can imperil any vessel afloat, and they regard themselves quite legitimately as very nasty customers indeed for an enemy to tangle with in a close engagement.

The submarine is also an excellent long-distance scout; it is used to locate enemy fleets, to observe enemy ports and coasts, and to disrupt enemy trade. We were intrigued by the distinctive black-hulled vessels lying mostly under water, and interested in their "toothpick" periscopes showing above the thin superstructure deck and conning tower.

The submariner believes that his ship is the safest type of vessel afloat because it is practically impossible to capsize it, and in case of a hurricane or typhoon he can submerge below the swirling water and find peace in the quiet sea one hundred feet below the surface.

First Steps to Becoming a Submariner

The Navy does everything thoroughly and efficiently, even to simply conducting a sightseeing tour around a sub base.

Anxious to see the various stages of training to which a submariner is subjected, we were first taken to the decompression escape chamber located in the small examination room at the base of the training tank. No chances are taken on the stamina and the physical condition of the men who must meet the rigorous emergencies of submarine life. The physical checkup covers eyes, ears, nose, throat, heart, and lungs. Special attention is given to the teeth to be sure they are in good condition for holding the mouthpiece of the Momsen lung apparatus.

The "Torture" Chamber

After the physical examination the men fit for underwater tests are placed in the compression chamber. This huge thermos bottle affair accommodates about fifteen students and two instructors. In it is given the real test to determine whether the men can take it!

We looked into it warily at first, then pulling our skirts together went through the hatch to investigate. We were thankful not to have to take the test, since the sight of this famous torture chamber gave us a violent attack of claustrophobia. It is often called the ear-cracking machine, and many dire and dreadful stories have had their beginnings in its interior.

This may or may not mean anything to you, gentle reader, but "the normal air pressure at sea level is 14.7 pounds per square inch, and in this chamber as a test the pressure is stepped up to 50 pounds, which is the equivalent of the pressure at 110 feet below the surface of the water."

If a man can't take the pressure, and becomes ill or faints, he is removed from the inner chamber to a small outer chamber, where the pressure is gradually brought back to normal. The instructors tell some droll stories about the consternation and fright of the mess attendants on their first tests; however, everyone who serves in a submarine must take the tests, even if his main job is making coffee and spreading sandwiches.

The Momsen Lung

The Momsen lung is so called after its inventor, Rear Admiral Charles B. Momsen, USN. It was given the name "lung" because it really acts as a third lung. As the word is monosyllabic, it lends itself well for quickly conveying to the minds of the submarine crew, in case of accident, that they are to equip themselves with the device and be prepared for individual escape.

The lung itself looks like a large hot-water bottle made of stockinet with one strap which fits around the neck to hold it up, another strap which fits around the waist to hold it down, and two small metal clamps by which it is clamped to the trousers to prevent its floating upward on the wearer's body when he is submerged.

Have you ever had a basal metabolism test? Well, the rest of the apparatus, from the rubber tube that fits in the mouth to the sturdy clothespin clamps that fit on the nose making breathing through the nostrils impossible, resembles that complicated piece of machinery employed in hospitals for such tests.

The explanation of the innards of the lung—and believe it or not, that almost human thing has "a heart which is a canister filled with soda lime" to absorb the carbon-dioxide generated in the lungs of the user—is much too complicated, with its various cut-off and flutter valves, for me to go into. Suffice it to say that "its function is to maintain equilibrium at all times between internal pressures and pressures of the surrounding water, thus keeping the bag at buoyancy irrespective of the depths of the water from which the ascent is made." The lung is designed to furnish a respirable supply of air during ascent and decompression by utilizing, in conjunction with an initial oxygen inflation of the bag, the air which is compressed in the wearer's body when a submarine is flooded preparatory to crew escape.

Tank Training

Now for the escape training tank!

Of course there is a spiral stairway winding around the tank, but the day was hot so we chose the elevator in the adjoining tower to carry us up to the top.

Once inside the cylindical tank, we walked around the enclosed circular platform at the top of the pool and stared down into the tube of fresh water one hundred feet deep. It looked very cool and inviting on such a hot day. The water is filtered through sand, chlorinated, and kept at a temperature of 92 degrees. A dozen or so students are sent to the tower at a time to begin lung training. This is one of the first steps toward qualifying as a submariner. Not cheerful, but a wise procedure.

The student must first learn how to make an emergency escape from a sunken submarine; and not only a student but every submariner from Admiral to the lowest-ranking mess attendant must repeat his training and "come up in the tank" to requalify once a year. There are three levels in the tank, 18, 50, and 100 feet. At the 100-foot level a picture of an alluring mermaid is painted on the wall of the tank. A very impressive certificate is presented to the 100-foot ascenders. The student is introduced to his escape training by easy stages. Standing by at all times are expert swimmers and divers, the instructors, and a medical officer.

A detailed explanation of every part of the lung, what it is for and how it is used, is given by the instructors. Demonstrations in the use of the lung are also given by the instructors. Preliminary ascents by students are made from various shallow depths, not greater than eighteen feet. At some time during this stage of training the student is required to make at least one stop between eighteen feet and the surface, for a period of about thirty breaths, to insure his proper breathing in the lung, all the time holding on to the ascending line. Having experimented, so to speak, with the lung, the student gains confidence when he finds how easy it is to breathe under water when wearing this device.

After having qualified in the use of the lung, all submarine personnel are required annually to make an ascent from the eighteen-foot depth. There are two side locks in the escape training tank which permit ascents from eighteen and fifty feet. There is also a submarine compartment at the hundred-foot level. All ascents from the hundred-foot side lock are voluntary. The lung not only enables a man to escape from a sunken submarine but will support the wearer as a life jacket when he reaches the surface. The process of emerging from a sunken submarine is the same as that which submarine personnel experience in emerging from a side lock or compartment at the escape training tank.

To ascend too rapidly, even from a shallow depth of fifteen feet, might prove fatal. In 1931 a sailor wearing a Momsen lung merely held his breath and allowed himself to shoot to the surface like a cork in a fraction over two seconds. The post-mortem report was as follows: "The deceased, after appearing on the surface, closed the shut-off valve and then reached for the ladder to ascend the float, but was unable to grasp it and fell backward. He breathed a few times and expired. The autopsy revealed numerous hemorrhages throughout both lungs, etc. The right ventricle of the heart was definitely dilated."

All of which is a technical way of saying that his lungs exploded.

Students are warned about the danger of making quick ascents, and also about the fact that their safety depends upon carrying out directions to the letter.

The Rescue Chamber

The submarine rescue chamber, another ingenious device, was responsible for saving the lives of thirty-three members of the ill-fated *Squalus* in 1939. It is an immense steel structure 10 feet high having a weight of 18,000 pounds. It is designed to be hauled down on to the hatch of a sunken submarine by a wire attached to the hatch. A total of nine men may be taken aboard the rescue chamber at one time. Once contact has been established, the chamber may make repeated trips from the surface to the submarine quite rapidly. To get a good idea of the prodigious job accomplished in rescue work and in raising a submarine from the bottom of the sea, see the various works of Commander Edward Ellsberg, who is an authority on the subject. He has directed and taken an active part in the raising of several sunken craft.

DEEP-SEA DIVING

The movies have a way of making deep-sea divers very romantic and glamorous, but there isn't anything especially romantic about weighting oneself down with 195 pounds of equipment and floundering about in the mud on the floor of the ocean. After being lowered into the water, the diver inflates his suit with air and floats, then slowly lets out the air and settles to the bottom. There is no trick in sinking, but great care is necessary when he is ready to make his ascent.

While the diver is at work, he is dependent upon the crew above on the submarine tender. Someone is holding his life line and air hose, and altough there is telephone communication, the diver isn't very talkative. The heavy air pressure makes it difficult to talk and also tends to make him a bit groggy.

The great danger is a form of paralysis known as "the bends" or caisson disease. It is the dread of all men who work far beneath the water. Here is the way an old-timer describes the bends:

Under the air pressure the blood is full of air bubbles. If a diver returns to the surface too fast, bubbles remain in the blood stream, collect and settle in a certain area, such as the leg, back or arm. The victim of the bends is stricken suddenly with severe pain which may jump from one section of the body to another. One of the men described it as an almost unbearable pain, as of needles sticking in the body, or severe cramps. Oftentimes, the victim loses consciousness. The only relief is to get under pressure in a decompression chamber, where the pressure is built up as fast as possible. In some cases, it is necessary for the patient to remain in the decompression chamber for several hours. If the attendant has to stay in the decompression chamber too long, he is apt to become a victim of the bends himself—upon leaving. In a severe case of bends, the diver's body remains sore for several weeks. The sore muscles and tissues are like a sprain, caused by the expanding air bubbles.

The world's record dive, without artificial breathing aids, was made in Hawaii in 1915 at the time the F-4 was lost in 300 feet of water about a mile from the docks in Honolulu. It was made by Frank Crilly, a commercial diver, who located the F-4 nearly a month after she went down.*

Tea on Board the Submarine *Gudgeon*

On January 25, 1941, one of the authors of this book had the honor of christening the *Gudgeon*, one of our largest submarines. Almost a year later she was invited aboard the *Gudgeon* and was kind enough to include her collaborator in the invitation.

A submarine is divided into eight or ten compartments and the conning tower; each is separate, watertight, and capable of sustaining human life for many hours, possibly days.

The duties of each officer are highly specialized. It is obvious that the amount of responsibility placed on the junior officers is tremendous. If and when a submariner transfers back to the line, he is usually in demand for key positions because of his command experience while serving in submarines.

Having entered the conning tower from the bridge we went below to the control room by way of a vertical ladder. (By all means wear low-heeled shoes if you visit a submarine.) The control room is the diving station of the ship, where, during a dive, the diving officer watches intently the "Christmas Tree," a broad panel of red and green electric signals, to insure that all hatches and hull openings are secure.

We were next escorted into the officers' country. We marveled at

* Virginia Hill, "Workers under the Sea," in the Feature Section of the Honolulu *Star-Bulletin*, Saturday, November 8, 1941.

the modern last-word equipment. The whole interior resembled the accommodations of a Pullman car. Not a single inch of space was wasted, from the compact galley with the kitchen utensils stowed away in the smallest space to the tiny narrow sleeping rooms shared by two officers. The Captain rated a tiny cubicle to himself, and the wardroom was furnished with a dining table which seated six comfortably, and eight at a pinch. The sides of the wardroom above the built-in comfortable leather seats were lined with cabinets holding the linen, silver, dishes, and glassware used in the mess. On a small built-in serving buffet an electric appliance kept coffee hot at all times for the officers. On the wall hung a picture of Mrs. Pye, the sponsor, taken at the christening of the *Gudgeon*. Directly beneath was a brass plaque which read:

U. S. S. GUDGEON
KEEL LAID NOVEMBER 22, 1939
AT NAVY YARD MARE ISLAND
CALIFORNIA
LAUNCHED JANUARY 25, 1941
SPONSOR
MRS. WILLIAM S. PYE
COMMISSIONED APRIL 21, 1941

Air conditioning added greatly to the comfort of the ship, and on this particularly hot day we were served delicious iced lemonade and cookies in the wardroom before continuing our tour of the ship.

We passed on to the crew mess where quarters were available for the men. (The crew also had bunks located in forward and after torpedo rooms.) This was called the after battery, because the area was located over the rear batteries of the ship. Bunks seemed to fold up into the most unusual places, but each was furnished with a rubber air-foam mattress, the last word in downy sleeping accouterments. Both officers and enlisted men enjoyed the showers with hot and cold running water. The men not on duty were quite happy and at ease as they sipped cups of steaming coffee and played the old Navy game, acey-deucy. Other members of the crew, on duty, were busy at their individual posts.

The engine room would have made the heart of any chef take a turn, for it somehow had the glistening beauty of a big kitchen. The engines, believe it or not, were immaculate white beasts, and the room itself, aside from the necessary lubricating oil, was beautifully clean. But oh! the noise!

The torpedo room, with its torpedoes nestled down in their cradles, waiting only to be loaded into tubes and to have the firing key pressed to send them streaking through the water, was really not very interesting until suddenly we realized that here was the whole reason for this thing. Extra torpedoes were packed into converted space, and the crew had their bunks practically on top of the torpedoes. Nice little bedfellows! The men were busy preparing exercise torpedoes for firing. Practice torpedoes have yellow heads, so that after exercise runs, when floating on the water they are more easily visible.*

Submarines are named for fish. For example, *Cat Fish, Sea Leopard, Capitaine, Entemedor, Pomfret, Segundo, Char, Flying Fish, Diodon, Sea Devil, Trumpetfish, Perch,* and *Tile-fish.* Submarine tenders or auxiliaries are usually named for submarine heroes or stars.

The Submarine Service is a highly specialized and progressive branch of the Navy, and great strides are being made in the experimental field. Some of the newly developed types of submarines are as follows:

1. Nuclear submarine: The Navy's first nuclear-powered ships (*Nautilus, Sea Wolf*).
2. Fast attack submarine: Ships designed and built after the end of World War II, containing most of the improvements World War II submariners desired including snorkel, latest electronic devices, and high submerged speed (*Trigger* and *Gudgeon*).
3. Guppy type submarine: Streamlined modifications of World War II submarines with snorkel added (*Trumpetfish* and *Clamagore*).
4. Radar picket submarine: Developed for aircraft control work in operations with carrier task forces (*Redfin* and *Ray*).
5. Antisubmarine submarine: Fitted with ultrasensitive sonar equipment to track down enemy submarines (*K1* and *K2*).
6. Guided missile submarine: Designed to carry and launch Navy guided missiles (*Cusk* and *Cargonero*).
7. Cargo and transport submarines: Designed to carry troops and equipment for advanced amphibious landings (*Sea Lion* and *Perch*).

* The *Gudgeon* was lost in 1944.

Submarine squadrons are currently based in New London, Connecticut; Norfolk, Virginia; Key West, Florida; San Diego, California; and Pearl Harbor, Hawaii. Bill will be asked while at Submarine School to indicate his choice of area assignments and will be ordered to the place of his choice if it is at all possible.

Submarine Service, a Friendly Service

It is good to know that the custom of exchanging calls has been revived among submariners. New arrivals should call on their Squadron Commander and the Division Commanders of their squadron. The purpose of the exchange of calls is to permit the newcomer to become acquainted. Calls should normally be made within two weeks after reporting aboard. They should be made again when there are changes in the senior officers mentioned above. Calls should also be exchanged between other officers on the staff, plankowners making the first call on the new arrivals. (A plankowner is an officer longer in residence on the station than the newcomer.)

Junior officers should call on their Commanding Officer and Executive Officer, and should also exchange calls with shipmates, plankowners always making the first call on new arrivals. Here are a few general rules of calling procedure:

All calls should be returned, within ten days or two weeks.

Officers leave one calling card for each adult member of the family.

Officers' ladies leave one calling card for each adult lady of the family.

Hours for calling are from 4 to 6 P.M., though on some stations evening calls from 8 to 9 P.M. have been inaugurated.

A call should last not more than twenty minutes or less than fifteen minutes. Should the volume of return calls become too great, "at homes" will probably be utilized.

It is a custom in both commissioned and noncommissioned circles of the Navy to make newly joined members of an organization feel at ease and at home. It is proper and commendable for everyone to make an effort to help the new arrival become adjusted.

Atomic Sub Crews

The U.S.S. *Nautilus*, whose keel was laid in June, 1952, at Groton, Connecticut, will be the first submarine to be propelled by a nuclear power plant. No, we do not understand anything but the words either, but perhaps your submariner husband will read you in, especially should he be selected to take training. The instruction includes theory, design, construction, and operation of the nuclear submarine propulsion machinery. The trainees stand machinery watches and perform emergency drills exactly as they will in the completed submarine. The schools are located in Pittsburgh, Pennsylvania, and at Arco, Idaho.

Guided missiles launched from submarines promise to be major offensive weapons in case of war. A missile of this type is said to travel to its distant destination under unerring electronic orders.

Chapter VII

THE MARINE CORPS

From the halls of Montezuma
To the shores of Tripoli;
We fight our country's battles
In the air, on land and sea;
First to fight for right and freedom
And to keep our honor clean;
We are proud to bear the title
Of United States Marine.

Marine Hymn

THE Marine Corps is one of the most colorful branches of the United States Military and Naval Service. Rear Admiral Lovette has put it strikingly: "Marines have been landing as sea soldiers from ships of war on foreign shores since the dawn of recorded history. It is written that the Marines of Phoenicia, Greece, Egypt, Carthage and Rome had similar duties to the Marines of today, in that they were the soldiers on board fighting ships, and were usually the 'spear head' in landing operations." *

The Continental Congress on November 10, 1775, authorized the raising of two battalions of Marines, and for that reason November 10 has been officially designated as the birthday of the Marine Corps and has been so observed by the Corps since 1921.

Marines played a vivid part in the War of 1812, and in 1846 they marched to Mexico and stormed the Castle of Chapultepec in the most spectacular battle of the Mexican War. Out of this encounter they brought home two mementos: the first line of the Marine Hymn, "From the halls of Montezuma," referring to the Mexican chief and his castle; and the red stripe, worn on the blue trousers of officers and noncommissioned officers, commemorating to this day service in that war.

* Leland P. Lovette, *Naval Customs, Traditions and Usage.* United States Naval Institute, Annapolis, 1934.

Marines served in the Civil War. Under Colonel Huntington they took Guantánamo in the Spanish-American War in 1898, landing from the U.S.S. *Marblehead*. They were with Admiral Dewey the same year, and in 1900 in Peking they helped suppress the Boxer Rebellion. Since 1900 they have operated in China, Korea, Siberia, the Philippines, Hawaii, Cuba, Mexico, Nicaragua, Hati, Dominican Republic, France, and Germany. They were ashore at Vera Cruz in 1914, and in 1915 they occupied Haiti, where they stayed until 1934. Many uneasy and volatile West Indian and Central American republics have become acquainted with them in a professional way.

In World War I the Fifth and Sixth Regiments of Marines at Belleau Wood and at Château-Thierry established an enviable record for their corps. General A. W. Catlin tells the story of some distinguished visitors who were passing the cots in a military hospital in France. On one of the cots lay a man, quite still, with his face buried in a pillow. Something about him caused one of the visitors to remark, "I think this must be an American soldier." From the depths of the pillow came a muffled voice: "Hell, no; I'm a Marine!"

In World War II, the Marines were the first to land in every island-hopping operation from Guadalcanal to Okinawa. They established a reputation for efficiency in the conduct of amphibious operations which all the world's military forces envy. They proved the worth of troops trained specifically in the conduct of amphibious operations and established beyond a doubt their right to existence as a separate corps. Even the earlier superb record of the Marines was embellished by their achievements in World War II.

Every capital ship carries a detachment of Marines. The rank and file are good enough Latinists to know the meaning of *"Semper fidelis,"* which is their slogan, and they are proud to live up to it. Detachments of Marines also serve at American embassies all over the world.

Marine Corps Organization

The Marines are essentially ground forces with a strong aviation component, trained specifically for the conduct of amphibious operations. They are organized as a Corps under the Secretary of the Navy and, for purposes of administration, discipline, and training in land warfare, constitute an independent branch. Their training for amphibious operations is co-ordinated with that of the Navy under Naval Amphibious Training Commands. Marines normally serve with the Navy but, as in World War I, by direction of the President they may be assigned to service with the Army. Except when serving with the Army, the Corps is governed by Navy regulations.

The Marine Corps Headquarters is in the Navy Department in Washington, D.C. The Commandant has the rank of General.

The organized fighting forces of the Marine Corps compose Fleet Marine Force. Fleet Marine Force Atlantic, with headquarters at Norfolk, Virginia, includes the 2d Marine Division, Marine Corps Base, Camp Lejeune, North Carolina; the 2d Marine Aircraft Wing, Marine Corps Air Station, Cherry Point, North Carolina; and the 3d Marine Aircraft Wing, Marine Corps Air Station, Miami, Florida. Fleet Marine Force Pacific, with headquarters in Hawaii, consists of the 1st Marine Aircraft Wing, the 1st Marine Division, and the 3d Marine Division, all stationed in the Far East.

The Marine Corps Wife

This topic is in itself well worthy of a special book, but suffice it to say that the wives of all Marines are made of pretty stern stuff! They have to be, in order to be good helpmates to the men they marry. Definitely, the Marine Corps is no place for the hothouse-plant type of wife.

Every Marine wife is as completely proud of the Corps as the Marines are who perpetuate its fine reputation. The Marine creed is "Not to let a fellow Marine down on the battlefield." A Marine wife's creed is "Not to let *her* fighting man down while *he* is on that battlefield." Accordingly, a Marine's wife must accustom herself to "carrying on" for long periods alone, just like the Navy wife, the Air Force wife, and the Army wife of today. Because Marines through the years have been the "first to fight," Marine wives have always had to adjust themselves to sudden moves and departures. Nothing in the way of unexpected orders surprises them.

The Marine Uniform Today

The field uniform of the Marine Corps is forestry green for winter and khaki for summer. The insignia of rank for commissioned officers corresponds with the relative rank of officers of the Army. The dress uniform is the famous dark-blue blouse (known as serge-blue) with the yellow-and-red sleeve markings and chevrons, the light-blue trousers (known as sky-blue), the white cloth belt with highly polished buckle, the cordovan shoes and visored cap.

The summer dress uniform for officers is white, and similar to the dress blue in design. On the enlisted dress blue uniform, the insigne of rank is in scarlet and gold (official Marine Corps colors). On the officer and enlisted blue trousers (NCO's above the rank of corporal) there is a scarlet stripe. This is in commemoration of the blood that was spilled in the Battle of Chapultepec during the Mexican War.

The rank of NCO (or noncommissioned officer) is shown by the chevrons worn on both arms of the blouse and overcoat, and on the sleeves of the khaki shirt. Chevrons are stenciled on the combat utility uniform. However, in the Marine Corps no insigne is needed, since an NCO is known by his bark and his bearing.

PRINCIPAL MARINE POSTS AND STATIONS

Marine Corps Base, Camp Pendleton, near Oceanside, California
Marine Corps Base, Camp Lejeune, near Jacksonville, North arolina

Marine Corps Air Station, Cherry Point, North Carolina
Marine Corps Air Station, Miami, Florida
Marine Corps Air Station, El Toro, Santa Ana, California
Marine Corps Air Station, Kaneohe, Hawaii

Marine Corps Recruit Depot, Parris Island, South Carolina
Marine Corps Recruit Depot, San Diego, California

Marine Corps School, Quantico, Virginia
Marine Corps Clothing Depot, Philadelphia, Pennsylvania
Marine Corps Supply Center, Barstow, California
Marine Corps Supply Center, Albany, Georgia

CAMP PENDLETON

Camp Pendleton is a wartime development provided for the housing and training of a large number of troops. It extends along the coast highway, U.S. 101, for a distance of nearly twenty miles between Oceanside and San Clemente. It comprises an area of nearly two hundred square miles, most of which is the former Santa Margarita Ranch.

On-station housing is good, consisting of 332 housing units for officers and 2,378 housing units for enlisted men; 3,076 housing units are available off the station.

There is a school on the base at Pendleton which is operated by the Fall Brook School District.

The Santa Margarita Naval Hospital is located within the limits of the base and has a section available for the treatment and hospitalization of the dependents of Marine Corps personnel.

Recreational facilities include an Officers' Club, tennis courts, and a golf club which is under construction. Sea bathing and fishing are available for those who enjoy such sports.

CAMP LEJEUNE

Camp Lejeune, at New River, North Carolina, was established some years before World War II for the housing and training of a Marine division on the Atlantic coast. The reservation consists of about 85,000 acres and has a water frontage of eighteen miles on New River and fourteen miles on the Atlantic Ocean, with a continuous stretch of beautiful beach. Most of the reservation is wooded, and every effort is being made to preserve as many trees as possible so as to retain the natural beauty of the place.

On-station housing consists of 883 housing units for officers and 4,026 units for enlisted personnel. Off-station housing offers 4,805 units in the towns of near-by Jacksonville, Morehead City, Surf City, Swansboro, Wrightsville Beach, and New Topsail Beach. In addition, housing is available in New Bern, New River, and Tarawa Terraces. This building program has greatly helped the housing situation for both officers and enlisted men. Splendid shopping centers have been set up in each community.

New Bern is thirty-eight miles northeast of Jacksonville. It is one of the oldest settlements in the state. The leading hotel is the Queen Anne.

Wilmington is fifty miles southwest of Jacksonville and has a population of 50,000. It has excellent railroad service, being on the Atlantic Coast Line R.R. route, and is also a bus terminal. There are good schools, a country club, two golf courses, and several libraries. Its leading hotel is the Cape Fear.

A private car is a necessity at New River. In addition to being the chief means of transportation, it will be a great source of pleasure

since there are many interesting places within easy motoring distance.
An Officers' Club, tennis courts, and a golf course provide recreation. The sea bathing and fishing are excellent. Bird and squirrel hunting are allowed on the reservation (with shotguns only).

CHERRY POINT, NORTH CAROLINA

Located fifty miles from Camp Lejeune is the Marine Corps Air Station at Cherry Point, North Carolina. On-station housing consists of 3,169 units for officers and enlisted men. The community supports 2,059 housing units. A fine Officers' Club and a beautiful NCO Club located on the river are available. The main drawback to Cherry Point is its isolation and lack of social life for unmarried personnel.

MIAMI, FLORIDA

There are only 215 housing units for officers and enlisted men on the Marine Corps Air Station but the community offers 1,523 housing units near by.

EL TORO, CALIFORNIA

The Marine Corps Air Station at El Toro is located between the coast and the town of Santa Ana. On-station there are 366 housing units for officers, 894 units for enlisted personnel. Near-by towns, including Laguna, offer 2,384 housing units. The naval hospital at Long Beach cares for dependents requiring hospitalization. Near-by March AFB Hospital at Riverside is also available in emergencies.

Recreation is afforded by an Officers' Club and at coast towns there is sea bathing and fishing.

KANEOHE, HAWAII

Known as the Leatherneck City is the Marine Corps Air Station at Kaneohe Bay on the windward side of Oahu. Activated on January 19, 1953, it is the home base of the crack First Provisional Marine Air-Ground Task Force, FMF. At present there are 286 on-station housing units, 481 off-station housing units. The on-station housing unit has been christened "Termite Village" by its inhabitants.

Marine air groups' Panther jets zoom through the air above Kane-

ohe Bay at speeds of over 600 miles an hour in all weather, day and
night.

MARINE BARRACKS, QUANTICO, VIRGINIA

The Marine base at Quantico, Virginia, was the first base established for training fighting units of the Marine Corps, but the Corps
has outgrown it, and such training is done at Camp Lejeune and Camp
Pendleton. Quantico is now the center of schooling for the Marine
Corps.

Located on the Potomac River about one hour from Washington
by automobile, the reservation comprises 6,000 acres. There are
a large number of married officers' quarters but not enough for
all. There are no hotels in the vicinity, and only a few small, unat-
tractive houses (furnished) in the village of Quantico. A few tourist
homes may be found at Dumfries, three miles from the post, but
most people who do not have quarters prefer to live in Fredericksburg
and commute. There are 590 housing units for officers and 851 units
for enlisted personnel. Off-station 634 units are available.

A modern brick school is located on the post with grades from
kindergarten through high school. There is also an excellent nursery
school. The schools are supervised by the Virginia School Board.
Transportation problems are solved by school busses.

A naval hospital on the post takes care of the officers and enlisted
men and their dependents.

For recreation there is an Officers' Club which serves regular meals.
There are tennis courts, a swimming pool, a golf course, bowling
alleys, and a skeet range, also a modern gymnasium available for the
use of officers and their families free of charge.

An outstanding development at Quantico is a $750,000 Hostess
House. It serves as a hotel and is equipped with a cafeteria, a gymnasium, bowling alleys, a well-stocked Post Exchange, and cobbler
and tailor shops. It also houses a thrilling exhibit of Marine uniforms
on wax figures, and relics and documentary history dating back to
1775. The center of the building is occupied by an air-conditioned
auditorium with a seating capacity of about 3,000. There is a large
stage on which the latest movies are shown, besides plays, radio programs, and road shows.

Though the climate is very much like that of Washington, D.C., the summer heat is less oppressive. Except for short periods there are no extremes of temperature.

RECRUIT TRAINING DEPOT, SAN DIEGO

The Marine base at San Diego, now called a Recruit Training Depot, was the original Marine training center on the west coast. Owing to the increased size of the Corps and the extension of training activities, it became inadequate and such training is now conducted at Camp Pendleton. Activities at San Diego are restricted primarily to the basic training of recruits.

There are only 44 housing units for officers at the Recruit Training Depot, with 408 available housing units for enlisted personnel. Off-station housing offers 1,185 units. Marine personnel attached to the base usually live in or near San Diego, Loma Portal, and Mission Hills, popular suburbs. There are few apartments, and the many small houses of the bungalow type available for renting are hard to get because of the demand. It is desirable to obtain a house with adequate heating facilities. Remember the old saying of the tourist who "went to California for the winter—and *got* it."

A car is most desirable, although there is good bus service. The Bank of America furnishes an excellent map of the city, which is an absolute necessity, as you will find when you try to ferret your way around the numerous canyons on your way to call or shop.

There aren't any servants except for those persons who can afford to pay California taxes and are down to their last yacht. The best most people can do is a part-time maid. Wages are high even for these, and a trained general servant's wages are exorbitant. If you have a good servant, by all means bring her with you.

As few families live on the post, the principal recreation facilities are those normally found in a city. There are, however, two excellent Officers' Clubs, one at the Marine base and one at the air station, on North Island, which is reached via Coronado, across the bay from San Diego. There are several popular hotels and civilian clubs in San Diego.

RECRUIT TRAINING DEPOT, PARRIS ISLAND

The Recruit Training Depot, Parris Island, provides basic training for Marines recruited in the eastern portion of the United States.

Parris Island is located about sixty miles south of Charleston, South Carolina. The nearest towns are Beaufort and Port Royal.

Available at the Depot are 111 housing units for officers and 215 units for enlisted personnel. Officers' families which cannot be housed on the post usually live in Port Royal or Beaufort. A causeway connects Parris Island with the mainland in order to facilitate communication.

Being some distance from the nearest city, the post has been made self-sustaining by providing a Commissary store, Post Exchange, laundry, tailor shop, and similar services.

For recreation an Officers' Club, swimming pool, tennis courts, and golf course are available. Hunting and fishing are good.

MARINE DEPOT, PHILADELPHIA

The Marine Depot, Philadelphia, is an equipment depot where all articles for the use of the Marines are assembled for issue to the various posts and organizations as may be required. In addition, there is a factory, familiarly known as "the pants factory," in which all Marine uniforms are made.

Officers attached to the depot live in Philadelphia or near-by suburbs.

THE MARINE CORPS PERSONNEL

Many Marine officers are Naval Academy men who upon graduation chose the Marine Corps as the branch in which they preferred to serve. The great majority are college graduates who during summer vacations qualified for appointment as Marine officers by attending Platoon Leader Training Courses, which are conducted annually. Others are former members of the Marine Corps Reserve who during the war demonstrated such high efficiency that they were transferred to the Regular Service. And many others are men who while serving as noncommissioned officers proved their ability as leaders of men and showed the efficiency and excellent character required of commissioned officers.

The reputation of the Marines as "tough fighting men" and their smart appearance and strong morale appeal to the highest type of American youth. As a consequence, the standard of recruits is very good. There is no finer body of fighting men.

Women in the Marine Corps

During World War II women were enrolled as officers and enlisted in the Marine Corps Reserve. Although women have served as "regulars" in the Marine Corps only since Congress authorized their permanent status on June 12, 1948, their service in the Corps began in 1918. A few hundred uniformed enlisted women reserves filled clerical billets in World War I, and in World War II a peak strength of 18,838 officers and enlisted women reserves served in hundreds of capacities. Their slogan was "Free a Marine to Fight."

Although most of the women were demobilized at the end of the war, a trained nucleus was retained which proved itself ready when rapid mobilization was ordered at the outbreak of fighting in Korea in June, 1950.

To be eligible for enlistment, a girl must be at least eighteen but not yet thirty-one years old, single, with no dependents, a high-school graduate, a citizen of the United States (or, if an alien, approved by the Commandant of the Marine Corps), and of excellent health and character.

The training center for enlisted Women Marines is at Parris Island, South Carolina; for officers, at Quantico, Virginia. After six weeks of intensified training, in which the enlisted woman is taught the fundamentals of Marine Corps administration, history, military justice, customs and courtesies, and other subjects designed to prepare her for her role in the military establishment, she is assigned a job at a Marine Corps post or station. She may be assigned to any type of duty except actual combat.

Women Marines are currently serving in the fields of administration, supply, motor transport, disbursing, communications, classification, recruiting, public information, photography, special services, and aviation. As a private with less than four months' service, a Woman Marine earns $75.00 a month; $80.00 when she has served over four months.

A Woman Marine with a college degree or the ability to pass a four-year college equivalency test and meeting the other requirements (i.e., physically qualified, a United States citizen, unmarried, and between twenty-one and twenty-seven years of age) may apply for a commission into officer ranks. The Women Marines have proved their worth.

Chapter VIII

THE COAST GUARD

T HE United States Coast Guard dates from August 4, 1790, on which day President Washington signed the bill authorizing Alexander Hamilton, the first Secretary of the Treasury, to construct "ten boats" to be operated with the objective of suppressing smuggling along the coast and of insuring the collection of tonnage dues and import duties from vessels entering United States ports.

During the early years of its existence, this organization was called the Revenue Marine; later, the Revenue Cutter Service; and since 1915, the Coast Guard. Because the Continental Navy was abolished at the end of the Revolutionary War and not re-established until 1798, the Coast Guard is claimed to be the oldest of the nation's seagoing armed forces as they exist today.

Immediately preceding and during the Revolutionary War, as a protest against British "Taxation without representation," smuggling had been encouraged in order to deprive the British government of the duties upon imports into the colonies imposed by the British Parliament. By the time the Revolutionary War was over and the United States of America created, the habit of smuggling had become so general that many citizens continued to avoid paying taxes and duty upon imported goods.

This wholesale smuggling was robbing the Treasury, and it was Alexander Hamilton's duty to correct the situation. He took his headache to Congress, and immediately that worthy body of lawmakers appropriated money for ten cutters, which were to be used to suppress smuggling and piracy. They were small craft, but they patrolled the Atlantic seaboard from New Hampshire to Georgia and managed to "put a crimp into the smuggling business."

During the years 1798–1799, France was conducting an undeclared quasi war against United States shipping. More than 300 American vessels were seized by French privateers. In 1798 the regular Navy was re-established, and in 1799 Congress passed a law stating that "Revenue Cutters shall, whenever the President of the United States shall direct, cooperate with the Navy of the United States."

Even before this law was passed, President John Adams had directed that the cutters be placed under control of the Secretary of the Navy. In 1799, four fleets, totaling twenty ships of the Navy and the Revenue Marine, operated at sea against the French privateers. Well over half of the French ships captured by these fleets were taken by the cutters.

Again, in the War of 1812 the Revenue Marine made a notable record. The *Jefferson* took the first prize of the war, and altogether, fourteen enemy ships were captured by the cutters. Following the War of 1812 the Revenue Marine was assigned the duty of suppressing piracy and the slave trade, a job which took them more than twenty years.

As was the case within the other armed services, at the beginning of the War Between the States many officers and men of the Revenue Cutter Service resigned and joined the Confederacy. Five cutters joined the Confederate forces, but the majority remained loyal to the Union and performed valuable service in enforcing the blockade of the coast of the Confederacy and in supporting the Army and Navy along the coast and on the interior waterways.

During the War with Spain, Revenue cutters operated in the blockade of Havana and in patrolling on our west coast.

At the beginning of World War I in 1917, the Coast Gaurd, so renamed by Act of Congress January 28, 1915, was placed under the jurisdiction of the Navy Department. At that time it consisted of 15 cutters, 200-odd officers, and about 5,000 men. The cutters were employed primarily in convoying cargo ships and screening transports. One of the Coast Guard Divisions became a famous antisubmarine unit.

When war broke out in Europe in 1939, President Roosevelt proclaimed the neutrality of the United States and directed the Coast Guard to carry out extensive patrols to insure that foreign vessels did not violate it. On November 1, 1941, the Coast Guard was again placed under the Navy Department. From our entry into World War II until 1945, the growth of the Coast Guard in material, personnel, and activities was tremendous. Its activities included sea frontier patrols, convoy and escort duties, antisubmarine operations, and the manning of many of the landing craft that hit the invasion beaches— such beaches as Guadalcanal, Anzio, Iwo Jima, and Okinawa.

At the end of World War II the Coast Guard was manning 802 vessels (over 65 feet) of its own, more than 350 Navy craft (many of which were of the destroyer type), about 300 Army craft, and nearly 1,800 shore stations and lightships. Of its more than 170,000 personnel, about one-half were serving in ships. The present military strength of the Coast Guard is 29,000 officers and men.

CURRENT PEACETIME DUTIES

In the more than 160 years of its existence the Coast Guard, in addition to its original objective of preventing smuggling, has been assigned many new duties and has absorbed the former Lifesaving Service, the Lighthouse Service, and the Bureau of Marine Inspection and Navigation of the Department of Commerce.

In general terms the basic duties of the Coast Gaurd embrace the following responsibilities:

1. To enforce or assist in the enforcement of all applicable federal laws on the high seas and waters over which the United States has jurisdiction, with particular reference to those laws relating to navigation and shipping and other maritime activities.

2. To promote the safety and efficiency of merchant vessels—with the object of preventing avoidable casualties—through the approval of plans, materials, and equipment used in their construction, repair, and alteration, the periodic inspection of merchant vessels and the licensing of their crews, and the enforcement of regulations for operation of motorboats.

3. To develop, establish, maintain, and operate aids to maritime navigation such as lighthouses, lightships, lights, radio beacons, loran (long-range navigation) and radio direction finder stations, buoys and unlighted beacons, as required to serve the needs of commerce and the armed forces.

4. To perform any and all acts necessary to rescue and aid distressed persons, vessels, and aircraft and to provide maximum protection to life and property on the high seas and waters over which the United States has jurisdiction, including operation of ocean station vessels and the International Ice Patrol.

5. To maintain a state of readiness to function as a specialized service in the Navy in time of war, and to maintain and train an adequate reserve force.

To accomplish these tasks, the Coast Guard maintains a seagoing fleet of 345 larger cutters and patrol craft; icebreakers; lightships; tenders; numerous smaller motorboats for harbor patrol duties; and a large number of motor lifeboats and surfboats. These surface craft are assisted in search and rescue operations by a Coast Guard aviation arm comprising 11 air stations and more than 125 aircraft. To knit together this wide-spread service, the Coast Gaurd maintains a vast communication network, which, due to the similarity of its training and procedure can be readily integrated into the Navy in time of war.

ORGANIZATION

In time of peace the Coast Guard is under the jurisdiction of the Treasury Department and operates under the immediate control of the Commandant of the United States Coast Guard, whose headquarters is in Washington, D.C. The Commandant holds the rank of Vice Admiral in time of peace. During World War II, when the Coast Guard was expanded for war, the Commandant held the rank of Admiral (four stars).

For more detailed local control over the activities of the Coast Guard, the area of the United States, including Alaska, Hawaii, and Puerto Rico, is divided into twelve districts, whose limits dovetail nicely into the limits of the naval districts. The headquarters of the Commander of each district is located in the most important city within his district.

Coast Guard officers are assigned to a particular type of duty, but, with the exception that only qualified aviators are ordered to duty involving piloting an airplane, an officer may be assigned to any type of duty.

COMMISSIONED PERSONNEL

Since 1920, the commissioned officers of the Coast Guard have held rank similar to that of officers of the Navy. There are on active duty fourteen officers with the rank of Rear Admiral, employed in important administrative offices in Coast Guard Headquarters and as district Commanders.

Other commissioned officers, from Captain down to Ensign, are apportioned in percentages in the same manner as in the Navy. Like the Navy, the Coast Guard has Chief Warrant Officers who are commissioned officers and rank with but after Ensigns.

As of today, commissioned officers for the Coast Guard are obtained from graduates of the Coast Guard Academy at New London, Connecticut, from young officers of the United States Merchant Marine, or from Warrant Officers or specially recommended enlisted Coast Guardsmen. Those of the latter two classes are appointed only after stiff competitive examinations.

THE COAST GUARD ACADEMY

Formerly, officers of the Coast Guard were appointed from experienced seamen of coastal vessels, transferred from the Merchant Marine, or detailed from the Navy. This method proved unsatisfactory, and in 1876 a law was passed for cadet training for the Coast Guard. For many years this training was accomplished in the bark *Chase*, but in 1912 such training was transferred to Fort Trumbull, New London.

The seven main buildings of the present Academy were opened as a unit in 1932. It occupies a beautiful site overlooking the Thames River. The four-year course is a stiff one. The Cadets study mathematics, English, chemistry, physics, radio, electrical engineering, naval construction, navigation, ordnance, seamanship, and surveying. A well-rounded course in physical training and athletics completes the program.

However, life for the Cadet is not all work by any means. New London and Connecticut College with their respective quotas of attractive girls add to the social life. Throughout the year there are formal and informal dances which culminate with the famous "Ring Dance," similar to the one held at the Naval Academy. During the practice cruises held each summer the Cadets visit such foreign ports as Amsterdam, Copenhagen, and Oslo and the ports of the Canary Islands or the Caribbean. After four years of hard work, graduation finally arrives, and the Cadet joyfully changes his narrow stripe for the half-inch stripe of the ensign.

The Noncommissioned Personnel

The noncommissioned personnel of the Coast Guard correspond in grades, pay, and allowances with those of the Navy. The highest is the Warrant Officer, then the Chief Petty Officer, Petty Officers First, Second, and Third Class, and rated men. Service in the Coast Guard is voluntary. Upon their first enlistment, recruts are sent to one of the Coast Guard receiving stations, located at Cape May, New Jersey, and Alameda, California. Upon completion of "boot" training, the Coast Guardsman may be ordered to duty on board a cutter or patrol boat, or to the Lifesaving Service, or to the Lighthouse Service. Or he may be selected for further specialized training at schools maintained for the training of Petty Officers. The Coast Guard emphasizes brains as well as brawn.

The Coast Guard Reserve

Because of the tremendous expansion of Coast Guard duties in time of war, it, like the other military services, requires a trained reserve that can be called to duty immediately when necessary. There are two types of Reserve: the Ready Reserve and the Stand-by Reserve.

The members of the Ready Reserve attend weekly drills at Coast Guard stations, Naval Reserve training centers, or air stations. Also, they are required to attend an annual two-week training period ashore or afloat. They receive basic pay, according to their rank or rate, for each drill period and for the two-week annual training period. Advancement is based on regular attendance, marks, and proficiency in rating.

A member of the Stand-by Reserve is expected to attend twenty-four meetings a year and train under a program planned for that unit. Promotion in the Volunteer Reserve depends upon points earned for minimum drill attendance, a two-week voluntary training course, when available, and home correspondence courses.

Women in the Coast Guard

During World War II women were enrolled as officers and as enlisted personnel in the Coast Guard Reserve. Their duties were similar to those of Waves in the Navy. Women reservists in the Coast Guard were called Spars, a name derived from the Coast Guard motto,

Semper paratus, meaning "Always ready." After the war a few of these women reservists were taken into the regular service and still are on active duty. The excellent work done by the Spars during World War II makes it certain that in the event of another war this organization will be again increased to meet the wartime need.

THE LIFESAVING SERVICE

The first of the semi-independent services to be absorbed by the Coast Guard (then the Revenue Marine) was the Lifesaving Service. The earliest lifesaving organization was established in Massachusetts in 1785 and patterned after the Royal Humane Society of England. The first lifeboat station was located at Cohasset, Massachusetts. The crew of the lifeboat were volunteers. Although a few boathouses and surfboats were added as the years passed by, it was not until 1850 that Congress specifically appropriated money for "surfboats, rockets, carronades, and other apparatus for the better preservation of life and property from shipwrecks on the coast." In the seventy years of its existence up to 1941, the Lifesaving Service, aided in some instances by cutters, had rescued 203,609 persons from death and had saved nearly $2,000,000,000 worth of property from shipwreck and flood.

The surfman is usually an entirely different type of man from the sailor. He is practically an acrobat when handling his small boat in high waves. His success depends upon proper timing, speed, and balance. He must be an excellent swimmer and diver. The creed of all Coast Guardsmen is: "We must save life."

COAST GUARD AVIATION

With the development of large seaplanes, the Coast Guard was quick to see their adaptability for general coastal service in patrol and rescue operations. A number of Coast Guard personnel applied for aviation training. The Navy agreed to give Coast Guard personnel the same aviation training given to naval personnel at Pensacola, Florida. At present the Coast Guard has about 200 trained aviators and operates more than 125 planes.

Air stations are maintained on the seacoasts and Great Lakes for search and rescue, and to assist in the enforcement of laws relating to customs and revenue. The aviators who operate these planes are adept at making rough-water landings in daylight, or at night by the use of flares.

In case of desperate illness or injury on board a ship at sea, a doctor may board a Coast Guard plane and be flown to the ship to treat the stricken person, or he may transfer the patient to the plane and deliver him to a hospital. These planes frequently carry serums to isolated areas where an epidemic is spreading. Each plane carries food, a stretcher, blankets, and medical supplies ranging from first-aid kits to rattlesnake and tarantula bite antitoxins. They are really hospitals on wings. The pilots' labor is endless, but it is all in the day's, or night's, work to them.

THE LIGHTHOUSE SERVICE

The first lighthouse on the coast of North America was constructed by the Province of Massachusetts in 1716. Gradually others were constructed by the various Colonial governments, and later by the various states, as the need was demonstrated. The responsibility for the provision of lighthouses and other aids to navigation, such as buoys and beacons, was taken over by the federal government in 1789 and assigned to the Department of Commerce. In 1845 this responsibility was transferred to the Revenue Marine Bureau of the Treasury Department. For many years naval officers were detailed to duty in the Lighthouse Service. In 1939 this service finally was transferred to the Coast Guard, where it definitely belongs.

As aids to navigation in the coastal waters, navigable rivers, and the Great Lakes, the Lighthouse Service of the Coast Guard maintains more than 400 lighthouses and lightships, more than 20,000 buoys and beacons; 42 loran (long-range navigation) stations, and numerous direction-finder stations and radio beacons.

THE WEATHER SERVICE

To the navigators of transocean planes, and to ships at sea, accurate prediction of weather conditions is of the utmost importance. To make such predictions, information about the weather conditions at many points must be obtained nearly simultaneously and over as large an area as possible. In order to obtain such information from definite areas of the oceans, the Coast Guard maintains six cutters in definitely assigned sea areas. From these ships, the weather men of the sea forward the desired information every three hours to Coast Guard radio stations ashore, from which the data are transmitted to the Weather Bureau offices in Washington and San Francisco. To members of the Coast Guard, duty in ships assigned to weather stations is perhaps the most uncomfortable and hazardous duty. The Coast Guard broadcasts hurricane and storm warnings from the Weather Bureau and issues storm and flood signals. By these warnings many lives and much property are saved each year.

COAST GUARD WIVES

This chapter on the Coast Guard has been included in *The Navy Wife* for two reasons: first, we are of the opinion that the lives of Navy wives and Coast Guard wives are so similar that information provided to assist young Navy wives in making their married lives more agreeable and successful will be of equal value to newly wed Coast Guardsmen's wives; and second, if the Navy wife has an opportunity to know about the sister Service, the Coast Guard, there will develop a mutual feeling of respect and good-fellowship among the wives of Navy and Coast Guard personnel.

Ladies of the Coast Guard, you are the wives of heroes, and as such you carry a responsibility all your own. You have a serious life, but you also have a pleasant social life among friends who know your difficulties and share them. They are understanding friends—the best kind. They are ready to help you, and it is a good idea to accept their help. Also try to do your part to help them, such as looking out for their children while you watch your own; or sharing with them your television or radio; or offering to prepare jointly a buffet supper or picnic. Work together for the Red Cross and other relief organizations, perhaps learn to play bridge or take up some other hobby. Such occupations will help you while away many lonely hours when your respective husbands are at sea.

There is a national Coast Guard Wives' Club, with headquarters in Washington. It has two branches, Senior for wives of commissioned personnel and Junior for wives of noncommissioned personnel. Most cities where Coast Guard units are stationed have branches of this club. The regular meetings of the Senior and Junior branches are held separately. But in Washington about once a year there is a joint meeting of the branches. It is usually held at the Club for

Soldiers, Sailors, Marines and Airmen at 1015 L Street, N.W., Washington. Regular meetings of the Senior branch usually are held at one of the many officers' clubs in the vicinity, such as Bolling Field, the Naval Gun Factory, or Naval Medical Center, Bethesda, Maryland, or at times at civilian clubs such as Belle Haven or Columbia Country Club.

You seldom hear of heroes in the Coast Guard. Not that there aren't plenty—the Service is full of them—but heroism is everyday bread-and-butter stuff in the Coast Guard. Nor do you see the wives of Coast Guard personnel wearing any special medals, but theirs is a life equally dedicated to the Service.

The magnificent work of the Coast Guard is well known and constantly brings forth the admiration of the American people. It has a double duty of defending our shores in time of war and of serving humanity in time of peace.

Chapter IX

ENGAGEMENTS AND WEDDINGS

Sweethearts and wives! Fill up the glass
  with crystal clink and clatter
And drink the liquid jewels down ——
  May the former become the latter
When raging winds and waves unite
  to form a mighty chorus,
We know that loving hearts at home
  are nightly praying for us.

I T was a custom in the old Navy, previous to prohibition days, when ships were at sea to drink a toast at dinner on Saturday night to sweethearts and wives. This toast dates back to Lord Nelson's day, and the second stanza continues:

Sweethearts and wives, those precious names
  that make our hearts grow warmer
Through every storm on sea or shore ——
  May the latter remain the former.
When lightnings flash and billows roll
  and straining hawsers sever,
Our thoughts upon the reeling deck
  are with them both forever.

Perhaps you received your engagement ring only last night. It may be a miniature of his college class ring, or miniature of an Annapolis ring, the traditional diamond engagement ring—or with great sentiment your fiancé may have had the stone of his grandmother's or mother's engagement ring reset for you. Modern engagement rings may bear anything from a star sapphire to a square-cut emerald, one stone or a cluster of stones. It may be an nth of a carat or a soda-bottle chip, but if there is true love and romance the wedding band will encircle your happiness.

It is still customary in the best circles, and particularly in the Services, for a Navy man to call on the girl's father or mother or whoever is head of the family and ask for the girl's hand in marriage. This is truly a matter of courtesy and principle. Generally speaking, it is no surprise to the girl's family if the Navy man has been particularly attentive for any length of time.

If the parents of the girl approve the engagement, the young (white hat) or officer should acquaint his parents with his intentions if he has not already done so. He breaks the news of his happiness to his parents by a personal visit, a letter, or a wire, choosing the method best suited to his purse, and considering the distance involved. One enthusiastic young Ensign wrote ecstatically to his mother and father: "Dear Parents: Hang on to your hats! I'm going to be married." Then he told them all about Sally and her family. He was even thoughtful enough to send along a good picture of his "dream girl." The letter glowed with happiness, and his mother and father each wrote to Sally a cordial letter welcoming her into the family. They also wrote graciously to Sally's mother and father, since it was impossible for them to call personally. The family of the young man must always welcome the bride-to-be. It is customary for them either to call upon or to write to the future daughter-in-law.

If the young Navy man is an orphan, his nearest relative should welcome his fiancée into the family. A definite understanding should be reached before a formal engagement is announced.

YOUR NAVY CHAPLAIN

Young couples should always consult a chaplain when planning marriage, even if they don't plan to have him marry them. He can be of invaluable practical assistance in getting the license, birth certificate, blood tests, and in finding out about rules concerning marriage ages, parental consent, waiting periods, etc. It should be noted that families of enlisted men below the top three pay grades are not transferred at government expense.

Today, premarital counseling is the accepted practice. Often the chaplain you consult about your wedding will not be the clergyman who will perform the ceremony. This is of primary importance in the case of a second marriage or marriage to a divorced person. Many clergymen will not perform such a marriage at all, some will require proof of the innocent party, some will need a waiting period, and proof that the divorce is final should be required by any clergyman.

At the present time, premarital counseling is encouraged by nearly all churches and required by some. The form which this counseling takes depends upon the requirements of the church and the practice of the individual clergyman.

In other words, the Navy chaplain conducts marriage ceremonies under the following provisions: "A chaplain may perform the marriage rite provided he complies with the civil law of the place where the marriage is to be solemnized and provided all parties concerned have complied with the requirements of that denomination the chaplain represents, and with any direction that may have been issued by the command or higher headquarters."

ENGAGEMENTS AND MARRIAGES OF ENLISTED MEN

There are no longer regulations governing the marriage of enlisted personnel. However, a sailor in the grade of E-1, E-2, E-3, and E-4, unless he has an outside income, should think twice before asking the girl of his dreams to marry him. A Seaman Recruit (SR), Seaman Apprentice (SA), or a Seaman (SN), does not draw enough money to care for anyone except himself. If more discretion were used, the number of dependency and hardship cases among families of enlisted men in the lower four grades would be reduced . . . but not even the Navy can stop love! Of course, for the married men who are recalled it is a different story, and to these the Red Cross, Welfare Society, and Navy Relief are always ready to extend a helping hand in emergencies.

Overseas there are definite marriage regulations for all Navy personnel. For instance, Navy men must submit an application for marriage to the appropriate commander who is authorized to approve such applications.

THE ANNOUNCEMENT

Several days before the announcement is to appear in the paper, the bride's mother either telephones the various daily papers or sends a written signed notice to the society editors. Most papers require a signed statement in order to avoid future trouble in the way of lawsuits. Depending upon the social prominence of the families, reporters and photographers will be sent out to get more information. At the same time, a signed copy of the engagement announcement should be sent to the Service periodicals—*The Army, Navy and Air Force Journal,* 1711 Connecticut Avenue, N.W., Washington, D.C., and *The Army Register,* 511 Eleventh Street, N.W., Washington, D.C. Announcement of engagement for Service journals should be as follows:

Mr. and Mrs. Howard Calhoun Patterson announce the engagement of their daughter, Nancy Lee, to William Satterlee Tyler, Ensign, United States Navy, son of Mr. and Mrs. James Lewis Tyler of Baltimore, Maryland.

Miss Patterson attended Holton Arms in Washington and was a member of the 1954 graduating class from Wellesley.

Ensign Tyler is a graduate of the United States Naval Academy, class of 1953. The wedding will take place in the late fall.

Local papers may carry a much longer announcement; occasionally, however, a brief three-line announcement may seem quite sufficient. The engagement of a widow or divorcée is always announced as quietly as possible. She either tells her friends or writes a brief note to them; but the announcement of the marriage itself should appear in the papers and Service journals.

Should an engagement be broken, regardless of the circumstances it is always broken by the girl—at least as far as the public is concerned! A little delay in sending the second notice might be wise, in view of the bride's variability. (She might change her mind again!) The second announcement follows closely the form of the first:

Mr. and Mrs. Howard Calhoun Patterson announce that the engagement between their daughter, Nancy Lee, and Ensign William Satterlee Tyler, United States Navy, has been broken by mutual consent.

Don't announce your engagement farther ahead than six months; life is too uncertain! If it is an engagement of short duration, then allow the announcement to be made not less than six weeks before the wedding date.

Nine out of ten girls today skip the announcement party, but go ahead if this bit of fanfare will make you happy. Being a prospective bride puts you on a sort of pedestal, out of the realm of mundane things. Your family stands ready to give you the moon, and your relatives and friends are also standing by to help you make all your plans and dreams a success.

The proper form for announcing the engagement of an enlisted man is as follows:

> Chief Petty Officer and Mrs. John Todd announce the engagement of their daughter, Suzanne, to Jackson Ford, Boatswain's Mate, First Class, United States Navy, son of Mr. and Mrs. Nelson Ford of Detroit, Michigan.

SHOWERS

Parties of this sort always seem to spring into popularity when there is a war in the offing. Why, no one seems to know, unless it is war hysteria.

At any rate, showering is not to be greatly encouraged. Brides should limit their shower parties to two and never accept a third. Usually the same friends are asked, as only one's intimate friends are supposed to be invited. It is never given by any member of the bride's immediate family, but may be given by a close friend of hers or of her mother's. More than two shower gifts, in addition to a wedding present, run into money, and there is usually criticism, whether voiced or not. Certainly it is inconsiderate and not in good taste for the bride to impose on her friends; so if someone insists upon giving a party for you, let it be a luncheon or tea, but if possible veto a shower.

An appropriate shower for a Navy bride would be a linen shower or a personal shower, should the hostess consult you. Try tactfully to veto a miscellaneous shower, crystal shower, or kitchen shower. Whether you realize it or not, my darlings, you are entering a life of eternal gypsying. There will be times when you will need to set up for real housekeeping, but the dime store will be the solution to your problems because you will either sell or give the utensils away when orders come. Now is the time to become accustomed to traveling light. Learn to keep yourselves mobile. Don't start out by burdening yourself and your handsome Ensign or sailor with valuable though useless gimcracks. A set of Spode china is a glory to look at, a delight to eat from—and an invention of Satan to pack.

Showers usually take the form of a tea, after which the gifts are presented in some novel fashion. In smart circles showers are not as popular today as formerly; however, it is a matter of personal taste.

PERSONAL TROUSSEAU

If you are fortunate enough to know where Bill or Jack will be stationed the first year of your marriage, consult a bridal counselor concerning the type of wardrobe you will need. If it is to be foreign duty, you will have some general idea of the type of clothes. But don't overstock. Orders are often changed without notice and sometimes en route.

The first thing to do is to make an inventory of the clothes you have in your wardrobe, then another memo or shopping list to cover lingerie, hose, accessories (belts, purses, scarves, jewelry, gloves, shoes), blouses, coats, suits, daytime dresses, evening dresses, rain gear, and luggage.

Naturally your wedding dress and your going-away outfit will be highlights of your personal trousseau. The latter should be a suit or costume that you can and will be proud to wear for seasons to come. Have a nucleus of substantial clothes such as well-tailored suits; use the fur coat you have on hand. Styles change overnight, so buy only the essentials and save your money for future wardrobe necessities when you have to replace the trousseau you chose for Washington with a less formal summer wardrobe suitable for the tropics.

The following list is given as an average wardrobe for the Navy bride. She may add to or change the list to suit her personal preferences, her pocketbook, or the climatic conditions

1 topcoat or fur coat	3 evening dresses (if needed)
1 classic suit	2 dinner dresses (if needed)
1 raincoat; rain gear	2 cocktail dresses (if needed)
Sportsclothes	Beach clothes
Dresses, blouses	Day shoes, sports and evening
Shorts, slacks, sweaters	shoes, mules

1 winter dressing gown
1 summer brunch coat or duster
1 lovely negligee (the prettiest one you can afford)
1 hostess gown or TV pajamas

An adequate lingerie trousseau may include:

3 nylon nightgowns or pajamas	4 slips
4 pants	4 brassieres
1 dozen pairs of stockings, various weights	

Any number of interchangeable skirts, long and short, with jackets, blouses, and sweaters will add variety to your wardrobe. If you are the "pinafore" type, clever combinations can be devised with extra blouses and skirts. Beach clothes, shorts, slacks, swim suits, robe, beach bag may be important in your trousseau.

Study the fashion magazines. Plan your trousseau with the help of one of the experienced stylists or consultants that all large stores provide. Window-shop first; look about thoroughly, watch sales; then use common sense, make up your mind, know what you want, how much you intend to spend, and start out to shop. Everyone knows that the shopper on a small budget who must dress inexpensively has to be far more exact than the shopper who has unlimited money to spend. Keeping the wardrobe sparse, and adding to it when a definite need comes along, is far more exciting than buying everything at once and growing tired of it. It is odd, but a cheap dress with fairly good accessories will look fine while an expensive dress with cheap accessories will look cheap.

If you can sew a fine seam, you can cut the cost of your trousseau considerably. I repeat, however, do not stock up with a large amount of clothes. Fashions change quickly, and it is a far nicer feeling to have the money in your bank balance for wardrobe emergencies that will surely arise.

To this trousseau list you may add countless sets of lingerie or double the outlay of clothes if your taste and circumstances permit. It will probably be the only time in your life when you will spend so much money at one time on lingerie; but don't go on a lingerie-buying jag. Try to keep in mind that these pre-wedding days, redolent of lily of the valley, will be followed by bread-and-butter days when you may have to tub your lovelies in a Laundromat. It will not be good to wake up with a laundry headache and yards of point d'esprit that will never look the same until it is fluted again at an expensive French hand laundry.

Learn to buy by brand names when you are shopping for quality lingerie. This means you can buy with confidence in whatever city you happen to be; though name-known lingerie isn't necessarily the lowest in price, you can be sure the money you spend is getting the most, dollar for dollar. For example, it is wiser to buy three good slips than six cheap ones, because the good slips not only will outlast the others but will give pleasure in wearing.

The selection of your lingerie should not be totally emotional or from the *femme fatale* point of view! You are entitled to make it a bit out of this world, but don't forget it must lead your day-by-day life with you. And life may be rugged at your first station! If Oslo or Alaska is in the cards as a winter honeymoon, include some warm flannel pajamas in your most becoming pastel shades; also, long red flannels of the gay-nineties variety come in some amusing styles.

The most subtle compliment you can pay your fiancé is to plan your trousseau to please him. By now you have a pretty good idea what type of clothes he admires, so strive to complete his dream picture of you. There are certain things which military men like in women's clothes, and one thing they ordinarly don't like is anything that resembles a uniform or clothes regimentation.

Smart formal evening gowns are in order, and the more the better because on a small base you see the same people over and over. Breath-taking effects may be obtained with a minimum amount of good material, some fine ribbon, and flowers if you can sew. Not too minimum, or the breath-taking will be actual as well as figurative! It is wisdom not to spend too much or pay store prices for evening clothes unless you have an outside income or a rich fairy godmother.

Regardless of where you go, lay in a good supply of sturdy, comfortable shoes. Beware of clothes which need constant pressing and the ministrations of an expert cleaner. Take a dim view of the weather and go prepared with attractive rain gear.

If you can afford it, include one really super coat of peach-bloom camel's hair in palest lime, peppermint pink, tomato red, or café-au-lait beige. You can use it for every occasion, from sports right through the evening over your prettiest dance frock.

LUGGAGE

One of the musts in your trousseau is attractive, durable luggage, preferably of the airplane variety. Airplane luggage is the lightest and most durable on the market today. There are many good name brands.

Your wedding luggage should match; however, do not discard odd suitcases as they will be perfect for cross-country moves later by car. Your wedding luggage may include a combination hat and shoe trunk; the large size for large hats will prove a joy. These usually come with a tray to be used for accessories and lingerie. A sky-robe case with hangers, similar to the cross-country bag aviators use, saves arrival pressing. That plus a generous-sized train box or make-up box should be adequate for the honeymoon trip. Learn early in the game to travel light and plan your trousseau accordingly.

LINENS

"Trousseau" is a French word, meaning the little *trousse* or bundle which it was customary for the bride to carry to the house of her husband. Today the word has come to mean the bride's personal wardrobe and her household linens.

The list given may seem sketchy to your grandmother and even your mother, who had "hope chests" full of embroidered linens on which they spend their leisure time, but it should prove adequate for the needs of the average young couple.

Buy the best linens you can afford; good linens last indefinitely. It seldom pays to economize on this item. You'll be disillusioned with a bargain the first time it is laundered, because its beauty washes away with the sizing on its first trip to the tub.

White linens are the safest buy, though color co-ordination is increasingly a decoration must, and linens today are available in luscious pastel shades which make them very tempting. All that can be said is that it is a question of taste rather than of an accepted standard.

For 1 Double Bed
6 sheets 90" x 108"
12 pillowcases 45" x 38½"
2 heavyweight blankets 80" x 90"
1 lightweight blanket 80" x 90"

For 2 Single Beds
12 sheets 72" x 108"
12 pillowcases 45" x 38½"
4 heavyweight blankets 72" x 90"
2 lightweight blankets 72" x 90"

For 1 Bathroom
6 large absorbent bath towels 26" x 50"
8 regular bath towels 24" x 46"

 6 small Turkish towels, easy to launder, 16" x 27"
 6 small linen towels, guest size
12 washcloths
 3 bath mats

Percale or supercale sheets and pillowcases are very durable, although real linen is equally long-lived. However, the latter is too expensive for most budgets. Here is something about sheets: be sure to buy them long enough, so that there is plenty to tuck in, and to fold well over the blanket. If your better half has to yank them up around his neck, you can be sure they won't last very well. The more threads to the inch, the smoother, more fine-textured the sheet. Pillowcases should fit easily, but not so snugly that they will soon be splitting the seams.

A down-filled comforter, the Carlin or Eleanor Beard variety of exquisite beauty, might be added with a gift check. Handmade quilts are also a most welcome gift to the bride's trousseau. You may add blanket covers, mattress covers, and bedspreads, as you wish, to the list given.

Linens last longer, seem fresher, if you follow a regular rotation plan. The easy way to remember is to stack the freshly laundered sheets, towels, pillowcases at the bottom of each pile in your linen closet.

For the bride with a larger budget, I suggest planning your linens to include two or three bedrooms with corresponding bathroom linens as they will always stand you in good stead. Linen is usually the victim of a grinding process of slow attrition, and the better the quality, the longer its life.

You may mark your linen with either a monogram or an initial. Perhaps you are a gambler, and don't want to mark it at all. If you do, it is usually done by hand, though today machine-monogrammed bath towels, facecloths, and bath mats are popular. Avoid funny or would-be-cute ideas. They get as tiresome after a bit as an old shoe tied to your bridal chariot in the second week of the honeymoon.

Table Linen

1 linen damask dinner cloth, 8 or 12 matching napkins
1 buffet or supper cloth with 6 napkins, 8 or 12 preferred
1 luncheon or tea cloth, 8 napkins (12 preferred)

2 luncheon place-mat sets
2 breakfast cloths, 4 napkins
2 bridge sets, 2 tray sets
Place mats, 4 sets; can be linen, Indian head, straw, or plastic

For the Kitchen

6 glass towels	6 dishcloths
6 hand towels	12 dish towels

NAVAL WEDDINGS

Naval weddings differ but slightly from the usual formal wedding, except that they are probably more elaborate. In fact, a naval wedding, with the officers in uniform and shining swords, presents a striking background for the beautiful bridesmaids and the exquisite bride in her traditional white gown. For once the groom almost outshines the bride. It is the nearest approach to the glamorous court life of bygone days that remains today.

However, a formal naval wedding is a bit hard to plan unless an officer is on shore duty. When it is difficult to set a definite date, many brides consider it wiser to send out announcements rather than invitations. Of course an invitation is a nicer compliment than an announcement, and the words are self-explanatory, but *that's the Navy.*

It is not against any rule or regulation for a noncommissioned officer or enlisted man in the Navy to have a full naval wedding. If the groom decides to go formal, every Serviceman in the wedding party should be in uniform (with the exception of the bride's father if he is not a military man).

Decide first of all with your family what type of wedding you will have, whether formal, military, semiformal, or informal. Try to plan it without spending your father's next year's income or leaving your mother with a nervous breakdown. Next, your fiancé included, decide on the date and time. June is the traditional bride's month, though April and May are popular and the autumn season is increasingly fashionable. It is not appropriate or in good taste to plan a large church wedding to take place during Lent, Holy Week, or Advent (the three weeks preceding Christmas). Marriage license bureaus carry on a thriving business every day of the year, however, so the month and date are up to your personal taste and convenience.

WEDDING INVITATIONS

The bride and her mother should consult a good stationer and place the order for the wedding invitations or announcements with him. If you can possibly afford it, be firm about having them engraved; however, printing methods today have improved so greatly that often it is difficult to tell the difference unless one has a "sensitive touch." Avoid any fads of engraving or printing, quality and shape of stationery. It is a good idea to request that the envelopes be sent to you ahead of the invitations or announcements so that you can have them addressed and ready. The question arises whether to remove the enclosed tissue in invitations! Of course, it is obvious that the stationer places the tissue between the pages to protect the engraving. If you have the time to remove the tissues, do so but it really does not matter. Invitations should be sent out three weeks in advance of the wedding.

There are two forms for wedding invitations. For church invitations the form is "request the honour of your presence." If the wedding is to be at a club or in the home, the form is "request the pleasure of your company." Tradition demands the British spelling of *honour*.

Before the invitations can be ordered, the bride's mother must consider the date and the hour of the wedding and speak to the clergyman about reserving the church.

A reservation for the church, if it is a popular one, should be planned four months ahead. The wedding invitation should read:

Mr. and Mrs. Howard Calhoun Patterson
request the honour of your presence
at the marriage of their daughter
Nancy Lee
to
William Satterlee Tyler
Ensign, United States Navy
on Saturday evening, the tenth of June
One thousand nine hundred and fifty-five
at eight o'clock
St. Michael's Cathedral
Charleston, South Carolina

The invitation to the breakfast or reception is enclosed in the wedding invitation and reads as follows:

Reception
Immediately following Ceremony
South Battery

R.S.V.P.
62 Avalon Court

The announcement of a wedding should read:

Mr. and Mrs. Howard Calhoun Patterson
have the honor of announcing
the marriage of their daughter
Nancy Lee
to
William Satterlee Tyler
Ensign, United States Navy
Saturday, the tenth of June
One thousand nine hundred and fifty-five
Charleston, South Carolina

Sue and Jack's wedding invitation should read:

Chief Petty Officer and Mrs. John Todd
request the honour of your presence
at the marriage of their daughter
Suzanne
to
Jackson Ford
Boatswain's Mate, First Class, United States Navy
Wednesday evening, the third of June
One thousand nine hundred and fifty-five
at five o'clock
The Navy Chapel, 3801 Nebraska Avenue, Northwest
Washington, District of Columbia

On formal invitations, announcements, or calling cards full name and title should appear. Abbreviations are not correct.

CALLING CARDS

Even though calling is almost an outmoded custom in the Navy today owing to the great expansion of personnel, increased size of naval stations, and distances involved, still no commissioned officer or his wife can really afford to be without personal calling cards. You may go along for an indefinite period with no use for the cards, then suddenly be ordered to a small station where the calling policy is rigidly enforced. It is suggested that you order one hundred calling cards along with your wedding invitations. Officers always have their own personal cards. Your personal visiting card should read simply: Mrs. William Satterlee Tyler. Avoid using abbreviations or initials, such as Mrs. William S. Tyler or Mrs. W. Satterlee Tyler. Neither form is in the best taste. The entire name, regardless of its length, should appear.

Joint calling cards are growing in popularity, although formerly they were used only when sending gifts or in sending flowers for funerals. It is quite correct to use the following form on your joint calling cards: Ensign and Mrs. William Satterlee Tyler, or Lieutenant and Mrs. William Satterlee Tyler. The designation "Junior Grade" is omitted.

THE FORMAL NAVAL WEDDING

Assuming that it is possible for you to have an elaborate church wedding, let us follow a formal wedding through its various stages. This is given in detail only as a guide. A smaller or less formal wedding may be fashioned after it quite easily.

We will assume that the bride-elect is from a socially prominent civilian family. The setting is a historic old cathedral, at which the bride's family has always worshiped. Perhaps a Bishop will officiate, or some other high prelate assisted by several clergymen. A vested choir with a renowned soloist will furnish the music, and the entire church will be elaborately decorated by a florist. The chancel will be a bower of flowers, and the pews for the families and distinguished guests will be designated by ribbons or sprays of flowers tied to pew ends.

This seems a good place to stress the importance of a rehearsal. By all means, have a rehearsal "if only to get an estimate of the situation."

The bride may or may not direct the rehearsal. It is optional but rarely does she take part in it, as in the old days it was considered bad luck. Often the bride asks the chaplain to direct the rehearsal, after she has explained to him precisely what she has in mind. Certainly someone must have full command of the situation. The bride's family should be asked by the bride to help out. Fathers often have many good suggestions to offer! And Father will be flattered; after all, he is probably paying for the wedding. The organist, who takes a very important part, should most certainly be present. After many repetitions, the entire party should master the art of walking to the wedding march. The head usher will set the tempo for the organist and the ushers will march in with military precision, but bridesmaids and especially the bride must not give the impression of scurrying up the aisle or of doing the "hesitation step." The bridesmaids should understand the advantage of walking on a single line. Once mastered, this will insure an easy flowing movement.

White flowers on the altar, white flowers tied in sprays or bouquets in the windows, white flowers in small bunches tied with white ribbons to the pews against a background of green ferns and palms . . . all these, with lights, candles and music can make a beautiful setting for a wedding ceremony. The florist or the church will provide a white canvas strip for the aisle which is unrolled just before the bridal procession starts; also there will be a colorful awning or canopy leading from street to church.

All the officers are in dress uniform, and the ushers arrive at the church forty-five minutes before the ceremony begins. One officer should take charge as head usher in order that he may be free to escort distinguished and elderly guests, as well as to co-ordinate the duties of the other attendants.

An usher asks everyone whom he does not know whether he is a guest of the bride or of the groom (reminding one, somehow, of the old game of London Bridge). The family of the bride is seated on the left side, the family of the groom on the right.

If the parents of the groom are unable to attend, the groom may invite his Commanding Officer to sit in the front pew on the right. The wives of married ushers are seated in the second pew on the right.

Flag Officers and Commanding Officers should always be seated according to their rank; other officers may be seated indiscriminately except for the choice of bride or groom's side. When an usher escorts a lady down the aisle he offers her his left arm. If a gentleman has come with her, he walks behind them. When a gentleman is alone, the usher walks beside him.

Few people, except at very large, fashionable weddings enclose

pew cards in the invitations; the seating of guests is much more informal than it used to be.

When all the guests have been seated, the head usher escorts the
groom's mother and finally the bride's mother to their seats. The
bride's mother is the last person to be seated. Then the doors are
closed and no one is seated during the ceremony. The ushers march
in in pairs and station themselves on each side of the chancel steps.

Next come the bridesmaids in pairs or singly and at the chancel
they also divide and stand on the steps or go up into the chancel. In
a large church, it makes a pretty setting if the bridesmaids and ushers
alternate and stand on the steps leading into the chancel; or it is
equally effective if they proceed to the chancel and await the bride.

The maid or matron of honor is next in the bridal procession and
stands on the left at the foot of the steps opposite the best man. If
there are flower girls, they precede the ring bearer and separate at the
chancel steps, standing in front of the ushers and bridesmaids.

The bride and her father, who have driven to the church together,
wait with the bridesmaids until it is time for them to join the procession. The bride enters on her father's right arm—then poor Dad does
not have to stumble over a cascade of veil and train to get to his seat.
Authorities differ on this point, and for a bride to enter on her father's
left arm is equally correct. At the rehearsal try out both entrances.
Father will agree with the first plan, whether you do or not; but after
all, it is up to you. It is your wedding!

Musical selections should always be of the classical type. Often
music played at church weddings is the one false note in a lovely ceremony. During the half-hour preliminary period while the guests assemble, the organist may choose selections from the old masters, such
as Wagner's "Evening Star" from *Tannhäuser;* "Largo" from the
Fifth Violin Sonata by Bach, or "My Inmost Heart Rejoiceth" by
Brahms.

Leave all popular favorites to be played or sung later at the reception where sentimental tunes can be as light and gay as the dancers
desire. In *Vogue's Book of Etiquette* Millicent Fenwick lists the following pieces as basically unfit for a sacrament of the church:
"Because," "I Love You Truly," "Oh Promise Me," "Liebestraum,"
and "Meditation" from *Thais.*

The proper wedding marches are: processional, Wedding March
from *Lohengrin* by Wagner; recessional, Mendelssohn's Wedding

March. While these are also secular music, both are usually approved by modern churchmen, though not by the Catholic Church.

At the first strains of the Wedding March the bride's mother rises and the assembled guests do likewise. On the first note of the Wedding March the clergyman, followed by the groom and best man, step from the vestry into the chancel. The groom removes his right glove, holds it in his left hand, and stands at the head of the steps to await his bride. It seems more gallant, if there are several steps, for him to go down to the foot of the steps to meet her. The guests like to see him smile as he watches his bride come up the aisle. Some bridegrooms look glum and scared!

When the bride and her father reach the steps of the chancel, the bride is met by the groom. She changes her bouquet to the other hand and puts her right arm through the groom's left arm. Her father moves back, then steps forward again when the clergyman asks, "Who giveth this woman . . .?" The bride's father may say "I do" or "Her mother and I do." The father then joins his wife in the first pew.

At this point the bride and groom, maid of honor, and best man move forward to the altar. The bride hands her bouquet to the maid of honor while the clergyman asks the best man for the ring, or rings if it is to be a double-ring ceremony. During the ceremony, the clergyman returns the ring to the groom, who places it on the bride's finger at the words "With this ring . . ." In a double-ring ceremony, the clergyman hands the groom's ring to the maid of honor, who in turn hands it to the bride, who places it on the groom's finger, as soon as she has received her ring.

After the ceremony is over, the clergyman says a few congratulatory words in which he wishes them happiness; the handsome groom kisses his lovely bride and the recessional music begins. The maid of honor hands the bride her bouquet and straightens her train. The bride and groom leave the chancel, and at the head of the steps they pause a moment.

The bride should appear sweet and serious but not in the least self-conscious. While she does not, obviously, walk with downcast eyes, she meets none of the many eyes focused upon her except, for a fleeting moment, those of her mother. She is traditionally supposed to be moving at this point in a sort of luminous daze, and usually it isn't hard to act.

The best man escorts the maid of honor, and the ushers escort the bridesmaids to the vestibule where they break ranks to form the arch of sabers.

It is a fine custom and adds a military note if the head usher returns to escort the bride's mother, first, and the groom's mother. Of course, the mothers may prefer to walk out with their husbands. *All guests wait* for the parents of both the bride and the groom to leave; there is ample time for this courtesy.

The ushers form in two lines facing each other at the entrance of the church, and stand at attention as the guests file out.

ARCH OF SWORDS FOR OFFICERS— ARCH OF RIFLES FOR ENLISTED MEN

Only the bride and groom may pass under the traditional arch of steel; it is not proper for any other members of the wedding party to have this honor.

The arch is formed either on the steps outside the church or on the walk leading to the steps. It is not proper to have the arch formed inside the church, as is shown in the following:

The ancient and traditional ceremony of the bride and groom walking under the arched swords of the officer ushers is always expected. At some weddings you will see this ceremony performed in the church, but never in a Roman Catholic Church. Would you like to know the reason for this? The practice of drawing swords at the altar or in the chancel of the church is entirely wrong. Because of the old law of right of sanctuary and refuge, as well as the very nature of a church, it is considered a flagrant breach of military etiquette to draw a sword in church. The arch should be made outside the church if possible, but if inclement weather or street traffic should prevent this, then the crossing of swords may take place in the vestibule near the door. The senior usher should give the order, "Draw SABERS."— *Naval Customs, Traditions and Usage*, by Rear Admiral Leland P. Lovette

The flower girls, maid of honor, and bridesmaids wait until the head usher orders: "Return SABERS." *

* There are two schools of thought on the arch of sabers. The one stated refers to the Catholic Church and a naval tradition; however, in many Protestant churches the arch of sabers is formed in the center aisle as the bride and groom leave the chancel. After the bride and groom have passed under the arch and while the wedding processional proceeds to the vestibule, the ushers double-time down the side aisles to form a second arch on the church steps. If the weather is inclement, the second arch may be formed in the vestibule.

Everyone loves to see the bride enter her new life under an arch of swords or rifles; there is something romantic and beautiful about the ceremony.

The bride's father, if he is not in the Service, wears a morning coat or a cutaway with dark gray striped trousers. Very light gray buckskin gloves are usually worn.

The bride's mother is poised, serene, and radiant. She is the hostess of one of the most important events over which she will ever preside; and while she has all the responsibility of the wedding, she does not seem to take an active part. A bride's mother should have great dignity; she is the lovely mature forecast of her daughter in the years to come. She is the last person to enter before the procession, and she should be becomingly and beautifully gowned. The groom usually sends the bride's mother, also his own mother, a corsage.

Receiving lines are sometimes formed in the vestibule of the church or on the front steps should there be no reception planned or for some guests not invited to the reception.

Each Officers' Club and CPO Club should own a sword or saber to be used in cutting the traditional wedding cake at receptions held at the club by the bride's family. To procure a sword for cutting the cake falls to the lot of the best man.

WEDDING PICTURES

Definite arrangements should be made with the photographer before the wedding that no pictures are to be taken until after the ceremony. An exchange of wedding vows is a sacred rite, and certainly there should be no flashing of photographers' bulbs during the ceremony. As the happy couple walk down the aisle or leave the church is the appropriate time for the photographer to take their pictures.

THE RECEPTION

The first question in planning the reception is always the hour set for the wedding. If the wedding is at noon, it should be followed by a fairly substantial breakfast or luncheon.

An afternoon or evening wedding calls for lighter refreshments such as champagne or punch, sandwiches if desired, and the wedding cake. The party may be as simple or as elaborate as one chooses; if there is to be dancing an orchestra should be engaged.

At a bridal party it is customary to have a bridal cake, the first slice of which the bride cuts with her husband's sword, his hand over hers. It is also customary to drink a toast to the bride. This toast is usually proposed by the best man.

If there is dancing, the groom always dances first with his bride, then with the bridesmaids and maid of honor. For the reception at home, it is always easier to have a caterer handle the refreshments if you can afford it.

When the guest list is large, the weddding reception is often given at a club or hotel. All the details, such as decorations, menu, music, can be taken care of expertly by the club, and the bride and her mother are relieved of responsibility.

The receiving line, formed near the entrance, includes the parents of the bride, the parents of the groom, the bride, the groom, and then the bridesmaids. The ushers are not in the line, and sometimes the father of the bride prefers to mingle with the guests.

If there is to be a dinner, there is a center table—the bride's table— at one end of which bride and groom are seated. The bride's table must always be covered with a white cloth and the wedding cake is set in the middle of the table as the principal decoration. Low bowls of white flowers are spaced at intervals on each side of the cake.

At a small home reception the dining table is covered with a white cloth, and it gives a pretty effect to surround the wedding cake with a wreath of green leaves. With champagne glasses or a crystal punch bowl at one end, a coffee service at the other, and plates of sand- wiches at the sides the table is complete.

Champagne punch looks its best in a clear crystal punch bowl, and it is the simplest to make of all punches. Simply place a quart of lemon ice or sherbet and a quart of ginger ale in the punch bowl and over it pour two bottles of champagne. The yield is about twenty-four cups.

Of course, champagne or punch is not necessary at all, but it some- how seems to go with weddings. If you prefer a fruit punch with iced tea as a base, then stand by your principles and serve it.

THE INFORMAL WEDDING

Naturally, every bride wants to be married at her home church or in her own home, but to those young women who have pledged their troth to a Navy man this wish is sometimes impossible of fulfillment. Navy chapel weddings are becoming more and more popular. Should you be fortunate enough to be stationed in or near Washington, be sure to avail yourselves of the privilege of being married in the Navy Chapel located at the U.S. Naval Security Station, 3801 Nebraska Avenue, N.W. It seems a fitting way to start your life in the Navy, and it can be something lovely to remember always.

The bride or her family pays for all decorations for the church, flowers for maid or matron of honor, bridesmaids and flower girls, and the fees for the organist and soloist. Many brides and their families either through ignorance or indifference seem to think Uncle Sam pays for all of these extras and that being married in a chapel is an easy out. I assure you, he does not, nor should the groom or the chaplain's fund be expected to pay any of these bills.

The bride and her mother should meet with the groom, the chaplain, and a recommended florist at the chapel a week or two before the wedding. The florist will want to know how many candelabra are available, and you can make your decorating and wedding plans all in one visit. At some stations—say, in California where flowers are plentiful—florists produce beautiful wedding effects for as little as twenty-five dollars. If a reception is to follow at the club, and you wish table or room decorations, this is the time to arrange for it. The bride's family also pays for the reception and decorations used, just as would be expected were the reception held in the bride's home.

THE HOME WEDDING

A home wedding may be as simple or as elaborate as you choose; but try to keep it from freezing into a stiff pattern. Home should stand for gracious and affectionate living. The dining room table pushed into a corner and the kitchen range draped with bridesmaids' wraps are poor aids to an overly formal service. Don't try to turn a duplex apartment into a Paris cathedral!

MARRIAGE AT PARSONAGE OR MAGISTRATE'S OFFICE

This ceremony is not a wedding, but merely a marriage. Street clothes are usually worn. The groom may wear uniform, though civilian clothes might be less conspicuous and preferable.

THE SECOND MARRIAGE

A second marriage for a man does not in any way affect the ceremony, but a second marriage for a woman can never be like her first. Many war widows, who had to forgo the formality of a white wedding owing to the exigencies of war, still cherish the idea of a real wedding with white satin dress, train, and veil. Everything is against it, my dear!

Since the days of the ancient Romans white has symbolized virginity, and the wearing of it should be reserved for the first-time bride alone. Weddings are formed upon just such charming traditions. It is perfectly proper for a young widow to send out engraved invitations or announcements of her wedding, but the remarriage of a divorced woman or of an older woman is always less elaborate than that of a young widow. The standing rule is, no woman rates two white weddings!

THE WEDDING DRESS

> Something old, something new,
> Something borrowed, something blue,
> And a lucky sixpence in your shoe.

Brides who dress in accordance with this old rhyme (and most brides do) usually wear some treasured heirloom of lace or jewelry and borrow a handkerchief. The blue is often a garter. If your bank is fresh out of sixpences, a shiny new dime will do.

And now to the selection of the *pièce de résistance*, the bride's dress! She is the central figure; it is the big moment of her life and no one can or should try to eclipse her.

Satin is still the classic material for the wedding gown, but sheerest lace is also highly favored. Frosted white organdy and marquisette are two leading fabrics for spring wedding gowns.

For the home wedding white bengaline, velvet, crepe, or any of the summer materials such as organza, *mousseline de soie*, or chiffon are appropriate.

The conservative bride with an eye to the future will choose a dress of such material and style that with slight alteration it can be converted into an evening dress. Sometimes the gown is made so that the train can be detached. If the bride wishes for sentimental reasons to keep her wedding dress, she may make it as elaborate as she wishes.

Often she chooses to be married in her mother's wedding gown, and if there is not too great a difference in style and length, this is a perfect solution. The veil may be of rare lace, an heirloom in the family, or it may be layers and layers of tulle or illusion arranged with orange blossoms, pearls, or shirring.

There is a tendency in modern fashion for brides to choose pastel shades, such as ice blue and petal pink, and this is entirely a personal matter; yet tradition decrees that white is really the color of the wedding gown.

FLOWERS

Although the bride may select the flowers and make arrangements with the florist, the groom pays for:

Flowers sent to the bride
Corsage sent to the bride's mother
Corsage sent to his mother
Corsage for his sisters and hers if they are not in the bridal party
Boutonnieres for his father and the bride's father

Wedding flowers do not have to be orchids or expensive camellias; florists can arrange beautiful effects in less expensive flowers. The bride's family pays for:

All flower decorations for church, home, or club
Flowers for bridesmaids
Flowers for flower girls
Flowers for maid or matron of honor
Fee for the organist and soloist
Fee for the choir

GIFTS TO THE BRIDESMAIDS

The custom of giving gifts to the bridesmaids is gaining in popularity, but it is by no means obligatory. Depending upon the bride's circumstances, she may give some little trinket, but it is nice to give something lasting, no matter how small. One recent Navy bride gave each of her attendants a miniature silver pin in the shape of a spoon that was a replica of her pattern of silver. Evening accessories often are given, or something that is to be worn in the wedding by the bridesmaids. Evening bags are popular, as are fans, charm bracelets, compacts, or some similar trifle. The groom usually gives to his groomsmen some small gift—studs, links, cigarette cases, or leather traveling accessories.

WEDDING PRESENTS

If wedding invitations have been sent out three weeks before the wedding date, gifts will begin to arrive soon thereafter. If announcements are sent, the gifts will arrive probably before you return from your wedding trip. Provide yourself with a gift book, which can be bought at any good stationer's, and as each gift arrives, you or your mother should fill in the date it is received, the article, the name and address of the donor, where bought, and the date the gift was acknowledged. This is a systematic and methodical way to keep a record, and it will be a wonderful help when everything seems to arrive at once and you feel overwhelmed. If the presents start coming in too fast, put them in a special room and do not open them until you are free to make a record of them. Thank-you notes are easiest to write while you are in the first glow of enthusiasm over each wedding gift. You *must* write a note of thanks to every person who sends a gift. The omission of this courtesy is the one thing the sender may forgive but never forget, and your youth will not excuse you. Always mention the present *specifically* in your note, and if possible tell how you plan to use it. Try to write graciously and appreciatively, and avoid using the word "little." There is nothing more deflating to the person who has spent his all on your gift than to receive such a note as this after sending, shall we say, a sizable silver salad bowl:

Dear Commander and Mrs. Thomas:
  Thank you so much for the dear little silver bowl you were so sweet to send us.
Sincerely,

Perhaps the persons who sent it sacrificed something they wanted very much in order to send you a present they hoped would add to your happiness. Of course, you would never be guilty of sending an engraved card of thanks or a typewritten thank-you note.

A thank-you note takes little enough time, for the long and pleasant echo it leaves in people's minds. Don't use stereotyped phrases.

Think a moment and put down some fresh phrase that you might use in talking; your thanks should sound not only spontaneous but sincere.

Upon the receipt of a wedding gift, a thoughtful gesture is to detail some member of your family to pinch-hit as your secretary in sending a small printed card to the person who sent the gift, saying their gift arrived, the date of arrival, and that a letter of thanks will follow soon. This is important to many people who like to pay their bills promptly but sometimes are inconvenienced and wonder if the gift was delivered.

Sterling silver is the most practical of gifts, and your flat silver is a necessity. Choose a pattern you really like, and one that won't be too expensive when you are ready to add to it. Even if you have to start out with two knives and forks, better to have four of the essential pieces in sterling than round dozens of everything in plated ware. Here is a list of what you should get with the checks you receive, or if relatives ask you frankly what you would like in your pattern of silver:

Flat silver in sterling:

    4 luncheon-size knives and forks
    4 bouillon spoons
    4 butter spreaders
    4 salad forks
  12 teaspoons
    3 large table or serving spoons
    1 steak or carving set

Later you can complete your service to twelve, also filling in with iced-tea spoons, cream soup spoons, ice-cream forks, after-dinner coffee spoons, and large-size dinner knives and forks.

In hollow ware or a good heavy plate you can use:

  1 silver meat platter
  1 silver vegetable dish with 2 or 3 compartments
  1 silver bread tray
  1 or more silver sandwich trays

Of course, some fairy godmother may present you with a silver tea service complete with tray. Be grateful . . . but the first thing to do is to insure it and then relax.

How to Mark Linen and Silver

Formerly only the bride's initials or monogram were used, but to-day it is considered proper to use the bride's future initials. Simple block letters are considered smart or a single Old English initial.

As for china and crystal, if you have any choice in the matter, select open patterns, in consideration of breakage in frequent moves.

Your Wedding Trip

Your first journey together, whether your honeymoon is to be for a week end or a month, will be a unique experience you will never forget! There will never be another trip to compare with it, so forget everything once you are on your way and be happy.

After you have discussed finances, and how much your husband not wants but has to spend, then decide what sort of trip you will both enjoy most. Consider your tastes when you map out your honeymoon program.

Of course, at this joyful period in your life you are both filled with starry-eyed good will and eager to agree to anything, but don't forget travel brings out the best in some people, the worst in others. Some people are born sightseers and others would be bored with the Taj Mahal. The only thing worse than being dragged through cathedrals and museums is being forced to follow a foursome around a hilly golf course while wearing high-heeled platform pumps. If you know anything about golf courses, you will know that this is taboo, and an easy out for you.

If you two are like most people, somewhere in the middle between extremes, you should be able to agree on a lovely trip that will be unforgettable. Even if you aren't movie-camera enthusiasts be sure to take along a camera.

Chapter X

BUSINESS OF THE NAVAL HOUSEHOLD

SUCCESSFUL Service women are probably, as a group, the most resourceful, efficient, and brilliant leaders in the entire field of homemaking. Although there are certain basic problems in any household, the wife of a Navy man has an entirely different set of housekeeping problems from those of her Air Force and Army sisters or civilian friends.

Hers is an itinerant household. What she calls home is literally the place where she hangs her hat. It may be a room in a modest hotel, or it may be a tiny "efficiency" apartment. Again, it may be a furnished bungalow with which she will hate to part. A wonderful offer may even present itself in the form of the lease of a luxuriously furnished estate, staffed with expert servants. At some time her husband will probably be attached to the Naval Academy, to a Navy yard, or to a naval station. There she may be furnished quarters and will enjoy for a time the compensations of a pleasant, predictable social life.

During her husband's many years of service she will probably run the gamut of living conditions. If she starts where most Navy wives do, her first abode may be a boardinghouse, or a tiny apartment in the purlieus of Long Beach, San Diego, or Norfolk; if she is very lucky, her husband may finally reach the post of command of a naval district, with a large, well-appointed home and usually a fine vegetable and flower garden. But whatever the location, whatever the difficulties, her job is to make the place into a home.

To do this the Navy wife must be nothing short of a genius. First of all, she must be a financier. This is a requisite, what with the Army, Navy, Marine Corps, Coast Guard, and Air Force still carrying on and trying to keep up a standard of living necessary to the morale of the armed forces. Somehow, the Navy wife manages!

Unless there are outside resources, the maintenance of a suitable standard of living and the making of adequate financial provision for the future necessitates scrupulous care and efficient planning. In other words, in addition to being a financier and a business manager, the Navy wife must be a culinary expert, an interior decorator, an expert in marketing and buying, a competent chauffeur, a perfect hostess, a devoted wife and mother, a social success, and a woman who can make an Ensign's pay stretch from the east coast to the Pacific frontier without ever breaking. A rather large order, isn't it?

However, it has been done and is being done every day by Navy wives—this living and getting along on a shoestring! When you see a group of Navy women at a social affair, they are always well dressed and beautifully groomed. In diplomatic and civilian circles experienced Navy wives are as much at home as among the members of their own set. More than that, they know what to say to Lord Montrose, how to encourage Congressman Smith to indulge in his own favorite monologue about "what I am going to do for the Navy," and how to listen interestedly, intelligently, and flatteringly to the most stodgy old-timers, be they civilians, Generals, or Admirals. They get along well with servants and speak the kitchen lingo. They have a perfect treasure store of foreign recipes for dishes which they can prepare and serve themselves. They love to travel, enjoy different people and change of scene; but most of all, they love the Service. They are true cosmopolites!

THE BUSINESS OF BEING "MRS."

When you became a Navy wife you accepted a definite responsibility. You cannot meet this responsibility by love and kisses alone, and whether you are legally experienced or inexperienced you have entered into a partnership business with your husband. Brace yourself, because it is bound to touch on such unromantic things as getting the floors waxed and the windows washed, how much it will cost to give a party, how long a sheet can be expected to wear. If you have an outside income, your business will be run on a large scale, and probably you won't have to worry about the longevity of sheets. If you are like most of us, however, you will have to meet large problems with a small income.

The first need in a good partnership is mutual understanding. In marriage, as in bridge, a team must play the same conventions to avoid going down. The time to bring up money matters and to reach some sort of agreement is before you reach the altar. It will be too late on the honeymoon. For some reason, it is difficult to speak of money matters just after the ceremony. Why, I don't know. Yet in those first few weeks of married life you may form habits and set up standards for keeps—for instance, the habit of living on an irregular amount irregularly handed out.

You will be wise to decide on a joint bank account, and many wives like the idea of having a separate savings account for emergencies. Of course, in the days of *Life with Father* you would have had difficulty putting this across, but today it is easier.

Many girls have had experience in the business world and know the value of a dollar. Certainly, feminine dumbness is not considered cute by men when it comes to money matters. Be most careful never to undermine your husband's confidence in the way you spend money. Unless you keep an eye on the bank balance and a close tab on check stubs you are headed for TROUBLE.

The Value of System

Every successful business in the world is built upon the foundation stones of system and records. Without these a business cannot continue to thrive. The Navy household is a business, and since your husband will be at sea a large part of the time you necessarily are the business manager.

Be Your Own Executive

One of the wisest and best investments for a portion of your leisure time is a good secretarial course. Enroll in a short course if there is a possibility of your having to pick up stakes and move; then, if there is more time, continue your study. In such a course you will learn not only typing, but the value of system, methods of filing, and the use of records. Such a course will make your Navy life easier going. This is merely a suggestion, but it is one based on the experience of hundreds of women who have tried it out. Some will always prefer the trial-and-error method. They have to learn the hard way. If that is your disposition, go to it.

To accomplish the maximum in assisting your husband to complete a successful naval career, it is essential that you keep certain records. Some of the records herein proposed must be kept with absolute accuracy; for others their extent and the degree of accuracy depends upon conditions which you will learn only by experience. The records you are advised to keep may seem at first unduly extensive, but none is recommended which will not prove to be worth while in insuring against financial embarrassment, in preventing neglect of social obligations, in increasing your future happiness, and in retaining your husband's respect, love, and devotion.

System in the Navy Household

Marriage means more than establishing a love nest. It implies creating a successful home, and a successful home is built by sound financing. Records show that money problems form one of the biggest causes for divorce today, and debt is something that is feared by all officers of the Service. The government instructs its employees that all official bills be paid by the tenth of the month and all other bills not later than the fifteenth of the month.

To know where the money is to go is the A B C of business. First of all, as the business manager provide yourself with the proper equipment. If a desk is part of your household furniture, take it over; if you don't have one, set up a bridge table or use the dining-room table. If you are using a roomy desk, have special drawers for files, document boxes, and household inventories. There should also be space for account books, cookbooks, a card catalogue, and a typewriter.

If the bridge table is your lot, you will need two tin boxes: the old-fashioned strongbox type or lockbox, large size, plus a fisherman's tin box for tackle converted to hold desk equipment. Your small box or desk might be equipped with the following:

pens	stationery	scissors	paste
pencils	post cards	tape measure	glue
clips	stamps	checkbook	mucilage
thumbtacks	scratch pads	stapler	ink

Should space be a factor, with your two tin boxes and a shelf or table you can set up your office anywhere. The strongbox should be large enough to hold a loose-leaf binder of standard dimensions—8½″ x 11½″. In this box you could also keep all the legal papers which it is necessary for you to have at hand at all times.

Your Business Log

"Log" is a Navy term; it is "a record of facts." It is in no sense a diary and should be kept free of sentiment and mental wanderings. Your log should be a record of events to which, in the future, it may be necessary or desirable to refer in order to refresh your memory. It is especially important when moving from one station to another, or for any day in which there occurs any important or unusual event. It should contain data for at least five years; often it is necessary to check income-tax returns, and sometimes they are subject to a call for verification of statements made in your joint income-tax returns. Notes can be made in a notebook in pencil, then transferred to your log at the first opportunity.

First of all, buy yourself a standard loose-leaf binder. There should be at least six heavy separation sheets, each with a tab to show the nature of the records on the pages immediately following. These tabs should be labeled in order: Automobile, Legal, Financial, Social and Dates (calendar, not social), Inventory.

Here are some of the items you might record in your log:

1. Departure from a permanent station, stating date and hour of departure, means of transportation used, and names of dependents makin the trip. Such data are required in making a claim for reimbursement by the government for the transportation of dependents.

2. Expenses during a trip by automobile from one permanent station to another—for gas, oil, tires, repairs, etc. If your husband, traveling under orders, makes the trip with you in the car, he is entitled to claim as deductions from income his actual travel expenses, i.e., the cost of gas, oil, etc., for a mileage equal to that between stations. If a wife travels without her husband in the car, travel costs are not deductible from the income. Of course, dependents are not considered in determining per diem allowances on a trip.

3. Hotels, motels, and eating places used en route. It is remarkable how often some article of value is left in a place where one has eaten a meal or spent the night. If the name of each place is noted, such lost articles can frequently be recovered.

4. Leases or other written agreements made. Anything of a legal nature should be recorded in general terms and in more specific terms in the legal section of your records.

5. Social obligations incurred and returned. This is for no thought of "an eye for an eye, or a tooth for a tooth," only as a matter of record.

6. Interesting or prominent people you meet. To recall past friendships, nothing is more important than records. Record the names and addresses of people you would like to remember, and they will probably be legion. Here's a tip! Always write down the names of your host's children wherever you visit. When your better half starts out on a cross-country to a distant base mentioning that he may see the O'Connors, be sure to brief him on Mrs. O'Connor's first name and the names of the little O'Connors. It always pays off; and should he be too busy to listen—I always found a little note slipped into my husband's pocket with the necessary data was read and used very gratefully once he arrived at his destination. Should O'Connor have changed wives, I always tried to remind him of that, too, but not on paper! Husbands have a careless habit of leaving embarrassing notes in the wastebasket, and, as you know, some women are as curious as cats.

7. Important events in family life. These will include engagements, weddings, births, christenings, illnesses, injuries, and deaths. Dates and hours of births and deaths may in later years be of unexpected legal importance.

AUTOMOBILE LOG

Your automobile record should contain a complete indentification of your car, including, besides all the data contained in the registration card, its color, equipment such as radio and heater, and identification numbers of tires. Then there will be license data, date of expiration, cost and number . . . of tag. The most important of all is the location of the ownership certificate, from what state the present ownership certificate was obtained, and when. You will also want to record auto insurance carried, kind, amount, company, and date of expiration.

LEGAL RECORD

In your legal section should be recorded in full any matter which might lead to legal complications, such as:

1. Wills. The date and substance of your latest will and your husband's will should be recorded here, also a statement of where the original wills are kept, preferably in a safe-deposit box at some bank.
2. Leases. The substance of any lease by which you have agreed to rent property from or to another. Copies of leases should be kept with you in your strongbox.

3. Purchases. Notation of property purchased with full description, date, purchase price, down payment, and monthly payment required.
4. Policies—a list of insurance policies carried by you or your husband.
5. Pension data for widow.
6. The date and hour of employing or discharging a servant, in states where an employees' compensation law is in effect.
7. Federal and state income-tax data.
8. Notation of inventory of furniture and equipment of any furnished apartment or house rented by you, and of the checking and release when leaving. Such inventory should be kept in your lockbox.

Also to Be Kept in Lockbox

1. Canceled checks for current year
2. Your power of attorney for your husband
3. Automobile ownership certificate
4. Auto insurance policy
5. Copies of leases
6. Receipts of bills paid with cash
7. Storage or warehouse receipts

Safe-Deposit Box

Every family should maintain a safe-deposit box in some bank or trust company vault and should keep in it all legal papers, such as birth and marriage certificates, wills, insurance policies, and other valuable property.

There are three ways in which a title may be taken to a safe-deposit box; each has its merits, and each its disadvantages. The first is individual ownership, in which case the box is absolutely private to the owner; in case of death, it can be entered only in the presence of a representative of the probate court.

The second method is joint tenancy for a husband and wife, in which case either may enter the box independently of the other. However, if either party dies, the box is sealed and may be opened only in the presence of a representative of the state tax commission, the purpose being to discover any assets which may be held subject to inheritance tax.

The third method and probably the best for Service personnel who are married is "individual ownership with appointed deputy." This is similar to the first method except that the box owner appoints a deputy who may enter the box. This method is advantageous to officers and families leaving for occupation duty. A relative or attorney may be appointed as deputy and may open the box in case necessary papers need to be forwarded.

LIFE INSURANCE

Insurance is one of "the first things that come first." Every young seaman, Petty officer and Navy officer with a wife, and particularly with a wife and family, should provide for their protection before all else. Straight life and endowment insurance is considered a good investment, and here are four good reasons:

1. The investment is as well protected as is humanly possible.
2. Insurance commits you to a plan of saving.
3. It means ready money in case of the death of the earner.
4. It serves as an investment fund against which you can borrow if necessary.

National Service Government Life Insurance for $10,000 is made available to every serviceman on active duty without cost.

How much additional insurance should be carried? This and many other questions do not have a stock answer. They will vary with the individual, his income, and his family needs. Normally, a husband takes out insurance for his wife, who is known as his beneficiary. With the birth of each child, it is well to increase the insurance if possible.

To get a clear picture of your husband's insurance program, sit in on the next conference he has with his life insurance agent. The agent will be glad to explain the program, and it is only right that you know your husband's plans and wishes should anything happen to him. Insurance experts advise that, whatever amount of insurance is carried, it be bought with the understanding that in case of death some of the principal, *but not all,* will be paid to the widow at once. Their experience has been that when a widow with little knowledge of how to invest, or handle fairly large sums of money, turns it over to a "friend" to invest, sometimes a charmer of the opposite sex, she loses part or all of the principal. The safest way is simply not to have all that money at one time.

A better plan is to have the major portion of the money paid to her in monthly installments over a certain number of years. This monthly income is distinguished from an annuity in that the latter is more expensive and continues for the lifetime of the beneficiary, while in an insurance benefit the monthly payments end when the amount designated has been paid.

If your husband's insurance policy is set up to pay you a lump sum, you will have the responsibility of investing it wisely enough to have an income from it. This is extremely difficult to do today, and you will probably need the services of a banker, a lawyer, or a broker. All of this is expensive and you will have to make decisions. You will be in a much better position to make these decisions if you and your husband are sensible and talk over your financial affairs frankly during his lifetime. Do not be sensitive about raising the subject. It is for your own good and that of your family. In addition, it will give your husband a certain peace of mind to know that you are provided for in an emergency, and that you will carry out his wishes.

WILLS

The mentioning of a "last will and testament" is a very ticklish proposition in some families, and yet every well-advised officer should talk it over with his wife. Many wives also make wills—a wise precaution if they have certain bequests they desire to make. Personally, I think that every wife should make a will, no matter how little of this world's goods she may have to bequeath. At the time of death, and in the stress and strain of readjustment, often a husband will dispose of, by selling or giving away, valuable possessions that the deceased would wish to be given to particular friends or to members of her own family.

In addition to discussing wills—while it is not a very cheery subject—officers and wives should come to some decision as to where they wish to be buried. If there are children, family burial plots should be considered. A Navy man should decide where he wishes to be buried and leave written instructions to this effect. He may make one of three choices, subject to local health laws and sanitary regulations: (1) at the place of his death; (2) at his home; (3) in a national cemetery. Where death of an officer occurs suddenly, it is difficult for his widow, stunned by grief, to make important decisions. This extra hardship can be averted if the husband has been thoughtful enough to discuss these important matters during his lifetime.

A will sounds like a formidable instrument. Really it is nothing more than a legal document whereby a person disposes of his property in the manner he wishes.

A testator is the person who makes and leaves a will in force at his death. A codicil is a postscript or an addition to a will that must be executed with the same legal formalities as the will itself. An executor or executrix is the person designated by the testator to carry out the provisions of the will. The wife may be chosen as the executrix of the husband's will.

It is well to consult an attorney for the preparation of a will, but if that is not possible, then make out a very simple one. An attorney will acquaint you with statute laws of the state in which the will is to be probated, and of any legal angles on which you should be informed.

When one dies without leaving a will, the law considers him to have died intestate. Then the state steps in and distributes the estate through an appointed county administrator, and according to the then existing state laws of descent and inheritance—a share for the wife, shares for children, shares for parents, etc. This method may or may not suit, but even if it should, it is expensive to resort to such litigation. A publicly appointed administrator is entitled by law to fees and is usually disinterested in economical handling of property.

Short Form of a Simple Will

All my estate I devise and bequeath to my wife, for her own use and benefit forever, and I hereby appoint her my executrix, without bond, with full power to sell, mortgage, lease, or in any other manner dispose of the whole or any part of my estate.

Dated April 10, 1955   WILLIAM SATTERLEE TYLER

Subscribed, sealed, published, and declared by William Satterlee Tyler, testator above named, as and for his last will in the presence of each of us, who at his request and in his presence, in the presence of each other, at the same time, have hereto subscribed our names as witnesses this April 10, 1955, at the city of San Diego, California.

....
Witness   Address

....
Witness   Address

The marriage of a man and the birth of his child, subsequent to the making of a will by him, have the effect of revoking such a will in many states. A new will must be made.

Remember if cash is deposited in the bank in the husband's name only, his wife cannot draw it out until the will is probated, even though he left it to her by will.

Another technicality in regard to bank accounts is this: It is possible in most states to carry a joint bank account and most banks have a specially prepared contract form setting out the legal status of the account. Such an account is the property of both parties (husband and wife). The contract should contain the provision John Doe and Mary Doe with right of survivorship and not as tenants in common.

If a bank account is in one name only and that individual dies, then the account is frozen and the deposit put in the hands of the executor or administrator.

It is wise to talk these matters over with an officer of the bank with which you are doing business. Banking laws in different states and possessions vary, but the subject is current with the bank's officials, and they can offer positive and valuable advice.

Necessary Papers for Personal File

Many government claims are unduly delayed because of not having at hand properly certified copies of birth and marriage certificates and divorce decrees. Usually a Navy man takes care of each of these items and does not leave the responsibility to beneficiaries. However, it is good business experience for a Navy wife to know exactly how to handle her business affairs in case of the death of her husband.

First of all, she should know exactly where all the necessary papers, including legal documents such as birth and marriage certificates, insurance policies, etc., are filed. If an officer is a member of the Navy Mutual Aid, this organization will take care of all such papers and will also assist the widow in filing her various Government claims. It is wise for a husband and wife to read over and check the following points:

1. Last will and testament. I have made a will. Check when accomplished and where it is filed.
2. U.S. Government life insurance policy.

3. Commercial insurance. Forms required: Proofs of death, obtainable from company when death occurs. Beneficiary's age must be proved if insurance proceeds are payable as life income.

INFORMATION IN REGARD TO BIRTH AND MARRIAGE CERTIFICATES

Probably 75 per cent of people over thirty-five years of age are under the impression that they cannot obtain birth certificates. An officer or enlisted man does not need a birth certificate except in cases of obtaining a passport; however, it is always desirable to have it on file. Practically everyone can obtain a birth certificate if he writes to the proper office of record.

No governmental agency will settle a claim without the proper certified copy of the record of birth and marriage, if it is possible to secure same. From this it may be seen that church records, records of family Bibles, affidavits of parents, "the beautifully engraved certificate given you by the minister who performed the marriage ceremony" are all inadequate. What you *must* have is: *certified copies of birth and marriage records* issued under *seal* by that office.

If a record of birth is absolutely nonexistent, and according to the book, *Custodians of Public Records,* it is shown that state records were not kept previous to certain dates, then other proofs are acceptable. In these cases, where other proof, in the form of affidavits, is accepted, accompanying the affidavit must be a certified statement from a state or county official verifying that no public record of the birth or marriage is obtainable for the period in which the birth or marriage occurred. That being established, it then is permissible to establish proof in the following ways:

1. *A certified copy* of a church record if the child was baptized in a church. Many churches maintain such records and the present registrar of the church will make a sworn statement of the record.
2. *Sworn statement of doctor who officiated at the birth of the child.* In many cases this cannot be obtained, owing to the death of the doctor or removal from community. If obtainable, the doctor must swear to it before a notary.
3. *Sworn statement of two witnesses present* at the time of the child's birth. This affidavit must be made by individuals who knew both parents at the time of and before the birth. They do not actually have

to have been present at the birth itself, but must certify that they knew of the birth and of the naming of the child.

4. *Notarized certificates* from entry in family Bibles of the birth. There are many avenues for fraud in making certificates from entries in family Bibles; therefore, such certificates may be refused and other proof required. Or the family Bible may have to be produced.

5. Request Veterans Administration to obtain from Bureau of Census the record of the family from first record of the Census which was made *after the birth of the child*. This method is used only as a last resort.

There is an unending delay in the settling of claims while waiting for proofs of age, so all of these details should be in order and in the business file of the officer or enlisted man.

PHOTOSTATIC COPIES

Again, there is much bad information and misunderstanding in regard to photostats. They are acceptable only when made from the official record by the Bureau of Vital Statistics or other official agency in charge of public record. Before a photostat is made, a marginal endorsement must certify that it is an official photostat of the public record. It then must be signed under the seal of the issuing office.

Whenever a widow is claiming pension or compensation for the death of a husband, and it is shown that either the deceased or the widow or both had a previous marriage, a certified copy of the divorce proceedings must be obtained and submitted before the right of the claimant can be established. This copy should be obtained from the court which granted the divorce. It is wise to get this record at once, when it is easiest, as many cases are on record of courthouses burning and records being destroyed.

HEALTH INSURANCE

With many government hospitals being inactivated, owing to the economy program, it is impossible in many places for dependents today to receive medical service or hospital care. Everybody wonders about the extra expense (or ought to) involved in a serious illness or in having a baby. It is good sense to write these off in adance by carrying health insurance.

The Blue Cross Hospital Plan of the Associated Hospital Service offers one of the finest types of protection to Service personnel. It (1) covers hospital bills; (2) covers medical-surgical bills while you are hospitalized; (3) covers medical-surgical bills when hospitalization is not required. A patient is allowed to stay in the hospital up to twenty-one days, and maternity cases are kept ten days. The Blue Cross pays the hospital direct, so there is no embarrassment about collecting the money from the insurance company. It is considered the most satisfactory health insurance available.

Fire and Automobile Insurance

Fire insurance is a must in the Service. If your husband does not have the maximum amount to cover your possessions, do not delay getting it. Write at once to the Army Cooperative Fire Insurance Association at Fort Leavenworth, Kansas, for necessary blanks and information. The yearly premiums are nominal, and it is splendid protection.

Automobile insurance, at least against public liability and damage, is imperative. The United Services Automobile Association of Fort Sam Houston, Texas, is a mutual company of long standing, organized and managed by Army personnel. Its premiums to Service personnel are lower than those of most automobile insurance companies and its service is of the highest. Educational insurance will be covered in Chapter XIII.

Income Tax

It is a common and erroneous belief in civilian circles that Service personnel are exempt from taxes. Under the present federal personal income-tax law a husband and wife may file a joint income-tax return. If the wife has an income from any outside source, she must keep an accurate record of sums received, with the date of receipt and source of such income.

Pay, not allowances, is subject to tax. Allowances include quarters allowance, ration allowance, and per diem.

Should a Wife Work?

Homemaking is a full-time job, and a wife should not work unless there is a real need for the money she earns. Of course, there are extenuating circumstances, where an aged or ill parent must be supported, but simply to improve one's standard of living or to buy a piano, silver, or a car is not a very worth-while reason, if such work in any way jeopardizes your home responsibilities.

If you do work, always remember that your husband and your home should come first, and it is not cricket to expect your husband to accept a slapdash sort of housekeeping. Also, never use your job for an alibi. Above all, whatever temptation you may have felt to be a martyr, banish it forever.

While there is no regulation against a Navy wife's working on a station, some Commanding Officers have serious objections, and will not allow it. Before accepting a position of any kind, find out the CO's wishes in the matter. This does not hold true on overseas bases where the extra services of teachers, secretaries, clerical workers, and PX personnel prove a blessing.

The reasons against wives' working on the station are obvious. Female workers can prove either a mercy or a nuisance. First of all, a great deal depends upon the attitude of the worker. She must keep her home and personal affairs out of the office, and she must consider all office and official matters *strictly confidential*. If she isn't careful how she talks both *during and after* office hours she will probably be eased out; also she can expect a certain amount of jealousy from the civilian employees, who are too ready to feel that favoritism got her the job. Even at best, a job on a station is not too easy . . . for a married woman!

A young married couple should never scale their living expenses to a double income because if the wife has to stop work they are really stuck. The basic expenses should be the husband's problem; he is the permanent earner and is legally responsible. By basic expenses I mean food, rent, and clothing. If the wife earns extra money, it makes for a better feeling to put it in a joint bank account; "this is the kind of thing that takes two individuals and merges them into a family team."

Savings and Investments

Foresight demands the immediate initiation of some form of savings plan. In these days of low interest on savings accounts, the Ensign will be wise to purchase government baby bonds. Each bond costs $18.75 and is redeemable for $25.00 ten years from date, thus yielding nearly 3 per cent per year at compound interest. Such bonds are redeemable at any date, in case of necessity, but at a reduced interest rate. The cost of purchase of one such bond per month is not too much to put into savings.

It takes will power to save money, but the pleasant satisfaction a bank account gives you more than makes up for the minor self-denials to which you condition your character. There are all sorts of attractive savings plans which your banker will be glad to recommend. Many Navy personnel try to keep the equivalent sum of a month's pay in their savings account for emergencies such as a change of station.

Investments should not be made without consulting your banker or broker. His sound advice may save you many dollars. However, if you have extra money with which to speculate on the stock exchange or "play the ponies," that is your own affair.

BORROWING

It is a poor policy to borrow money from friends or relatives. A bank or finance company is the proper place to borrow money. Avoid all unknown loan associations or "loan sharks." Apply first if possible to your own bank or to the Federal Services Finance Corporation. This is a reliable organization and is accustomed to handling Service loans. It has branches in nearly all places where a large number of Service people are situated.

POWER OF ATTORNEY

In order to permit the wife to obtain automobile licenses, etc., and to dispose of joint property in an emergency, she should be furnished with a duly certified "power of attorney" to act for her husband. Legal blanks for this purpose are available at all Navy yards.

BUYING A CAR

Although an automobile is not absolutely essential in all stations, it is a great convenience. Modern life seems to center around a car, and the Navy family usually owns a fairly good one even if the home is a one-room apartment. Very often it is bought on the installment plan. Often a second-hand car will serve the purpose of a short stay.

A definite sum of as much as $30.00 per month should be set aside with a view to the purchase and operation of a car.

If the wife is given power of attorney it is desirable that the car be registered in both husband's and wife's names as joint owners.

Look Before You Lease

Just as it is highly important to read over every clause of an insurance policy, so it is equally important to read over every sentence of a rental lease. In view of the temporary plans, both civilian and naval, most landlords rent apartments on the basis of at least one month's occupancy, after which at least ten days' notice is required to terminate the contract. The present shortage of houses and apartments is making it increasingly difficult to rent without a lease.

In leases extending for more than a month you should insist on a Navy clause which reads about like this:

In case the said ———— ————, Lieutenant, USN, is detached from his present station, or the ship in which he is serving is permanently detached from the Naval force based in this area, this lease may be vacated upon ten days' notice.

Avoid breaking a lease, for such a procedure is legally and ethically wrong. In addition, it may bring upon you a lawsuit which will have a serious effect on your husband's record and bring discredit upon the Navy. Frequently it is possible to sublet or obtain a new client for your landlord who is willing to take your lease.

Operation Efficiency: On Shore Duty

When all is said and done there are four musts in the daily routine regardless of what you are doing with the rest of the day. They are:
1. Bedmaking
2. Dishwashing, tidying up
3. Meal planning and marketing
4. Preparation of meals

Learn to enjoy doing a good job at your housework; have respect for your job and a mature pride in your home. There is nothing menial in housework if you have a sincere love for and a genuine interest in your home. But remember, to have an orderly, attractive, well-kept home requires daily routine.

When You Are Your Own Maid and You Probably Will Be!

Depending upon your hours of rising and the time of breakfast, after which you see your hero off to work, two hours should give you ample time to do your daily routine housework thoroughly. Of course, if you stop to finish a detective story or go back to bed for an extra nap, remember to deduct it from your leisure instead of skipping your household duties.

If you want to do a good cleaning job, get set for it by wearing comfortable and practical clothes. With all the good-looking play outfits on the market, you might as well choose an attractive combination such as shorts and shirt, slacks (if you have the figure for them) and shirt, pedal-pushers and shirt, or an attractive utility house dress. There's no point in looking like a scrub woman when it is possible to look pleasing. Here is a check list that may help.

1. After removing breakfast dishes, put butter and cream in refrigerator, then clean living room and dining room. (You may have early-morning callers, and it is disconcerting to have a disordered living room at any time when visitors arrive.) Assemble in a basket anything left in the living room that belongs in the other rooms. A special wastebasket on rollers for papers, discarded flowers, and ashes will save you steps. If you're a soap-opera addict, tune in on your favorite program and enjoy it while you work!

2. Make beds and tidy bedroom and bathroom. Fold towels neatly on racks. Clean lavatory and tub, check supply of soap and toilet tissue. Replace soiled towels with clean ones.

3. Return to the kitchen, check over menu for the day. Check refrigerator for leftovers and, if necessary to market, make list. Prepare vegetables for lunch and dinner and do any long-in-advance cooking preparations for dinner while washing last night's dinner dishes and the breakfast dishes. (Of course, some housekeepers may be horrified at this. For my money, twice a day is enough for any bride to wash dishes. The brides think so, too!) While drying the dishes, perhaps you can tune in on a foods program which will give you ideas in planning your meals and tell you the prices of foods that are in season and plentiful.

4. If it is convenient to market early, this is the best time for

good fresh buys and you will beat the crowds. Of course, you will not need to market every day. Once or twice a week should be sufficient.

5. Prepare lunch for yourself on a tray, if your husband does not come home to join you. Wash or stack your dishes; your kitchen will be neater and more inviting if everything is washed before you prepare dinner.

6. Learn to budget your time, so that you can include rest, recreation, personal beautifying, and mental improvement in your "design for living."

7. If your menu calls for a simple dinner which will not require your attention until an hour before mealtime, you will be free until late afternoon. Plan ahead if any food conditioning is necessary such as crisping vegetables for salad and thawing frozen foods. Set your table attractively. Arrange the living room for evening enjoyment, such as laying the fire, adjusting the window shades, and setting out the equipment for making drinks, if your husband wishes to serve a cocktail before dinner.

Dinner should be a restful meal, gracious and peaceful and not interrupted by frequent trips to the kitchen. A weary husband may enjoy a cocktail or highball before dinner, or it may be equally restful for him to have a quiet talk with you as an unhurried companion. Sometimes he may like to listen to the radio, and make informative remarks on the news to you. Even if you don't agree with his views, save your comments until after dinner. A good meal improves a man's disposition. You can make this before-dinner interlude a period of charm and relaxation to which your husband will look forward if you plan intelligently. Have your domestic machinery so well oiled that you can take it easy before dinner.

8. After serving dinner, clear the table, stack the dishes in a covered container. (Never ask your husband to help you with the dishes at night; he has been working for the government all day. If he enjoys drying the dishes and offers to help or to do them, that is something else! Be agreeable and don't fail to be appreciative; but don't expect him to do your work in addition to his own military duties.)

There is nothing effeminate about a man's helping about the house. If your husband likes to cook, surrender the kitchen whenever he offers to take over. Illness or some unforeseen occasion may arise and it is good if a husband is capable of carrying on in your place. I still believe, however, that just as a Navy man keeps his job separate from his home life, so should a Navy wife keep her housekeeping job separate from her homemaking.

SUGGESTIONS ON DAILY ROUTINE

1. Go over entire quarters daily. Learn to finish one room before going on to another.

2. In your daily care, it is easiest to dust first, straighten, then run your carpet sweeper or vacuum and dry mop.

3. Before going to bed, straighten living-room furniture, put away newspapers, cards, card table; empty ash trays and dispose of glasses so that the sight of the living room will not overwhelm you the next morning. It takes only a minute to empty the contents of the ash trays into a paper bag and to quick-rinse the glasses and bottles; the polishing can wait until morning. Plump up the pillows, open the windows, weather permitting, and you will have a much more cheerful view of life in general the next morning.

In the management of your household, remember that the small decisions are yours. Don't worry your husband with such trivialities as the bakery or dairyman's passing you by; learn to keep these petty annoyances to yourself. No man likes to clutter his mind with such details, and little irritations like these all come in the realm of housekeeping and are the gremlins that beset every housewife. He has his own pet gremlins to contend with in his work, but ten to one he never mentions them to you. Be adult, and do likewise!

YOUR WEEKLY ROUTINE

There will be certain days that you may set aside for special cleaning, baking, mending, just as your mother and your grandmother did before you; but it will help greatly if you will be methodical and use a little will power about complying with the routine schedule you make for yourself.

Monday: Regular daily routine plus! Monday spells washday to many housewives; I like the first day of the week to get organized for the days coming up. It is a good day for general cleaning and checking. If the laundry is to be sent out, it should be listed and counted. If it is to be done at home, it will be easier if it is separated. Check and straighten linen closet. Check supplies of all types; bath, kitchen, laundry, and needs of household.

Tuesday: Laundry and part of ironing. Defrost refrigerator.

Wednesday: Thorough cleaning of bedrooms and baths including clothes closets.

Thursday: Mend, remove spots from clothes, brush clothing, clean silver.

Friday: General cleaning of living room, hall, dining room, downstairs closets, and kitchen. Introduce fresh flowers for week end.

Saturday: Market early, then after routine work enjoy the week end with your husband.

YOUR MAID IS A VIP

If you are fortunate enough to have a full- or a part-time maid today, it stands to reason that you must pay standard wages and have your home equipped with modern appliances and labor-saving devices.

One of the reasons many young women do not wish to go into domestic service is that they feel there is a social stigma attached to it. This attitude can be eliminated if you fulfill the following points as an employer:

1. It is mandatory by law that you have social security insurance for household employees. They contribute one-half of the 3 per cent, but as an employer you are responsible for sending in the entire amount to the Collector of Internal Revenue.

2. Arrange specified days and time off.

3. Schedule your maid's work.

Make your maid feel at home and comfortable; the more you can do to make her feel at home, the more permanent and rewarding your association will be. Her room should be attractive. It might be a bed-sitting room and include a comfortable studio bed, a good reading lamp, a desk, a radio, and closet space. Good sense and common decency will make the wise employer look after a maid if she is ill. If there are children in the household, your maid's good nature and dependability contribute enormously to your peace of mind and the happiness of your family. When you choose a maid, you are really choosing a member of the family.

Planning Meals

Menu planning saves time, money, and the need of thinking each day what to have for the next meal. Try making out practical menus for a week and you will be sold on the idea. Always plan meals when you are hungry, not after having eaten a hearty dinner!

It is a good idea to shop personally at least once a week and to become acquainted with your grocer, butcher, and baker at the market where you do most of your buying. If you market at the same grocery regularly enough, the staff will learn your needs and preferences and will value your patronage. You can save money by watching the daily papers for sales of foodstuffs. Stock up on staples and canned goods during sales.

Today the only advantage in commissary buying is the convenience of shopping on the station, if you reside there. Prices are the same as those of downtown stores.

A Few Tips on Marketing

1. Check your staples once a week. When you open the last bottle of catsup or vinegar, can of coffee or box of salt, list it, and reorder.

2. Have a standing order for milk, butter, and eggs.

3. Don't fail to ask the price of things before you buy.

4. Learn the different cuts and grades of meat. Cheap cuts can be delicious if properly cooked. Ask for the bones that come with all your meat, so you will have the makings of bouillon, soup, or a savory gravy. Save out bits of vegetables here and there, such as celery tops, a carrot, four or five string beans, outside cabbage leaves, and you can make a wonderful vegetable soup. Learn small economies as you go along.

5. Special sales can save you money, but be sure the quality is high even though the price is low. It is usually safe to buy your favorite name brands.

6. Plan your vegetables so that you will use the more perishable items like spinach, lettuce, and tomatoes first. Reserve cauliflower, cabbage, and squash for the last of the week.

7. In buying fresh fruit and vegetables, watch the market. Read the ads; listen to the radio.

8. Give yourself a good course in marketing from books. There

is no use learning the hard way when experts have tested and worked out an easy way that is yours for the asking at any library.

YOUR EMERGENCY SHELF

In the Navy there is no such thing as an unexpected guest. Once he arrives and accepts your invitation to share potluck, it is up to you to use your ingenuity in preparing a good luncheon or dinner. Your emergency shelf will prove the lifesaver. It should be kept well stocked with standard canned goods and a few delicacies that will turn a plain dinner into a company dinner and make your husband marvel at your cleverness. With no mental road blocks as to your culinary ability, a pantry well stocked with the right cans and seasonings, a basic knowledge of the principles of plain cookery, and a true incentive to supply your husband with the food he really likes, you will go far!

Most men like oyster stew, kidney stew, broiled sirloin steak, French fried potatoes or baked potatoes, rib roast of beef, French fried onion rings, green apple pie, and strawberry shortcake. For emergency use, it is a good plan to keep two cans of Madrilene or jellied consommé in the refrigerator along with two packages of frozen vegetables. Your emergency shelf might include:

Canned soups

Canned meats (whole chicken, ham, corned-beef hash)

Canned fish (tuna, salmon, lobster, crabmeat, sardines, caviar, anchovies)

Canned vegetables (peas, mushrooms, asparagus, artichoke hearts)

Canned fruits (pineapple, pears, peaches, apricots, whole greengage plums)

Canned juices (tomato, grapefruit, grape, lime, lemon, orange, sauerkraut)

Crackers, cookies, pretzels, popcorn, peanuts, potato chips in cans, olives, pickles, brown bread, sandwich spreads, plum pudding, jellies, preserves, mints, candy, nuts

Chapter XI

CHANGE OF DUTY

NOTHING is more exciting in the Service than "receipt of orders." They may come without any previous notice, but usually in peacetime an officer has the privilege of asking for certain assignments for which he feels he is especially qualified. The Supply Officer will be not only your best friend but your real source of information in regard to the move. He is an expert on travel and shipping your household goods; he knows the ins and outs of travel by private car, rail, ship, or MSTS transport, MATS or commercial air travel. It is best to consult him early in order to avoid many complications. He will furnish the required forms for requesting transportation of household effects.

By "scuttlebutt" or the grapevine you may receive rumors of orders, or your husband may receive official information as to his next duty before he receives orders. Don't hit the panic button but use this extra time to collect all the information you can on your new station. You will find all kinds of advice freely given; listen attentively but absorb only the information you will need. For overseas stations, the Navy Department issues interesting pamphlets. Another excellent source of information is the AFHA (Armed Forces Hostess Association), Room 1-B-877 in the Pentagon, where a complete file on overseas stations is kept.

If you are moving to a new place in the United States, write the Chamber of Commerce of the city to which you are going; the American Automobile Association will also be glad to furnish information to members; the large oil companies, in addition to road maps and travel information including transient accommodations, give helpful counsel. If you need help on living conditions, schools, housing, write the Supply Officer or Housing Officer at your new station.

Before you actually start packing, visit the hospital to see if the

Medical Department will release to you any X-rays or medical history that you might need in the future, as well as prescriptions for medicine and glasses. If you are going overseas, order extra glasses to take with you, also an extra set of dentures should you wear them. Inoculations or "booster" shots should be started. You should also check and examine your insurance policies, especially accident insurance and any on your household effects and car. "Change of address" cards should be filled out and mailed to business firms, any institutions from which you receive regular reports, magazines, newspapers, and book club publishers.

The Navy Supply Department attends to the packing, crating, hauling, shipping by freight, and delivery, plus unpacking at your destination, of your household goods. If they are to be moved by van, an estimate will be made first of the entire shipment. Van service today is wonderful; expert packers are employed and the old saying "Three moves are as good as a fire" is no longer applicable. Remember, don't heckle the packers with your suggestions!

An officer or enlisted man is entitled to shipment of a definite weight (according to rank) of household effects at government expense. "Professional books and papers owned by Naval Personnel may be shipped without charge against the weight allowance." (Manual Bu S & A.)

The weight allowances of effects, packed and crated, are:

Effective 1 July 1954 (date of shipment of HHG)

	Navy Weight Allowance		Permanent Allowances Increase	
	Temporary	Permanent	5%	40%
Admiral	2000	11000	11550	15400
Vice Admiral	1500	11000	11550	15400
Rear Admiral (upper half)	1000	11000	11550	15400
Rear Admiral (lower half) and Commodore	1000	11000	11550	15400
Captain	800	11000	11550	15400
Commander	800	10000	10500	14000
Lieutenant Commander and Warrant Officer (W–4 pay)	800	9500	9975	13300

Effective 1 July 1954 (date of shipment of HHG) (*Continued*)

	Navy Weight Allowance		Permanent Allowances Increase	
	Temporary	*Permanent*	*5%*	*40%*
Lieutenant and Warrant Officer (W–3 pay)	600	8500	8925	11900
Lieutenant (j.g.) and Warrant Officer (W–2 pay)	600	7500	7875	10500
Ensign, Officer Graduate of the Coast Guard Academy, Warrant Officer (W–1 pay), and Officer Graduate of USNA	600	7000	7350	9800
Enlisted Personnel (effective 3 May 1954)				
E7 CPO	400	6000	6300	8400
E6 1c	400	5500	5775	7700
E5 2c	400	5000	5250	7000
E4 3c (7 or more years)	400	4500	4725	6300
E4 3c (less than 7 years)	400	3000	3150	4200
Aviation Cadet	400	400	420	560
Civilians (with dependents 8750#)				
(without dependents 3125#)				

2/7 or 40% (frt. or express)
1/21 or 5% (van, intra-city moves and auth stg)

Household effects may be packed, crated, and shipped as soon as orders have been received and proper application made, even previous to the detachment of the officer or enlisted man; or, if preferred, they may be delayed a reasonable length of time after detachment.

It is not essential to send all household effects in one shipment. They may be divided into several shipments, each or any of which may be sent to any one of the authorized destinations. The latitude allowed in the points to which shipments may be made, and in the number and times of shipments, is of great assistance to families.

The Permanent Change of Station

A permanent change of station usually involves a complete uprooting and transplanting for the family. The term "station" means, in the case of an officer on sea duty, the home port or the home yard of the ship to which the husband is assigned. Transportation for dependents is furnished by the government when the permanent station is changed. When an officer is ordered to sea duty, his dependents may choose the home port or the home yard as their destination. This alternative should always be kept in mind when making a change from shore duty to sea duty; for although the home port is normally the better destination for the family, a current or approaching overhaul period may make the home yard the better choice.

There are two great differences between travel performed in making a permanent change of station and travel to a port for a short visit or to the home yard for an overhaul period. The first is: The government furnishes dependents with necessary rail and steamer tickets; or within the continental United States, if dependents travel by automobile at their own expense, the government will reimburse the officer after his dependents have completed the trip. The second is: In many cases the officer in making a permanent change of station is able to travel with his dependents.

When household effects are to be shipped by the government, the following points should be kept definitely in mind: The owner is responsible for supervision of the carrier's inventory of the goods shipped—for seeing that such inventory properly describes the condition and quantity. Examine the inventory before your effects leave your home and, if not satisfied, request that the inventory be amended. However, do not attempt to dictate to the packers; instead, contact your Shipping Officer immediately. The government does not insure shipments of household goods and the carrier's liability in the event of loss or damage is limited to 30 cents per pound per article for van shipments; 10 cents per pound for rail or motor freight shipments; and 30 cents per pound for uncrated household goods via freight forwarded.

Private insurance may be obtained, but be sure that you understand the "co-insurance clause" contained in most of such policies; it means, in effect, that you will receive in case of loss or damage only a pro-rata share of the loss, such pro rata being equal to the ratio of the amount of insurance carried to the full value of the goods so insured. Hence, if you intend to insure your property, insure it for its full value.

You should always sign the government bill of lading after the delivery of your goods, writing upon the reverse side of the bill a note of any loss or damage.

Prior to making your shipment, if possible, read the pamphlet *Household Goods Shipment Information* published by the Bureau of Supplies and Accounts. The Supply Officer can get you a copy.

REIMBURSEMENT FOR AUTOMOBILE TRAVEL

Dependents may travel within the continental United States by private automobile if they so desire. Upon completion of such travel, the officer or enlisted man is entitled to reimbursement of the amount such travel would have cost the government if performed by train. It usually requires a month or six weeks before the submitted claim for reimbursement is settled. As the cost of shipping an automobile is high, many families prefer to proceed to the new station by auto.

One other important advantage of traveling by automobile is that the head of the family not only saves the cost of his trip by rail but also is allowed as a deduction from income on federal and state income tax returns the cost of actual travel by car, provided it does not exceed cost of travel by rail. This includes gas, oil, a reasonable amount for car and tire depreciation, and cost of lodging and meals for the distance and time consumed in normal automobile driving between new and old stations.

In this case, it is imperative that expense deductible from income be meticulously recorded. If the family, without the officer or enlisted man, proceeds by car, no deductions are allowed, and the entire sum received as reimbursement for dependents' travel must be recorded as income.

RAILROAD TRAVEL AT GOVERNMENT EXPENSE

When a Navy man is ordered to a new station, his dependents are entitled to transportation by rail for the necessary travel within the continental limits of the United States. If such transportation is desired, it must be requested. Upon approval of the request the dependents will be furnished railroad tickets and first-class Pullman car accommodations on any regular-fare train on any regularly traveled route. An extra-fare train or any desired unusual route may be used by paying the difference in cost. Dependents must pay for meals except in commercial steamer travel, where meals are included in the fare.

TRAVEL BY COMMERCIAL STEAMER

If you are sailing in a commercial steamer your reservation will have been made for you, and you will be informed where to call to obtain your ticket. On commercial steamers meals are included in the fare, but you will be required to pay for any extras such as drinks and steamer chairs.

TRAVEL BY GOVERNMENT TRANSPORT

If overseas travel is involved, dependents are often required to make the sea trip in a government transport. Because of the infrequent transport trips, your husband may be required to precede you by other naval or by commercial transportation. In case you are to travel by transport, you will be informed by the Bureau of Naval Personnel as to the name of the ship on which you will embark and the day and approximate hour of sailing.

Since March 1, 1950, all former Army transports have been operated in conjunction with the Navy transports by the Military Sea Transportation Service, under the control and management of the Secretary of the Navy.

To accomplish its mission, MSTS has a fleet of C-4 and P-2 class ships, some completely air-conditioned. All are clean, modern, and relatively fast and comfortable. The MSTS is operated under strict regulations which are rigidly enforced. For instance, in your packing don't include intoxicating liquors since the introduction, possession, or use of these on board government transports is prohibited.

There are four ports in the United States from which personnel are shipped overseas: New York, San Francisco, Seattle, and Hampton Roads, Virginia. Persons going to Europe, Africa, the West Indies, and the Canal Zone leave from New York; from San Francisco go passengers to Japan, Okinawa, Guam, the Philippines, and Hawaii; Seattle operates vessels to Alaska and Japan.

Preparation for a Trip by Transport

Usually transportation for dependents by transport is authorized only when the orders received by the officer or enlisted man direct his assignment to, or detachment from, a ship or station outside the continental limits, and even then only to such places and under such conditions as may be prescribed by the Navy Department. Normally, transportation of dependents is not authorized unless the head of the family is expected to remain abroad for more than one year. On some occasions, however, transportation by transport from one coast of the United States to the other is authorized. The first step is for the officer or enlisted man to request such transportation for his dependents, through the proper channels.

The following advice is addressed to the Navy wife who does not have the benefit of her husband's presence during her preparation for a trip by transport.

Once your transportation has been authorized, you will receive a sheaf of travel orders. Guard these with care, for eventually you may be required to show or to surrender each of the dozen or so copies of the original order. This is part of the tape that is known as *red*; however, you will find that one of the mimeographed sheets will prove an open-sesame when you arrive at your port of embarkation.

By telegram or by letter from the transportation officer of the naval district in which you reside you will be advised as to the date, port of embarkation, and place where you should report for your transportation overseas. You will be furnished commercial rail, air, or motor transportation between your home and your port of embarkation, unless you prefer to drive your own automobile or travel by commercial means at your own expense. If you choose to go by train the transportation officer makes your reservation and presents you with your ticket. Your railroad ticket permits you to check up to 350 pounds of baggage, and a half-fare ticket, 175 pounds. Should your baggage be in excess of these weights, you must pay the charge for such excess. Again may I remind you to carry your travel orders with you on the entire journey. Various officials will require copies to substantiate many acts of assistance.

Three Important Don'ts!

Don't report to the embarkation port until you have been notified when to do so. Don't fail to notify the transportation officer should illness or other unavoidable circumstance make it impossible for you to report as directed. And don't fail to notify the transportation officer immediately should there be any change in your address.

Medical Certificates

As soon as you receive your travel orders, arrange with the nearest naval dispensary, or if none is available with an Army or Air Force dispensary, for immunizations. They will be given free upon presentation of your travel orders.

All persons traveling on MSTS ships must present medical certificates proving that they have been inoculated against smallpox, typhoid, and paratyphoid, within twelve months prior to departure. Typhus immunization also is required, and certain inoculations, particularly for diphtheria and whooping cough, are advisable for children. Infants under one year of age are exempt from smallpox vaccination. If you are bound for South America, a medical certificate on trachoma is required; and if to the Orient, cholera shots are advised. No female dependent who will have gone beyond the seventh month of pregnancy at the scheduled date of arrival at her destination will be carried by the MSTS.

Passports and Visas

There are four classes of passports: diplomatic, special, regular, and dependent. If you travel beyond the continental United States, Alaska, Hawaii, Canada, or Bermuda, a passport is required.

To apply for a dependent passport you must submit a letter of authorization from the oversea commander to whose area you are going. This letter arrives before your orders so that you will have sufficient time to apply and to have your passport at the port before you arrive. Complete instructions are given, and you must follow them or you won't get a passport.

You may apply at a State Department office in Washington, D.C., New York, Boston, Chicago, New Orleans, San Francisco, or at a state or federal court authorized to naturalize aliens.

You must submit two passport photographs of yourself, 2½ by 2½ inches, full face. If you have children under twelve years of age, they will be included on your passport. Your picture should include all minor children.

You must submit a birth certificate or other birth evidence for yourself. Your birth evidence will be retained by the State Department. Forms of birth evidence other than a birth certificate are a baptismal certificate with the seal of the church imprinted on it, and a notarized affidavit executed by a parent, guardian, or the physician who attended your birth, or by a reputable person who has knowledge of the facts which enables him to testify as to date and place of birth.

If you are a naturalized United States citizen, you must submit your naturalization certificate with your application. Your naturalization certificate will be returned to you by the State Department.

You must also pay the fee of $1.00 for having your passport application executed. This means you take an oath of allegiance and sign your application before a State Department agent or a clerk of a state or federal court authorized to naturalize aliens.

Your passport application and supporting documentation will be sent to the State Department in Washington. This is the last you will see of it until you reach the port of embarkation, and a complete passport with visas, if necessary, will be handed to you before you board the ship or plane.

Baggage—You Can Take It with You

The first thing you should decide is what you need to take with you and how you are going to pack it! Take everything you need and *only* what you need. The trick is to avoid duplication, yet provide for a versatile wardrobe. If you take two suits instead of four, or five dresses instead of ten, and a minimum of comfortable shoes, you'll have more space for accessories and the little extras that are so convenient.

The fifth freedom for travelers everywhere is "freedom from baggage worries," so pack sensibly, taking a minimum of luggage. If you have traveled to any extent by air with a baggage allowance of sixty-six pounds, you will have small difficulty on water transport. Each member of your family is limited to two pieces of standard hand luggage (not foot lockers) which will go into the cabin. In addition, you are allowed a make-up box for toilet articles, and you will be wise to select a roomy one to include such essentials as you may need should your other baggage be checked through and not be immediately available upon your arrival at the embarkation port. Any luggage which you expect to have in your stateroom should be carefully tagged with your name and the name of the transport on which you are sailing, and marked "Cabin."

A very convenient article with which you can equip yourself before sailing is an ordinary cretonne shoe bag—or better, an apron of this sort. There will not be wall space to which you can thumbtack a shoe bag on a crowded transport, but you can always tie it to your bunk or around your waist. It is ideal for holding toilet articles or manicure equipment and may serve as a sewing kit.

Another indispensable item is a small bag of the knitting type. Carried on the arm it will not be considered luggage, even if you are flying. It proves its worth in helping you keep small articles, such as sunglasses, hair nets, playing cards, bridge scores, books and writing material, with you when on deck.

In order to avoid damage or loss of baggage, be sure your pieces are sturdy and durable. Easily identified baggage saves time for everyone, so here are a few pointers:

1. All baggage other than that you are to have in your cabin will be stored in the hold and probably will not be available during the trip. It is to be marked "Hold."

2. Remove all stickers and travel labels; erase or paint over old markings now on your luggage which is to be stored in the hold.

3. On each container to be stored in the hold stencil or paint, in letters one inch high or larger, on each side, top, and end, your address as follows, for example:

TO: PORT TRANSPORTATION OFFICER
SAN FRANCISCO PORT OF EMBARKATION
OAKLAND ARMY BASE
OAKLAND, CALIFORNIA

FOR: NANCY P. TYLER
LIEUTENANT WILLIAM S. TYLER
(his Navy identification number)

MANILA, PHILIPPINE IS.
PRIORITY 12345 June (from your orders)

Remember this is but a sample address; you might not be sailing from San Francisco, nor be bound for Manila.

4. It is a good idea to place a copy of your travel orders in each piece of luggage for identification.

5. In case your cabin or hold luggage does not accompany you, it is recommended that you forward it by express prepaid to the Port Transportation Officer, allowing plenty of time for delivery at least seventy-two hours before your reporting date.

6. A wise traveler carries his personal luggage with him and never permits it to get separated from him.

Remember that only two pieces of real luggage are allowed in the stateroom, but all women have hatboxes, jewelry cases, and small packages, which are allowed within reason. However, keep in mind that there is no better place to apply the golden rule than on a transport. One inconsiderate, selfish person can ruin the trip for all of those with whom she shares a stateroom or compartment.

Private Automobiles

Privately owned automobiles are not shipped to the port of embarkation at government expense, nor may an automobile be shipped under the classification of household effects. However, the government recognizes the urgent need for an automobile, and if there is space available in the transport, it may, at the discretion of the Port Transportation Officer, be transported overseas free of expense. Should you desire your car to be crated, that expense must be borne by you.

Mail and Money

Mail to be delivered at the embarkation port prior to sailing should be directed to the person, the name of the transport, and the port of embarkation, thus:

Mrs. John Steele
U.S. Transport *Upshur*
San Francisco Port of Embarkation
Oakland, California

All correspondents should be informed of your new address, which should be written thus:

> Mrs. John Steele
> c/o John Steele, Gunner's Mate 1 Class
> (his service number)
> U.S. Naval Station Guam
> via Fleet Post Office San Francisco, California

Overseas mail for stations in the Pacific is handled by the Fleet Post Office in San Francisco; for overseas stations in the Atlantic by Fleet Post Office, New York City.

It is suggested that banking accounts be maintained in the United States. Since personal checks cannot be cashed on board transports or at the port of embarkation, you should plan to have on hand cash, traveler's checks, or U.S. postal money orders to cover all expenses while waiting departure of the transport, and to pay subsistence charges while on board. Allow for at least two days' expenditures at the port of embarkation, to include food, lodging, local transportation, entertainment, and purchases of personal items ashore and on board ship.

Not more than $50.00 in currency may be taken to overseas destinations by each person. But do not purchase foreign currencies before your departure, since the Navy provides adequate facilities for converting United States currency and dollar instruments into foreign currencies. Of course additional funds may be carried in the form of traveler's checks or postal money orders.

The Transport Voyage

There is nothing that quite compares with travel in a transport. To begin with, government transports have a habit of sailing if and when they choose; about the only thing you can depend upon is that they almost always sail at high noon. You are advised to arrive at the port of embarkation twenty-four hours ahead of scheduled sailing time, and it is wise to do so in order to check on the latest information. You may be delayed for days, or again you may sail ahead of schedule. Very aptly, transports are spoken of as "phantom" ships.

Anyway, they get you there, and in pretty fine style, though you shouldn't expect anything fancy like afternoon tea, cocktails, or morning bouillon. The food is splendid, and meals are served right on the dot. Being fifteen minutes late for a meal on transports means that you automatically skip that meal.

Your accommodations as to staterooms, seating in dining salon, priority for use of baths will be in accordance with the relative rank of your husband compared to that of the husbands of other wives on board. You will be required to pay for your meals at the rate of about $1.65 a day, and you will be able to buy cigarettes, stationery, candy, soft drinks, and numerous toilet articles.

HOME YARD AND HOME PORT

The most usual home yards for naval ships operating in the Pacific are Puget Sound Naval Shipyard, at Bremerton, Washington; Mare Island Naval Shipyard, at Vallejo, California; and San Francisco Naval Shipyard. Those for ships operating in the Atlantic are Portsmouth Naval Shipyard (submarines only) at Kittery, Maine; Boston Naval Shipyard; Philadelphia Naval Shipyard; Norfolk Naval Shipyard; and Charleston (S.C.) Naval Shipyard.

The usual home ports for vessels operating in home waters in the Pacific are at Long Beach and San Diego, California; and in the Atlantic, at Newport, Rhode Island, and Norfolk, Virginia. For many ships operating in the Pacific from Pearl Harbor or farther west the home port is Honolulu.

While their husbands are on sea duty, most Navy wives arrange for some kind of housekeeping at the home port or home yard. Normally, the home port is more desirable.

ATLANTIC PORTS

Newport, Rhode Island

Of the home ports on the Atlantic, Newport, Rhode Island, is perhaps the more desirable. The naval colony there is quite large, including in addition to the families of naval personnel attached to ships operating from there, families of officers on duty at the Operating Base, the Naval War College, the Naval Reserve Officers' Candidate School, and the Naval Hospital. There is an attractive Officers' Club beautifully located on Narragansett Bay.

Norfolk, Virginia

Norfolk is much larger than Newport. There was during World War II a great increase in its housing facilities. Living conditions are so satisfactory that many naval people are buying homes in and out of Norfolk. Virginia Beach is one of the communities. The Bolling Square Apartments convenient to the naval base rents furnished apartments by the week or month.

There are many recreational facilities both at the Operating Base and at the Amphibious Force Base near Little Creek, and several well-run Officers' Clubs. It is said that in the Norfolk area calling as a custom is returning.

PACIFIC PORTS

Long Beach, California

Before World War II Long Beach was the home port for all the large ships of the Pacific Fleet. The naval colony was large and gay. More recently, fewer ships have used it as a home port, but the number is increasing. In Long Beach there are many apartments, both furnished and unfurnished, and many small homes for rent. The beach is fine for surf bathing and there are many municipal recreation facilities. Los Angeles is within an hour's automobile drive.

San Diego, California

For families having San Diego as home port there are several choices as to where to live. San Diego, Coronado, La Jolla, Imperial Beach, and a number of other small towns are within easy motoring distance of the Navy landing. Only in San Diego are there many apartments, but in all the other places there are small houses suitable for naval personnel. Some of these are rented furnished, but most supply only gas or electric stove and refrigerator. Because of the tremendous increase in population of this area during World War II, suitable housing has been difficult to locate; however, the situation is improving. There are several comparatively low-rent government housing projects.

Visit to the Home Yard

The home yard is the Navy yard designated to perform the regular overhaul of the ship, which requires from two to three months at periods of eighteen to twenty months. Also, emergency repairs are usually made at the ship's home yard.

Regular overhauls are scheduled many months in advance. As such periods normally exceed any other continuous stay of the ship in any port, most wives, even when there are children, move then from the home port to the home yard.

Such a trip must be made at your own expense. It involves giving up your apartment or home in the home port and obtaining a new place to live in the vicinity of the home yard. With the present crowded conditions in the vicinity of Navy yards, to find any place to live is most difficult.

Usually one Navy ship is leaving the yard, completing its overhaul, as another ship of the same type arrives to begin her period. As the number of officers and enlisted men on each ship of the same type is approximately the same, there are usually about as many wives leaving as arriving, and prior to leaving they try to pass on their apartments to the new arrivals.

For those wives who have no experience in the details of closing a home or apartment, here is a check-off list for your convenience.

1. Never pick up stakes and start for a Navy yard city without being certain of a place to stay when you arrive. If you have been unable to obtain an apartment or a house you may be able to obtain hotel accommodations until other arrangements can be made, or you can wait at the home port until your husband arrives and obtains a place for you.

2. Notify your present landlord of your departure by as much advance notice as is required in your lease. You must avoid breaking a lease. Frequently a landlord will permit you to sublet or will terminate your lease if you can find a new tenant.

3. In case you have been occupying a furnished house or apartment, you should arrange with the landlord to check with you before your departure the inventory of furniture and equipment. You must arrange to have the house or apartment thoroughly cleaned, soiled linens washed, and blankets dry-cleaned. It will save you trouble if the landlord in lieu of such cleaning will permit you to pay a cleaning charge.

4. Notify the gas and electric light companies of your expected departure; also the telephone company if you have had a private telephone; and the municipal agent controlling the water supply if you have been paying for your water supply.

   At least forty-eight hours before your departure you should make arrangements for the final reading of the gas and electric meters on the day of your departure, and for paying the respective bills by making a deposit or by furnishing to the companies if agreeable to them the address to which they are to forward your bill. You will have made a deposit with each of these companies when its service was started; be sure you receive credit for such deposit.

   The telephone company normally requires payment for its monthly service in advance. You should therefore have a credit unless you have had excessive charges for long-distance calls.

   Unless you have been living in a house you probably have not been paying for the water; but if you have been, be sure to arrange for payment of any outstanding bill.

5. When moving to a home yard for several months' stay, your packing problem is complicated; you should:

   a. Put in storage any furniture or bulky articles not required during your stay at the home yard. Number each box put in storage and list the nature of contents of each in your log and legal record, stating date, place, and name of storage company.

   b. Pack your trip essentials in suitcases and hatbox. If you are traveling by car, try to make a place in the trunk compartment for a box containing such canned goods, condiments, spices, etc., as you may have on hand. A cardboard box containing such items will assist in setting up the new apartment and will save more money than one would suspect. Other articles you will require which cannot be carried in the car should be packed in boxes and sent by freight, or fast freight, to your destination. Fast freight is nearly as rapid as express.

6. Stop all regular deliveries of milk, eggs, newspapers, etc.

7. Stop all charge accounts you may have opened; notify stores of date of your departure and pay all outstanding bills before leaving.

8. Cancel any engagements you will be unable to keep.

9. Obtain card from post office on which you notify the postmaster of your change of address; if your new address is not known, have your mail sent to the ship in care of your husband. As an additional safeguard, it is desirable to ask a friend, neighbor, or accommodating landlord to forward any mail that may be left for you. Under any conditions you should leave a forwarding address with your landlord.

10. If you have a checking account in a local bank, it generally will be desirable to close it out.

Being able to follow the ship usually hinges on the same old story— Navy pay! Youth has a tendency to be unduly optimistic, especially in financial matters, but it should never forget that there is more unhappiness in the Navy from lack of financial foresight than because of temporary separations.

Nearly all Navy wives make some trips following the ship. We shall, therefore, discuss the most important activities connected therewith, namely, transportation and allied matters.

There are four general types of situations that may arise:

1. A short visit from three days to a week, usually involving a trip of several hundred miles, from the home port to another port on the same coast, to which your husband's ship is going to participate in a celebration such as Memorial Day, Independence Day, Armed Forces Day, or Veterans' Day, or for the purpose of granting leave and liberty.
2. A visit to the home yard where the ship goes for regular overhaul, usually extending several months.
3. A permanent change of station.
4. A trip overseas, such as to Honolulu or Panama, during the winter cruises of the fleet, which require no explanation as it will be at your own expense.

TRAVELING BY AUTOMOBILE

Frequently, long trips, such as to the home yard or even a permanent change of station, will be made by automobile. At first thought it may seem an extra expense to join the AAA (American Automobile Association), but it is considered advisable to do so if you contemplate frequent trips. The towing service provided in emergencies may be very welcome sometimes, and an AAA tag on a car provides a certain degree of protection against vandalism. For the novice, and as a reminder to the more experienced, here is a check-off list for desirable preparations for a trip by automobile. The longer the trip, the more important is attention to these items.

1. Try to get some other wife to go with you; most wives who have cars will want to drive their own cars but someone who has no car may be

glad to go with you and share expenses of fuel and oil. If you are unable to find a driving companion try to find several wives who are driving cars on the same trip and form a convoy or "driving caravan." Such a caravan, if well planned as to route, speed, and stops, permits a check of each car's progress and a possible reduction in expenses by sharing accommodations.

2. Plan your trip carefully. The following suggestions may help you:

   a. Decide upon your route. Obtain an automobile route book such as is published by the AAA, or a tour aid for the state or states through which you will travel such as are provided free upon request by some tourist bureaus and by oil companies. Consider routes with a view to the time of year, distance, and points of interest. If traveling in the West, you may arrange a visit to Yosemite Park, the Redwood Forest, etc.

   b. Decide upon your schedule. In scheduling a trip plan to get an early start each day, seldom base your schedule on an average speed in excess of thirty miles per hour, and avoid driving after dark, too long at a stretch, or too far in a day.

   c. Decide where you will spend each night and the hostelry you desire to use, and write or telegraph for a reservation. It is most undesirable for a wife traveling alone to find herself in a strange place without a reservation at a suitable hostelry. Be sure to inform your husband of your contemplated address at your destination. The information concerning lodgings and eating places is quite complete in many tour aids. In selecting places to eat and sleep many people have found very satisfactory advice in two books by Duncan Hines entitled *Adventures in Good Eating* and *Lodging for a Night*.

   d. If you are driving in a convoy decide upon the stops and the exact place at which all cars are to check in. Cars should always be checked in at the end of the day's drive, and preferably twice a day. It may be desirable for a caravan to consider stopping at some one of the better tourist courts or motels. Many such now have accommodations on a par with moderate-priced hotels, are cheaper, afford a solution to the parking problem, and are more convenient for making an early start in the morning.

   e. Decide upon the luggage you are to carry in your car. Try out, empty, the suitcases, hatboxes, etc., in the trunk compartment and determine the most satisfactory stowage. For long trips when your car is to be crowded this procedure will save much time and patience.

   f. Be sure that you have the following items with you:

      1) Registration card and valid automobile operator's license.

2) Insurance policy or card.

3) Your husband's card with his service number and the name of his ship, and your Armed Forces Identification card, in the container with registration card; also your own last address and future address if known.

4) Tools and spare parts, include a jack, wrench for wheel nuts, large screw driver, small chemical fire extinguisher, flashlight, and a spare spark plug. If traveling north or if anticipating mountain driving, consider the possibility that your car may require chains and your radiator an anti-freeze mixture. If your car is of ancient vintage include a spare fan belt.

5) A vacuum bottle filled with cold water.

6) Route maps and schedule for your trip.

7) At least one warm blanket per person and if traveling north a warm coat.

8) In your purse a duplicate insurance card or a card containing data in regard to your insurance policy, and complete identification data for your car, including license number, engine number, and the manufacturer's numbers of your tires, including the spare.

These identification data are essential in case your car is stolen or a dishonest garage shifts tires on it while it is put up for the night. It has been adequately demonstrated that dishonest garages take advantage of women traveling alone.

You should have in cash, preferably in small bills, a sum sufficient to cover one day's expenses, adequate traveler's checks to more than cover your trip expenses, and your checkbook. It is desirable that your traveler's checks be carried on a string around your neck rather than in your purse, so that a lost or stolen purse will not deprive you of money.

This check-off list may appear long and too detailed, but there is included not one item which, if neglected by you, may not result in delay, inconvenience, or possible embarrassment to you and your husband; for a wife's errors are usually charged to her husband's ignorance or inefficiency in instructing her in motoring.

The Trip

For you, Nancy Lee and Sue, as for many others, this may be the first motor trip you have made in which you have had the sole responsibility. May we give you just a few more items of advice as to your trip:

1. The early morning is the best part of the day for motoring unless you have retired late. There is less traffic and this early-morning period can be used for no other purpose than sleep, of which, if you turned in early, you should have had plenty.
2. Keep within the speed limit and watch carefully for road signs indicating curves, detours, and desirable shift of gears, i.e., as to shift to second in descending a steep hill.
3. Buy only nationally known brands of gas and oil and only from respectable-looking service stations, or you may get watered or otherwise faulty gas or oil. Never let the gas in your tank get below one-quarter full and have your crankcase oil checked each time you buy gas.
4. Check water in radiator frequently in hot weather and in mountain driving.
5. Check tires frequently in hot weather, especially in desert driving. Remember that heat expands the pressure and is the cause of many a blowout.
6. Take time to eat proper meals.
7. Carry no liquor in your car and never indulge in even one intoxicating drink, if at all, until your driving for the day is finished. Alcohol is responsible for many automobile accidents, and alcoholic liquor in your car or the smell of alcohol on your breath, in case of a collision or other accident, prejudices your case at the start.

Any trip that can be made by automobile can be made by train. But when traveling at your own expense, you will find train fare too expensive to permit many trips.

MATS (MILITARY AIR TRANSPORT SERVICE)

Air Transportation for Naval Dependents

Occasionally, air transportation overseas is authorized for dependents. It is provided by the Military Air Transport Service, organized in 1948. The new command, a consolidation of the Air Force's Air Transport Command and the Navy's Air Transport Service, is operated under the Secretary of the Air Force. From its headquarters at Andrews Air Force Base, near Washington, the MATS global air-route command operates three major transport divisions: the Atlantic, the Continental, and the Pacific.

Ports of Aerial Embarkation

Dependents traveling on MATS aircraft to and from foreign stations are processed at the embarkation port. Ports of aerial embarkation are located at Westover Air Force Base, Massachusetts, for Europe; Travis Air Force Base, California, for the Pacific; McChord Air Force Base, Tacoma, Washington, for Alaska; Brookley Air Force Base, Mobile, Alabama, for the Caribbean and South America; National Airport, Washington, D.C., for all foreign areas.

Processing of Dependents for Overseas Air Travel

Dependents arriving at any one of the aerial embarkation ports for overseas air travel are welcomed by the processing clerk in the Embarkation Section. Here is the procedure: Present a copy of your orders so that the clerk may check all the pertinent details. If you are going where warm clothing will be needed, the clerk directs you to the Supply Section with a copy of your orders, and necessary warm clothing is issued.

The dependent, or the person responsible for the dependents if there is a mother with children, then signs *three very important cards*: a baggage certificate (one hundred pounds is your allowance per person); a blue card (complete with detailed information which eventually becomes a permanent record. It is used to compile the manifest, so guard this with your life. First you will present it to the doctor for medical clearance. Dependents must have taken all required shots and physicals before reporting to the port); a white card, giving your mailing address and the person to be notified in case of emergency. When properly filled out, it is forwarded to the base post office, which assumes the responsibility of forwarding all mail to the family's new address.

If you applied for a passport to be picked up at the port of aerial embarkation, you will be directed to the Passport Section. A clerk must verify the passport picture, and if it is valid, you sign it in his presence and receive your passport.

Your blue card, having been initialed by each section you have cleared through, is now returned to the processing clerk, who turns it over to the Passenger Service Section, where you receive your plane reservation and a ticket stating flight number, date, and pickup time.

After being ticketed, the passenger is free until the trip is set up. The SOP or standard operating procedure of processing dependents is basically the same at all ports of embarkation. Currently passengers clear through the port in one day and go out the following day; however, the procedure is very fluid, and length of stay depends on the amount of traffic flowing through the port and on one's priority for travel.

In order to acquaint dependents fully with the accommodations available at the port and to give them an idea of the general routine while awaiting departure, the processing clerk gives a briefing on such things as accommodations, where to get meals, where to secure baby foods if needed, the amount of money to carry, how and where to get traveler's checks. The passengers, in turn, have an opportunity to ask about anything that is still puzzling them.

Enlisted men traveling with their families are informed of the consolidated mess available to them. Women traveling with children are briefed on the use of the nursery and available transportation. Everything possible is done to make the waiting period as comfortable as possible.

Information concerning the country to which the dependents are going is usually furnished at the time port calls are issued. Such data ordinarily originate with the overseas commands, and enclosed brochures are issued by each headquarters. But don't let it stop there. If you have an inkling in advance, go to the library. Reading is a handy device for gathering information.

Passengers are called four hours prior to take-off and brought to the passenger terminal for final processing and flight briefing. This preflight over-water briefing is given by the flight attendant. It includes an explanation of the emergency equipment, emergency flight procedures, flight times, and anticipated weather. One important point to remember is that passengers cannot be posted for shipment until all phases of the processing have been completed.

Information on trip accident insurance is available at the Passenger Service Counter in the terminal.

Facilities Available in Flight

The motto of MATS traffic personnel is "Passenger service is second only to flying safety," and every effort is made to keep all passengers as comfortable as possible. Of necessity, MATS aircraft operating on world-wide air routes are not as luxurious as commercial liners, but in-flight meals, hot soup and coffee, milk, and fruit juices are available. Pillows and blankets are also provided. The flight clerk has a hot cup that can be used to heat babies' bottles or to warm milk for older children.

It is suggested that you take an adequate supply of magazines and a book or two on the flight. Air travel with children is covered adequately in Chapter XIII.

How to Dress for MATS Travel

Women are advised to wear slacks when boarding aircraft, but they are not permitted to wear slacks in the Officers' Club at any time. MATS usually requires slacks so that Mae Wests or life preservers and parachutes can be worn decently; but unless you are specifically requested at the time to wear slacks, I think, for a flying start, a simple basic dress under a flaring short jacket travels better than a suit. If you find the high altitudes cool, you can slip off the jacket and roll up comfortably in your blanket. It might be hard to look glamorous in Alaskan flying apparel, outfitted in GI oversized trousers, Mukluks, parka, and mittens, but for a short flight to Hawaii of ten hours, you can arrive at Hickam Air Force Base looking very well turned out with a bit of planning.

Air travel tests your clothes sense. Wear a well-mannered girdle, not a new, stiff, uncomfortable one—if you come in the girdle category. Wear stockings that fit, low-heeled shoes, a taffeta petticoat to keep your skirts from "sitting out," and a smart print tie-silk or packable in a light color. This, with either a small or a large hat and a gay short coat over your arm, plus a roomy handbag, the shoulder-strap type if you like, will see you off the plane smartly anywhere in the tropics.

The trick, of course, is the co-ordination of everything to a master plan . . . a color plan. White, beige, all shades of green, bright blues, and yellow are your basic colors in the tropics accented with any exotic shade becoming to your natural style of beauty!

A hat with a separate veil so you can pin the veil on first and stay kempt even when hatless will be a delight, and be sure to choose a handbag more than big enough for your needs. Your handbag check list will include an American-money wallet, a foreign-money wallet, passport case, flying pen, pencil, small pocket diary with combination address book, a mirror, compact, lipstick, perfume flask, comb, sunglasses, cigarette case, lighter, and handkerchief. You will add six other incidentals peculiar only to you, if you are like most of us.

If you are the slender type for slacks, and "orders are orders" whether you are the type or not, invest in a well-tailored pair in gray or a dark color. Pastels are not to be desired, and certainly white slacks are appropriate only for sailing or yachting. A bright-colored silk blouse, or white with a gay scarf, plus a topcoat will see you off.

As for luggage, you will be allowed one hundred pounds, so carry light bags. Commercial air lines carry excess baggage at about $1.25 per pound; MATS may accommodate if the excess is slight or they may ship excess by cargo, but don't count on it. Weight-saving canvas or aluminum luggage is available. Another travel trick is to substitute a cardboard hatbox for your heavier make-up case for a short flight.

Chapter XII

ENTERTAINING IN THE NAVY

Jack dances and sings, and is always content,
In his vows to his lass he'll ne'er fail her,
His anchor's a-trip when his money's all spent—
And this is the life of a sailor!
(From Dibdin's *The Yankee Sailor*)

HERE are a few preliminary ideas which may help you either as a guest or when you are the hostess, and serve to give you poise and confidence. First of all, answer every invitation graciously and promptly. In Service circles being "fashionably late" is taboo. If you arrive even five minutes early, your hostess may not be ready to receive you, though she should be unless something has gone wrong with her last-minute plans. If an unavoidable accident delays you, you should phone if possible, and in any event your hostess will not wait at a formal dinner more than twenty minutes before dinner is announced. When you arrive you are expected to take your place and start your dinner at whatever course is in progress. It is not considered "smart," however, to delay your entrance just because you don't like soup.

The hostess must always be in command of the situation. An attractive table, congenial guests, and good food make up the recipe for a successful party, and if carefully planned it needn't cost a lot, either. Behind every successful party there has been a lot of constructive planning and, though the hostess pains belong to the person giving the party, guests have definite obligations to their hostess. First of all is punctuality; next, if there is a guest of honor, special attention should be paid to the honored one; it is assumed that all invited guests will be courteous and friendly.

In Navy circles there is a certain informality about extending invitations to small social affairs. However, if the entertainment is of an official nature, such as a reception, a dinner on board ship, or a formal "at home," then the greatest formality is observed, both in extending and in accepting the invitation.

FORMALITY VERSUS INFORMALITY

Very few formal, well-staffed homes today, in this land or even abroad, can accommodate the *"traditional thirty-four"* guests at one dinner table, or even half that many, in comfort. Formal dinners are so much trouble, so much expense, and require so many servants that even in their heyday they were given by great establishments only three or four times a year. Important hostesses today prefer to give small, frequent semiformal dinners or quite informal dinners. If the occasion really seems to demand a formal dinner, for visiting royalty or such, then a private suite in a hotel, a fashionable restaurant, or a club is usually the answer. If dining at home seems best, a competent caterer may be engaged who furnishes dishes, silver, complete service, and waiters.

Since formal dinners are given at embassies, and formal official dinners are given throughout the Service, it seems wise to include sections on formal invitations and formal entertaining just in case. At some time you might be required to marshal your forces as a hostess for a formal luncheon or dinner. Ten to one, you will go along your merry way enjoying informality in your entertaining, but there may come a day!

INVITATIONS

Formal invitations, whether they are engraved or written by hand, are always in the *third* person. Good usage demands that acceptances and regrets be written in the same person.

Few Navy people are so formal, except those on legation duty or in Washington, that they send out engraved invitations for dinner. An exception to this is a collective invitation such as the following:

The Wardroom Officers of the U.S.S. Iowa
request the pleasure of
General and Mrs. Eugene Stuart's
company at dinner
on Saturday, the twelfth of November
at seven o'clock

Ship's boat will leave from
Pico Landing at six-thirty

A formal invitation is always answered in handwriting, and the hour as well as the day is repeated so that there will be no mistake. For example:

> General and Mrs. Eugene Stuart
> accept with pleasure the kind invitation of
> The Wardroom Officers of the U.S.S. Iowa
> to dinner on Saturday, the twelfth of November
> at seven o'clock

If it is impossible to accept, the form used is:

> General and Mrs. Eugene Stuart
> regret that they are unable to accept the kind invitation of
> The Wardroom Officers of the U.S.S. Iowa
> on Saturday, the twelfth of November

A formal invitation by a group of officers will usually read something as follows:

> The Commander-in-Chief and Officers
> of the United States Fleet
> request the pleasure of your company
> at a reception
> to be held on board the U.S.S. Maryland
> on Saturday afternoon, the tenth of September
> from four until six o'clock

Boats leave from
Pier 10   R.S.V.P.

In the lower right- or left-hand corner, instead of R.S.V.P., may be written, "Please reply to flag lieutenant."

The acceptance or refusal, written by hand on a good grade of plain white notepaper, should read:

> Lieutenant and Mrs. John Pelly Bright
> accept with pleasure the kind invitation of
> The Commander-in-Chief and Officers
> of the United States Fleet
> to a reception to be held on board the U.S.S. Maryland
> on Saturday afternoon, the tenth of September
> from four until six o'clock

The partly engraved invitation when used is sent for big dinners of twenty or more and for formal dinners whether large or not. Traditionally, an engraved invitation meant full evening dress, and "Black Tie"—written in the lower corner—indicated an exception to the rule. Today, the black tie is the rule; "White Tie" shows the exception. "Decorations," * as always, means full evening dress. Formal invitations may also be written on any personal writing paper and need not be engraved. A formal invitation is never written entirely across the page, in longhand running style, as an informal invitation is.

The acceptance or refusal should be written within twenty-four hours and should follow the same form as the above. Delays are very annoying to a hostess, and she might like to ask someone else in your stead who has better manners. Under no circumstances should a dinner invitation be accepted conditionally, nor should you ask your hostess if you can give a reply later.

FORMAL AT HOME INVITATION

At Home
On Thursday, November the fifth
from five until seven o'clock
Chief of Naval Operations House
Observatory Circle

THE INFORMAL WRITTEN DINNER INVITATION

Dear Mrs. Tyler:

Will you and Ensign Tyler (or Bill) have dinner (or dine) with us on Friday evening, the sixth of June, at seven-thirty o'clock?

Looking forward to the pleasure of having you with us,

Very sincerely,
ANNE SINCLAIR BARRINGTON

If you accept, you write:

My dear Mrs. Barrington:

We shall be very happy to dine with you and Captain Barrington on Friday, the sixth of June, at seven-thirty o'clock. Thank you so much for asking us.

Most sincerely yours,
NANCY LEE PATTERSON TYLER

* The word "Decorations" as used here is only a term and does not refer to military decorations, although, as far as anyone knows, that's where it came from.

If you must decline, then it is imperative to state some reason. It is exceedingly ill mannered to decline without offering an excuse.

My dear Mrs. Barrington:
We are so sorry that we cannot dine with you on Friday, the sixth of June, as we are going to White Sulphur for the week end.
Thanking you for your kindness in thinking of us,
Most sincerely,
NANCY LEE PATTERSON TYLER

THE TELEPHONE INVITATION

Usually the Navy wife keeps an engagement book or social calendar near her telephone and makes a note of her engagements when she receives them. This also proves a good check when one is making up a guest list.

Invitations should not be left with servants and children, although it is quite permissible to leave your number and ask to be called. If you have any choice in the matter, do not indulge in long conversations. It is not considerate to use the telephone for social visits. It is very exasperating to try to get a number only to have it busy because some thoughtless person is chattering.

The telephone invitation may go something like this:

Mrs. Tyler, this is Elaine McComas speaking. Will you and your husband have dinner with us (or with Admiral McComas and me) on Saturday evening at eight o'clock at the Yacht Club?

ENTERTAINING IN THE NAVY

Young Navy couples are not expected to give large, expensive, formal parties, though they do have a very definite obligation to return in some way the social courtesies shown them. A formal dinner (should you be invited by a Captain or Commander) may be returned by a simple home dinner, a small dinner party at a club, hotel, or restaurant, or a buffet supper, a luncheon, a picnic, or a cocktail party.

Young Navy couples frequently meet in each other's apartments and cook dinner together. A movie, dancing, or bridge, often played "for love" (no stakes involved), usually concludes the evening. Navy people are generally very frank with each other in regard to finances, since everyone knows to the penny exactly what each officer in each grade draws as a salary. There is not competitive spending or dressing, no "keeping up with the Joneses"; and living beyond one's income causes nothing but adverse comment and criticism from one's contemporaries and seniors.

Reserve Officers and their wives sometimes find the required entertaining and repaying of social obligations a bit strenuous. The most important thing to remember is this: Every social obligation should be returned, but it is not necessary to *repay in kind*.

Your First Guests

Before you really have your bearings, some afternoon Bill will bring Miles Stearley and another classmate home from the ship with him quite without warning. Perhaps he will ask them by for a drink, but don't be fooled. What he really wants is to show them you and his recently acquired home. He knows you are wonderful. They will think so too if you can disappear into the kitchen for a moment, whip up some toothsome canapés and appear bearing the fruits of your morning's planning. A good trick is to keep a small covered dish of highly seasoned Philadelphia cream cheese in the refrigerator to be spread on crackers. With olives you have a feast on hand. Or you may have only that can of fresh peanuts on your pantry shelf, but it will be the little extra touch that turns the drink into a celebration.

There will be much toasting at this little impromptu housewarming, and Bill will probably lead off with the familiar Navy toast as he raises his glass to his guests and says, "Glad to have you aboard." The visitors' response is, "Glad to be aboard." Or Bill may simply say, "Here's how," the response being an answering "How."

This type of gathering often turns into a dinner party, and you will cordially invite Bill's shipmates to share potluck with you. When you say it, mean it. This is the supreme test of the seafaring man's wife—her welcoming of her husband's shipmates.

Your emergency shelf will prove a lifesaver, and even if it does make you exceed your weekly food allowance now and then, in the end it is cheaper than taking your guests to a hotel or restaurant for dinner. The plain dinner can easily be turned into a company dinner provided the *pièce de résistance* can be stretched to include visitors.

Your guests will be impressed with your culinary ability and ingenuity, your husband will marvel at your cleverness, and everything will be lovely.

COCKTAIL PARTIES

The cocktail party is one of the easiest and most popular forms of entertainment, though often rather expensive. It is a pleasant informal means of entertaining a large number of guests, if given at an Officers' Club. Smaller parties of this type may be given at home.

A caterer may handle the food, but if you prepare the hors d'oeuvres, it is wise to keep them simple. Men like good, filling appetizers—shrimp, with an accompanying bowl of piquant sauce, celery, small knobs of cauliflower, sliced raw carrots or potato chips to be dipped in Roquefort or Thousand Island dressing. Large pineapple and Edam cheeses with assorted cocktail crackers are popular. Some hostesses include a platter of assorted cold cuts or a baked ham or turkey with buttered slices of rye and white bread near by. The day of fancy canapés, those "dainty little tidbits over which a hostess and all of her friends used to spend the day laboring" have gone with the well-known wind. The hostess of today likes to enjoy her own party, and leaves the elaborate party sandwiches and canapés to experienced professional caterers.

Highballs of Scotch, bourbon, and rye take the lead in drinks, while martinis, gin and tonic, Manhattans, and old fashioneds head the cocktail list. Sherry is often served. Coca Cola, fruit juices, and tomato juice should be provided for nondrinkers. Never feel obliged to take a drink if you do not want it or if it is against your principles. Stick to your convictions and remember this: You will be better off if you never drink. This applies both to officers and their wives and to enlisted men and their wives. People will respect you for the stand you take, provided you are not rude or critical in regard to the drinking of others, or unfriendly and disapproving in your manner.

IF YOU SERVE LIQUOR!

Let's agree that you don't have to serve liquor if you don't wish to, but having a drink is fun and, for those who like it, liquor adds to a party. It is an excellent mixing agent!

Never insist even gently upon anyone's drinking. Certainly no one need drink at any time unless he wants to. Today, people usually do as they please. There are many who have never indulged in strong drink, and neither do they belong to a temperance union! Some of the older boys and girls who cut their adolescent teeth on bathtub gin bottles have given up the habit entirely. It could be that they are watching their figures or their ulcers. Sometimes, even without hypochondria, they see the folly of their ways.

By and large, few people include liquor in their budget, and the price of liquor plus mixers is something one seldom sits down and faces. For those who cannot afford to keep a stock on hand, it seems easier if a visiting fireman arrives unexpectedly to send up to the club for a bottle of Scotch. It is charged, of course, and forgotten until the first of the month; but there is always a day of reckoning, and if an influx of visitors occurs several times during the month, not even Einstein could balance your budget.

These suggestions were compiled with the help of a famous bartender of long experience and are taken from *The Household Manual* (p. 223):

1. Find out the cost of bottled drink and the different kinds just as you know the current price of butter and eggs.

2. Select what you can afford to serve, if any. Big stores often have special sales on standard brands. Watch for them. Decide before a party what you will serve and stick to it.

3. Serve drinks in adequate glasses but not oversized ones. If you do, you are asking for trouble!

4. Own a jigger. The professional bartender whistles softly at the idea of putting more than a jigger of hard liquor in a drink. Don't depend on that belated "when."

5. Without being obvious about it, see to it that you or your husband pours the drinks. It is the host's place to do so, anyway.

6. Keep the bottles preferably in another room. If you set the bottles down beside the visiting firemen, nothing can be done to space the drinks properly.

7. Finally, to be definite, if you cannot afford Scotch, don't apologize or feel embarrassed about it. The person serving the drinks should state: "We have Martinis and Old Fashioneds" or "Manhattans and Scotch."

8. If your guests come to your home for dinner and are offered chicken, they do not ask for turkey; well, it is the same idea.

9. It is very unfunny to "load" a guest's drink, particularly if she is *usually* a lady!

To sum it up: price the drinks
           plan the drinks
           measure the drinks
           space the drinks
and never serve more than two rounds before dinner.

How to Give a Cocktail Party

Unless a large number of guests is expected, it is better to have the cocktails mixed in the pantry and passed on trays. Should the guest list be large, set the dining table as for a tea, using either a novelty cloth or an elaborate one. Appropriate decorations should grace the table. Both the food and refreshment tables may be placed in the garden.

The first requisite for a cocktail party is good liquor. "Good liquor is not cheap and cheap liquor is not good." Everything for mixing drinks should be set up on one table. The six most popular mixed drinks are Bacardi cocktails, daiquiris, dry martinis, Manhattans, old-fashioned cocktails and whisky sours. Usually, and for even a fairly large party, provide dry martinis, whisky and soda for highballs, sherry, tomato and iced fruit juices, plus milk for those on diets who like to go to parties just the same. Offer something for everyone.

Be sure that hot canapés are served very hot. Cold things should be chilled and banked in ice when possible. An Old English silver hot dish keeps hot canapés at the proper temperature. Potato chips served hot in wooden bowls are tempting, as are hot roasted nuts.

Canapés should be small enough to pop into the mouth in one bite. They should be crisp, never soggy. Here are some suggestions:

Pepitas, Mexican pumpkin seeds
Shrimp, onion or chili Krispies
Oysters wrapped in bacon—broiled
Olives wrapped in bacon—broiled
Seasoned cream cheese wrapped in drief-beef funnels
Seasoned cream cheese thinned with mayonnaise for sauce in which to dunk
    cauliflower knobs, carrots, shallots, potato chips
Single spring onion rolled in bread-and-butter sandwich, held by toothpick,
    with green top of onion protruding from one end
Tiny hot biscuit with sautéed mushroom
Tiny hot biscuit with ham

Broiled chicken livers impaled on toothpicks
Large pecan halves sandwiched together with anchovy paste
Celery stuffed with Roquefort
Caviar, anchovy, hot cheese canapés
Spiced deviled eggs
Cheese, crackers, cold cuts, olives
Freshly roasted almonds, hot chestnuts
"Hush puppies"—made of water-ground meal mixed with finely ground
   bacon and onion. They originated at old-fashioned southern fish fries,
   when a busy cook would hurriedly throw a corndodger to the barking
   hungry hounds that were always underfoot. "Hush puppies" (or tiny
   hot corndodgers) are delicious!

Room temperature is an important feature in giving a party of any
kind; but particularly at a cocktail party be sure to open a window
which will not create a direct draft. An open fire is fine if there are
only a few people, but it can make guests uncomfortable if it isn't
controlled carefully. In giving a tea or a cocktail party, it is important
to be space conscious. Remove all but two or three chairs, so that the
guests when tired of standing will circulate. People like a crowd to be
a crowd, and they don't mind being almost suffocated if the party is
gay and they are having fun. But if it is to be a small intimate group,
then be sure to provide a seating space for each person invited.

If servants are to be hired for the party, it is wise to get the help
all lined up before you issue your invitations. Remember, it is easy to
get guests but not so easy to get servants. No one ever knows what a
cocktail party will turn into; it is a safe bet that it will run on into the
evening. If you feel so inclined, have a baked ham or a roast chicken
with rolls and coffee ready in reserve.

Whatever you do or whatever kind of cocktail party you give, avoid
being tricky or cute about yourself, your house, your drink, or your
food.

THE COCKTAIL SUPPER

The cocktail supper is becoming increasingly popular since it is
given usually preceding a dance, a reception or some social function
at the club. This type of party is to be encouraged; it starts the ball
rolling and everyone gets in the spirit of the evening. It is a stand-up
party!

It differs little from a regular cocktail party except that it is not necessary to serve a great variety of food. An elaborate party table might be planned with a turkey at one end, a ham at the other and plates of thin bread-and-butter sandwiches beside the platters. Also celery, olives, pickles, cheese and coffee.

THE FORMAL DINNER

Once in a while the problem of a formal dinner must be faced and, although at this point you are an invited guest and on the receiving end, still there are certain formalities you should know.

Wear your best dinner dress or formal evening dress. Some women feel that a formal dinner calls for bare backs and bare shoulders, but a gown with a suggestion of sleeves is also apropos. Gloves are always worn to a formal dinner and removed at the table. To me it is barbaric to leave them on the arms, tucking back the hands, suggestive of a surgeon getting ready for an operation!

Your husband will know what to wear: either formal uniform evening dress or civilian evening dress (tails) or, if he possesses neither, a dinner coat, though the latter is not correct, strictly speaking, except in tropical climates.

A few general officers and officers of flag rank who maintain well-staffed households entertain formally as in days gone by, but most formal dinners today are given at exclusive clubs or hotels.

The seating at a formal dinner in Service circles is always according to rank, with the exception of the guest of honor. The experienced hostess—and no one except an experienced social leader should attempt to entertain at a formal dinner—will draw up a seating chart. Undoubtedly she will have to consult the official *Register*, and if her husband is helpful he will assist in drawing up the seating arrangements.

Your hostess will be standing near the door and will greet you upon your arrival with some gracious remark and a smile of welcome. Remember this: The perfect guest owes his hostess the courtesy of entering into the spirit of the party and should strive to be entertaining and at his best. However, one should not attempt to "take over" or try to be the "life of the party."

Never be late to dinner. If you are invited at eight, be there at eight, not five minutes before or two minutes after. A formal dinner never begins before seven o'clock, and when it is set for this hour, it is because the guests are going on to another entertainment later, such as the opera or the theater. The usual hour for the formal dinner is eight o'clock or eight-thirty. It is a social sin to keep a dinner party waiting!

Your dinner partner is the gentleman on your left, but during dinner be careful to divide your conversation equally between the men on either side of you. Because the host should at the beginning of dinner direct his conversation to the guest of honor on his right, it follows that the other men must turn to the right also. If some one of the guests through thoughtlessness or preference concentrates his attention on the lady on his left, a guest is automatically left out of the conversation at one point or another. Every experienced hostess is familiar with the guest who gazes wildly into space, with the stricken expression of a castaway, while her partners on either side chat vivaciously with other guests. Should you draw for a dinner partner a Sphinx, who wishes to commune with himself and be left alone with his food, that is something else. However, you should make several attempts to engage him in conversation. If that doesn't work, you're on your own. Maybe you can horn in on the couple across the table.

After dinner, the American custom is for the ladies and gentlemen to return to the drawing room or living room for coffee and liqueurs. The European custom is that the men remain behind in the dining room for coffee, cigars, brandy, and talk while the ladies await them in the drawing room.

Guests at a formal dinner which has been followed by conversation alone usually leave at about ten o'clock. As a rule, not everyone leaves at once, but the ranking guest leaves first. The host and hostess rise when bidding their guests good night and go with them to the drawing-room door. As a guest it is enough to say, "Good night, and thank you so much." Then leave. The door dawdler is the bane of everyone's existence.

Entertaining at Dinners, Formal and Informal

For gay little informal dinners to which you invite one or two couples or several bachelors the table appointments may be very simple. Candles appear at dinner, and bread-and-butter plates are omitted.

Cream-soup plates are used instead of bouillon cups; otherwise, the service is the same as at luncheon. At the informal dinner the host may carve the roast or fowl at table; at the formal dinner the carving is done in the kitchen and all dishes are served by waiters. The use of place doilies for informal dinners is accepted, but regulation-size dinner napkins are preferable to luncheon-size napkins.

Seating

Ten is considered the ideal number for a seated dinner. Multiples of four—eight, twelve, sixteen, twenty and twenty-four—are awkward numbers if one has the usual rectangular table. It is impossible to escape having two men or two women at each end of the table. To avoid this embarrassing situation the only solution is for the host and hostess to be seated at the middle of the table facing each other. Any formal dinner of more than sixteen moves up into the pretentious class and usually takes place only in high social, diplomatic, or political circles.

Although a hostess may prefer to seat her guests on the basis of congeniality, at an official dinner especially in Washington or in capitals of other countries she must observe the immutable laws of protocol. At a formal dinner, the names in full are written on the place cards in script writing. The order of precedence for members of the armed forces follows the order of precedence of the Services: Army, Navy, Air Force. Officers of equal rank in separate Services are placed accordingly. For example, a Captain in the Navy, although of equal rank with a Colonel in the Army, is seated below him at the table. A Lieutenant General in the Air Force should be seated below a Vice Admiral in the Navy. Officers of equal rank in the same Service are placed according to the dates of their commissions. Here is where you need a *Register* of all three Services at hand!

It is important to remember in seating officials that the husband and wife are treated as equal in rank. In our country, the woman guest of honor is seated on the host's right; if a man, to the right of the hostess. But in some European countries the guest of honor is seated on the left. In Denmark, in addition to seating the guest of honor on the host's left, the hostess always enters the dining room last, and is the first to leave the table so she may stand at the door. As each guest passes, he thanks her for his meal.

The Formal Dinner

If you are eager to give a formal dinner, think three times before you plunge unless you are a victim of circumstances and it is part of your job. Remember, it has to be done perfectly—with the correct silver and china, and well-trained servants—or it will be a headache even to the guests. If all goes well, it is at best very likely to be dull.

Formal dinner service demands menservants and that is that! No dinner can be said to be formal if women serve it or assist in its service. Many hostesses when faced with giving a formal dinner take recourse to a hotel or private club, or call in a reputable caterer. When the dinner is to be given in a private home, it is quite a different matter.

Don't attempt a formal dinner unless you have an experienced cook, a butler, and two experienced servingmen for the evening. It is better to give a semiformal dinner, which is probably the most comfortable, the most practical, and the most pleasant way of entertaining.

At formal dinners the table should be covered with either an elaborate dinner cloth or a faultlessly laundered damask cloth, with a heavy silence cloth underneath. Even the most formal dinners of today consist of no more than five courses, and four are preferred.

1. Soup	1. Soup
2. Roast	2. Fish or entree
3. Salad	3. Roast
4. Dessert	4. Salad
	5. Dessert

Demitasse and liqueurs

The centerpiece, if it is a flower arrangement, should be kept low. See that the table has been extended enough to give the guests elbow room—twenty inches between places—and that there is enough space for the servants to pass the dishes. The dinner napkin, folded square, should be placed in the middle of the service plate, and if place cards are used they should be put on top of the napkins. The center decoration, candelabra, compotes holding salted nuts, salts and peppers, and individual ash trays are the only extra silver, besides the flat silver, on the table. Salts and peppers should be at every other place at table.

Suggested Menus for a Formal Dinner

Clear soup	Clams or oysters on half shell
Fish hollandaise	or
Filet mignon	Clear turtle soup with sherry
String beans	Roast duckling with orange sauce,
Carrots glacé	or quail or squab
Rolls	Green peas
Aspic salad	Artichoke hollandaise
Ice cream	Coffee ice-cream mold
Coffee	Coffee

At a formal dinner, the appetite should not be dulled by a heavy cream soup; a thin clear soup or some type of sea-food cocktail is more appropriate. Highly flavored Spanish, Italian, or Indian dishes are not appropriate for a formal dinner but are popular at an informal dinner or buffet supper.

Suggested Menus for Traditional Holiday Dinners

Thanksgiving

Tomato bisque
Roast turkey, gravy
Chestnut dressing
Sweet-potato pumpkins
Creamed onions
Avocado-grapefruit salad
Mince or pumpkin pie
Coffee

Christmas Buffet Supper

Hot strong bouillon
Cold roast turkey, sliced
Pickled peaches, cranberry jelly
Creamed oysters with ham and mushroom either en casserole or in individual ramekins
Hot biscuits
Aspic fruit salad, relishes
Eggnog ice cream
Christmas fruit and nut cake
Coffee

New Year's

Fresh tomato soup with chives
Wild duck, black currant jelly
Wild rice, string beans not cut or sliced, but whole in neat little bundles
Apple and celery heart salad
Pineapple sherbet with chocolate leaves
Coffee

Easter

Tomato juice
Baked ham
New peas in cream or in potato nests
Molded vegetable salad ring
Angel food cake with fresh strawberries or strawberry shortcake
Coffee

<table>
<tr><td align="center">*Fourth of July*</td><td align="center">*New Year's Reception*</td></tr>
</table>

Fourth of July	*New Year's Reception*
Jellied madrilene	Eggnog in large punch bowl
Broiled fresh salmon	Beaten biscuit, Smithfield ham or
New potatoes, green peas	ham spread
Cucumber salad, French dressing	Sandwiches, celery and carrot sticks
Watermelon	Olives, salted hot pecans
Iced coffee	Miniature mince pies—size of
	fifty-cent piece

The Semiformal and Informal Dinner

At a seated dinner be careful not to invite more guests than you can seat comfortably at your dining-room table. Nothing is more awkward than to try to eat a meal without sufficient elbow room, or with a table leg between the knees if one is wearing a narrow skirt. With more than six people, things will be greatly expedited by place cards.

One detail that distinguishes a formal from an informal dinner is the question of carving and serving at the table by either host or hostess. If the host carves at the table, the dinner is informal. It is customary to place the required number of hot plates in front of him, and the maid or waiter carries each plate to the guest, removing the place plate as she serves the meat course. This service is naturally slow, but if a second maid passes the vegetables to each guest served, the food will not grow cold. Another informal custom is for the host to carve at table and serve the dressing and gravy, then for the guests to pass the plate along to the hostess, who serves the vegetables. During this procedure the maid may pass the rolls, celery, and olives.

When the host is carving, family and guests should forget him. If he is in trouble, it will not help to give him the hypnotic eye. Carving is truly an art and calls for a few essentials on which the man of the house has a right to insist. First, he should have good tools—a standard carving set of good steel. If game is the *pièce de résistance,* a pair of poultry shears is a bit of required cutlery. The anatomy of a duck defies logical dissection, but shears make it easy. An acceptable Christmas present sometime!

A steak set also has its place. The knife should be razor sharp, and anyone caught cutting cord or the laundry line with it should be scalped! The platter should be large enough so that the guests will not shudder when the roast or chicken looks as if it is coming their way. A small platter garnished with potatoes, carrots and onions may make a beautiful magazine advertisement but it is an abomination to the carver. Skewers and cords should be removed in the kitchen, unless the rolled roast threatens to explode without them.

Coffee is generally served in the living room at an informal dinner.

At semiformal seated dinners rank is observed, though not so rigidly as in Washington. The first and second of rank are given the seats of honor, and after that the guests may be seated according to congeniality.

Menus for Informal or Semiformal Dinners

Clear soup	Shrimp bisque	Consommé
Leg of spring lamb or crown	Roast prime ribs of beef Yorkshire pudding	Roast duck, turkey, goose, or chicken
Mint jelly	Franconia potatoes	Dressing, gravy
New potatoes	Fresh asparagus	Wild rice
Fresh peas	Escarole, endive, chickory salad	String beans
Lettuce salad, water cress	Meringue with crushed fresh raspberries	Currant jelly
Cold lemon soufflé	Coffee	Mixed green salad
Coffee		Hot rolls
		Tangerine sections in sherry
		Coffee

One more thing about seating: If you want to be the family favorite, don't forget to place your husband's mother at the right of her darling boy and your father-in-law on your right. Remember, the first family dinner is the hardest. Serve good food, spread good cheer, but don't attempt anything too fancy that might not come off just the way you planned.

OTHER PARTIES

Morning parties usually include "coffees," "coke parties" in the South, and Sunday brunches.

At a coke party, cold "cokes" or other soft drinks are served with hot cheese sticks or Welsh rarebit on crisp wafers and cookies. With hot or iced coffee you might serve small doughnuts piping hot, or Danish pastry.

A brunch or breakfast is simply a stand-up luncheon, but the food is simpler. Provide large pitchers of orange juice, tomato juice, and pineapple juice, or a large, deep silver tray piled with cracked ice in which pieces of melon, luscious grapes, oranges, and other tempting fruits are kept chilled. The latter makes a pretty centerpiece.

Sausages and waffles, bacon or ham and scrambled eggs, or fried chicken and spoon bread are a few of the combinations you can serve. Have plenty of good hot steaming coffee. In winter, hot Tom and Jerrys served before a blazing log fire put everyone in a jolly mood, and in summer iced drinks may be served before brunch or breakfast is announced.

One of the simplest yet most congenial ways of entertaining is to have friends drop by after church for coffee, a piece of Danish pastry or coffeecake and that's all . . . period!

LUNCHEONS

Suggested Luncheon Menus

One hot course at a meal is always a wise procedure, as many people dislike cold food and it may not agree with them.

Borsch	Hot or jellied madrilene	Iced melon
Lobster tails	Squab	Lamb chop
Tiny roasted potatoes	Peas	Spinach ring
Tossed salad	Frozen fruit salad	Hot rolls
Vanilla ice cream	Hot rolls	Baked Alaska
Crème de menthe sauce	Coffee	Coffee

Mushroom soup	Vichyssoise
Cheese soufflé	Shrimp or crabmeat salad in half
Fresh fruit salad, French dressing	of avocado
Whole-wheat muffins	Shoestring potatoes
Iced tea or iced coffee	Rolls, coffee
	Raspberries with raspberry sherbet

The food you serve and the way you serve it are just as revealing of the kind of person you are as the house which is your background and the clothes you wear. It is fun to dream up new color combinations both in decorations and in foods.

Your First Tea

If a lovely tea service was among your wedding gifts, your easiest party will be a tea. The number of guests may be from two to a round dozen or more, and you may choose to serve in the living room before an open fire, or perhaps in the garden, or to convert the dining table into a tea table. Your loveliest cloth will cover the table, and at one end will be the tea service. A pretty flower arrangement will be in the center of the table, flanked by candlesticks or candelabra holding lighted white candles. To carry out certain color schemes, colored candles are often used, but white or ivory tapers are really in better taste. Have all silver shining. If you can't have it gleaming, then don't use it. Substitute crystal or china. If there is no servant, prepare everything beforehand except boiling the water for the tea.

Near the tea service arrange the required number of cups and saucers and teaspoons, or cups and salad plates. The latter are more satisfactory, as sandwiches may be placed on them. Arrange tea napkins near by.

Place small loaf sugar in the sugar bowl, and provide both cream and lemon. A pitcher of ice water and several goblets may be placed on a serving table or on the buffet.

Trays of sandwiches, cakes, and mints are placed on the table or passed by one of the younger guests you have asked to assist you. It is customary to ask the Commanding Officer's wife, or some older person to pour tea.

Three Suggested Menus for the Informal Tea

> Bread-and-butter sandwiches—cinnamon toast—tea
> Toast or muffins with jam or marmalade—tea
> Water-cress sandwiches—cookies—tea

Your First Buffet Supper

Beloved of the maidless for Saturday or Sunday night entertaining, beloved of everyone who enjoys the casual, a buffet supper is a sensible way to entertain a large group with little effort.

Right from the start, you must learn to let other people help you. Don't let all your guests jump up to help. Pick one or two and work them hard. They won't mind and it won't break up the party.

Suggested Menus for Buffet Suppers

Roast turkey	Creole shrimp	Chicken à la king in patty
Wild rice	Rice	shells
Peas	Molded salad	Asparagus
Salad	Sherbet, cake	Tomatoes stuffed with celery
Hot rolls		Dessert, coffee
Dessert, coffee		

Mexican Supper

Chile con carne
Mexican rice
Frijoles
Enchiladas
Tomato stuffed with guacamole
  salad
Frozen fresh pineapple soaked
  in rum
Coffee

Southern Supper

Country captain
  or
Southern fried chicken
Grits or spoon bread
Asparagus au gratin
Frozen fruit salad or
Green salad
Coffee

Chinese Supper

Chop suey
Rice
Sweet-sour
  spareribs
Green salad
Dessert, coffee

Curry

Chicken curry
Rice
Condiments
Salad
Dessert
Coffee

HOUSE GUESTS

Much has been written about the art of being a good host, but all too little has been written about being a good house guest.

First of all, no one should feel hurt when a hostess specifies both the time of arrival and the time of departure in the invitation. Sophisticated guests actually want to know what the arrangements are so they themselves can make plans in advance.

The host and hostess should be informed as nearly as practicable of the exact hour of your planned arrival and your departure. Never write or telegraph "Arriving on Thursday." That is too indefinite for your hostess. She may have a bridge or luncheon engagement or a beauty-shop appointment which will raise her metabolism to dangerous levels if she has to do shore duty waiting for your arrival. If a guest is this thoughtless and inconsiderate, the hostess is well within her rights to leave a note of welcome saying when she will return, then go on with her original plans.

Of course, there may be extenuating circumstances. If the guest is arriving by car, in accepting the invitation he might say so and add: "We expect to arrive at your home shortly after four on Friday afternoon and must start our return before nine on Monday morning. Thank you again for your kind invitation and we are looking forward with great pleasure to being with you."

Arrive as nearly as possible at the time you have given your hostess. Your delayed arrival may upset her planned entertainment; early arrivals are even less appreciated. Leave when you are expected to, regardless of the good time you are having. Benjamin Franklin put it right on the line when he said, "Fish and house-guests should never be kept over three days."

How to Be a Welcome House Guest

1. A guest must adjust to the conditions of the household. Emily Post says, "You take your meals at their hour, you eat what is put before you, and you get up and go out and come in and go to bed according to the schedule arranged by your hostess. And no matter how much the hour or food or arrangements may upset you, you must appear blissfully content. When the visit is over, you need never enter the house again; but while you are there, you must like it. You must like the people you meet and the things they do. That is the first inviolable law for the guest." She continues in a humorous vein, but she does suggest that you can *always* send yourself a *telegram* and *leave*. Regardless of how uncomfortable the visit has been, however, you must not even by a facial muscle betray to your hosts that you have had anything but a beautiful time when you bid them good-by. Your obligation extends further. Having broken bread in their house, you must never confide to anyone afterwards how desperately wretched you were on your visit.

2. A man guest should keep his things picked up and his room tidy, even though he is unaccustomed to doing so at home! He should leave the bathroom in the same or better condition than he found it.

3. A lady guest should take complete care of her room and be similarly thoughtful about the bath. In a servantless home, she should

share in the household work to the extent that is welcome or acceptable.

4. In a servantless home, it is a gracious gesture to offer to take your host and hostess and the children, if you wish and can afford it, out to dinner. If once proffered and declined do not press the invitation.

5. When you leave be certain no personal belongings are left behind for the host to package and mail.

6. Always ask permission to tip a servant. Some hostesses object to the practice. At any rate, be sure to thank the servants for courtesies they have extended.

7. A remembrance to your hosts given either before or after your departure always seems a bit more gracious than to arrive with gifts (like a social passport, as it were). The thoughtfulness of arriving with a little gift for each of the small fry is a nice gesture, however. Children love presents, and the most inexpensive gifts will please them and put you off on the right foot with the juniors.

A cause of embarrassment to both hostess and visitor sometimes is the question of payment for a telephone toll call. Imposition is a poor way to thank one's host. As soon as the call has been completed, the person making the call should ask the operator the charges, then leave the amount with a slip, giving the date and number called. Or if one has made many calls during a long visit, the complete list of calls and telegrams sent, with the amount of each and the total, should be handed to the hostess when one says good-by. This is the only way a guest can feel free to telephone as often as he may want to. If you fear that your hostess may not accept it from you, leave full payment in an envelope where it will be found by her. Blessings on the guest who leaves a clean trail of graciousness and fairness in his wake!

A day or so after your departure, a gracious thank-you note, sometimes referred to as a "bread-and-butter letter," is a *must*. Remember that even an elaborate, expensive gift does *not* take the place of this letter.

THANK-YOU TELEPHONE CALL

The day following a cocktail party, luncheon, or informal dinner it is a nice gesture to phone your hostess, thanking her again for including you at the party and extending a few complimentary remarks in regard to the success of the party. You might mention her artistic flower arrangements, the delectable food, if such, and the good time you and all the guests had.

ENTERTAINING IN ENLISTED CIRCLES

There are certain social talents so generally useful that if you have not acquired them, and wish to be a successful Navy wife, you should start now: the ability to introduce people, acknowledge introductions, accept and pay compliments, express gratitude, and know the few rules of etiquette that are based on consideration for others.

Every Navy wife owes it to herself to be competent in at least two social graces. These include being an average or better player in card games (bridge, rummy, canasta, or poker), being a good ballroom dancer, being able to play a musical instrument, and being socially athletic (at golf, tennis, badminton, bowling, table tennis, hiking, riding, swimming). If you are good at any two of these, you will pass muster! If not, get busy and it won't take long. The more strings you have to your bow, the better chance you will have of fitting into a wide variety of situations. And if people—lots of different kinds of people—genuinely like to have you around, your social success, which is so important to your happiness in the Navy, is assured.

Conversation

There are as many kinds of conversation as there are kinds of people; however, it might be noted that a good conversationalist is always a constructive listener. "One should cultivate alert, accurate, and sympathetic listening in conversation. By all means, one should be able to talk other than 'shop.' Trite expressions, attempts at fanciful language, profanity, coarseness, and bad grammar are the marks of poor manners and bad training."

Conversation is a considerate give-and-take, in which one tries to be as interesting as possible to the other person. The first rule for conversational behavior in company is: "Try to say and do only that which will be agreeable to others." The second rule is: "Try to draw the other person out and make him or her interesting." A bore is said to be "one who talks about himself when you want to talk about yourself."

Conversational Taboos at Social Gatherings

1. Vivid details of an operation, illness, death or funeral
2. Personal jokes of an embarrassing nature
3. Sneering remarks or attitudes
4. Destructive gossip and repetition of scandal
5. Discussion of personal money matters or the price paid for articles
6. Thoughtlessness of the feelings of others or tactlessness
7. Discussion of one's personal affairs with strangers or mere acquaintances
8. And unless the gathering is one of young mothers, forget the children!

Introductions

It is important that people be properly introduced to each other. One always introduces a man to a woman, a younger person to an older person, and one person to a group. There are several correct ways of making introductions. One may say, "Mrs. Thomas, may I present Chief Petty Officer Black?" Names should always be spoken very distinctly, so that they may be understood.

Another form is: "Mrs. Thomas, I should like to introduce Chief Petty Officer Black." This is considered less formal than the first form. Or, "Mrs. Thomas, this is Chief Petty Officer Black." The name of the person to whom the introduction is being made is always mentioned first.

In introducing a Warrant Officer, still another form would be: "Mrs. Thomas, do you know Mr. Thompson?"

When introducing members of the family, one avoids using titles as much as possible. For instance: "Mrs. Brown, this is my husband." "Mrs. Paine, may I introduce my daughter, Carolyn?"

A man should always rise when introduced to anyone, and men usually shake hands. A woman may offer her hand or not, but a man never offers his hand first. If a woman extends her hand, under no circumstances can the offered hand be ignored.

As you know, the correct reply to any form of introduction is "How do you do?" and it is courteous to add the name of the person to whom you are being introduced.

No woman is ever presented to a man, except to the President of the United States, a royal personage, or a dignitary of the church.

A hostess always rises to meet or to be introduced to a guest. Otherwise a woman does not rise to be introduced.

A man should never be guilty of introducing his wife as "the little woman," "the wife," "friend wife," or "the missus"; it is equally vulgar for a wife to introduce her husband as "the Chief," "my man," or "my hubby"!

It is no longer the best form to say, "Pleased to meet you" or "I am pleased to make your acquaintance." Again, the most acceptable form is "How do you do?" You don't need to answer that rhetorical question, of course, but may plunge into conversation at that point.

When one shakes hands it should be with warmth and firmness. A limp hand suggestive of a clammy fish is irritating. However, no one enjoys a bone crusher. Shake hands as though it were a pleasure, but not as though you were a drowning man going under for the third time.

CLUB PARTIES

On most naval stations there are two types of clubs for enlisted men which provide entertainment in the form of dances, bingo parties, suppers, and beer parties for the members and their wives or guests. The CPO Club is for Chiefs only; no enlisted man enters this club except on invitation from a member who must be a Chief. Then there is the Petty Officers' Club or the enlisted man's club (white hats) which takes care of the first four grades of Petty Officers and their guests.

EIGHT RULES OF SOCIAL CONDUCT FOR ENLISTED MEN

1. At a dance your primary mission is to show attention to your partner and see that she enjoys herself. You should introduce her to your friends and see that she dances as often as she wishes. You should not leave her entirely with your friends, but should dance with her at least several times.

2. You should dance at least once with your hostess.

3. After a dance with a woman who came with someone else, you should escort her back to her partner, or to her table, thank her for the dance, and leave.

4. Be sure to thank your hostess when you leave a party. You might say, "I have had a fine time here, Mrs. Jones. Thank you very much for everything," or anything along that general line. (Complete honesty is not always recommended in this case.)

5. Keep your voice low. Never be loud or boisterous. If you have had some drinks, try to remember that they may be making you talk too loudly and too much.

6. Never whistle at a woman. Leave that to the drugstore cowboys.

7. When you ask a woman for a date, give her a chance to get out of it if she wants to.

8. Avoid overstaying your welcome when visiting anyone.

A Sociable Cup of Tea or Coffee for Navy Wives

To ask a neighbor, a Navy newcomer, a young mother you met out baby-pushing in the park to drop in for a cup of tea is an easy, inexpensive, and simple way to make mere acquaintances into friends. A thin bread-and-butter sandwich with a dish of jelly or a pot of jam adds a festive note. You might invite your guest to bring her knitting or sewing.

If you favor serving coffee, then invite your new neighbor for a cup either in the morning or in the afternoon. You need not serve anything with coffee, though Danish pastry, small doughnuts, or cinnamon coffeecake is a nice addition.

Two Kinds of Entertaining

There are two kinds of entertaining: one you plan; the second is usually wished upon you. If you have a job, time (or the lack of it) may be the vital factor in your entertaining program. If you have a baby or babies, and washing is on your daily agenda, then effort and the strength expended may be vital factors. Baby-sitters come high, so Navy juniors accompany their parents and the kids have a field day. Usually a room is assigned to them for play.

On the social side, beer and the sailor "kinda go together," so one of the quickest and easiest ways to launch a friendly evening is as follows: Chill enough beer for the guests, far enough in advance to assure its being icy cold. Fix big mixed trays of the "four P's"— pretzels, peanuts, potato chips, popcorn (cheese and plain buttered). Hard-boiled eggs may be added, and pickles. Let the guests do the rest.

Variations on the Theme are as follows:

Substitute or add hamburgers.
Prepare a dressing into which potato chips may be dunked.

Set out the makings of "Dagwood sandwiches" and turn the guests loose on their own.

Fix some submarine sandwiches in advance.

A dish of assorted cheeses might be arranged with crackers.

With beer, a platter of cold roast pork sliced paper-thin and sprinkled with salt and lots of pepper, with a companion plate of buttered bread, will please the men.

Navy Wives' Clubs of America, Inc. (NWCA)

One of the finest of Service wives' clubs is that of the Navy Wives' Clubs of America, Incorporated, founded in California on June 3, 1936. It was the dream of two Navy wives named Grace Stahl and Catherine Pringle to organize Navy wives into clubs all over the continental United States. Mrs. Stahl's husband, Carl, advised them, in the early fall of 1935, to ask Mary Paolozzi to help them as she had vision and potential leadership qualities. She gathered about her a group of girls who formed a Navy Wives' Club in San Pedro, which was to be the forerunner of groups of Navy wives on naval stations and in every seaport.

However, five years earlier, in February of 1931, a Navy Wives' Club of Long Beach (California) had been formed to promote sociability and service among the wives of enlisted men. It was decided in 1935 that the San Pedro and Long Beach Navy Wives' Clubs should form a corporation.

During World War II, many Clubs were chartered which were later forced to disband when naval stations were deactivated. Today, charters have been issued to Navy Wives' Clubs of America in French Morocco, the Philippine Islands, and Puerto Rico.

Program of NWCA

While operating on the premise that "The Navy takes care of its own" and that "charity begins at home," still NWCA reaches out to take a helpful and humanitarian interest in near-by communities and towns if and when possible. This makes for fine public relations between the Navy and the community.

NWCA has a threefold program: to promote welfare, social, and educational projects.

A national project is the Scholarship Fund for the children of Navy, Marine Corps, and Coast Guard enlisted personnel. This is a most worth-while project. Two scholarships have already been awarded.

A cookbook is in the process of being published for the NWCA, with Mrs. C. Daryl Bailey, chairman of the Ways and Means Committee, and Mrs. Helen Walker, co-chairman, in charge.

Suggestions for classified activities are as follows:

On Your Station	*Off Your Station*
Navy Relief Society	Adopt group of local orphans at Christmas
Collect clothing regularly	
Donate to needy families	Visit crippled children's hospital; help entertain children
Furnish child care for hospitalized patients	Take Thanksgiving, Christmas, or Easter basket to home for aged
Collect magazines and books for patients	Toy tea for orphans' home
Furnish current magazines for maternity-ward waiting room	Visit local Veterans Administration hospital; ward party for patients with refreshments and prizes
Buy wheel chair for child polio victim on base	Collect used nylon hose, buttons and thread, magazines and books for home for aged
Wrap Christmas packages for seamen	Dress dolls for local Salvation Army
Make layettes	
Supply workers and flowers for Chapel Guild	
Sell Christmas and Easter seals	
Heart and Cancer Fund, Red Cross contributions	
Blood bank	
Pre-Teen-Ager Candy Pull	
Teen-Ager Hay Ride; Sleigh Ride	
Teen-Ager Back-to-School Dance	

Educational activities for the Club might include an informative film on parliamentary procedure; a film on Korea, Hawaii, the Philippine Islands; an informative film on cancer with lecture by a Navy doctor; an informative film on polio with talk by therapist or mother of victim. Encourage members to take Red Cross training, and to work with Scouts, Brownies, and Cubs.

Social Activities

Potluck luncheon or dinner	Fashion show	Hard-times party
Cosmetic demonstration	Dinner dance	Canasta, bridge, or
Hair styling demonstration	Square dance	scrabble party
Flower arrangement demon-	Lawn fete with	Beachcomber party
stration	bazaar and	Beach party
Cake decoration demonstration	fishpond	Spaghetti supper
Waffle brunch	Homemade ice-	Picnic, barbecue, or fish
	cream and	fry
	cake sale	

An installation tea with candlelight service for new Club officers and outgoing officers is always an interesting event.

Pledge

As a member of the Navy Wives' Clubs of America, I promise to uphold the Constitution and By-Laws, and to live up to the high standards and ideals of the organization.

I pledge myself to be *kind* and *charitable* to my sister members, to attend meetings regularly, to avoid gossip, and to join in all activities insofar as I am able. I promise to conduct myself at all times in a manner which will bring credit to the organization and to be ever mindful of the dignity of the position which I hold as the partner of a man serving the Flag of our Country.

The benefit you derive from your Club will be in ratio to the enthusiasm, interest, and work you put into it. Don't be timid about joining. It is a station activity which needs your wholehearted support, not so much financially as morally, socially, and in the spirit of friendliness which makes for pleasant and gracious living.

JANGO

The Junior Army-Navy Guild Organization, better known as Jango, was founded in March, 1942, owing to the efforts of Mrs. Robert P. Patterson, whose husband later was Secretary of War, and the late Mrs. Ralph A. Bard, whose husband was Assistant Secretary of the Navy.

A nonprofit organization, its aims and purposes are to form a link between the community and the armed services, to assist local charities, and to promote a feeling of family relationship and loyalty to the armed services. These aims and purposes have been well observed during the years of Jango's growth.

The membership, now about 500, is composed of wives, daughters, granddaughters, mothers, and sisters of commissioned officers who are serving or have served in the armed forces of our country. There are two groups—Juniors, ranging in age from fourteen to twenty-one; and Seniors, over twenty-one.

Jango is a working organization, presenting various "projects." A member may serve her volunteer hours in the project of her choice; Juniors, in the canteen at the Soldiers, Sailors, Marines, and Air Men's Club, as Nurses' Aides, or caring for children in the nursery of the Post Hospital at Fort Belvoir; Seniors, as hostess in the Bargain Shop, or as members of the Internation Hospitality Committee. The Bargain Shop is the main source of income.

Chapter XIII

NAVY JUNIORS

C HILDREN of naval personnel are always spoken of in the
Service as "Navy juniors," Army children are affectionately
called "Army brats," and Air Force youngsters are appro-
priately termed "Air Force fledglings."

Wise young couples have their children in the early years of their
married life if that is at all possible. Sometimes, when young couples
plan to have their families at some future date—for instance, "When
Jim gets to be a CPO" or "When Bob is promoted and we have
Lieutenant's pay"—"Man proposes, but God disposes." The couple
may lose the wonderful chance of fulfillment with which heaven
endowed them. The best advice is, don't delay.

WHEN JUNIOR IS EXPECTED

Bearing a child is a perfectly normal function, and you have nothing to fear but fear. Pay attention only to your doctor, and discard
all superstitions, strange ideas, and advice from well-meaning relatives and friends. You are performing the most important and the
most magnificent job of your life, the one for which you were
designed.

The waiting period should be filled with plans for the new baby,
which you and your husband will find pleasure in sharing together.
Don't forget it is his child too. There will be days when you are not
too comfortable. If you feel your sense of humor dwindling, by all
means invest in a copy of Rory Gallager's *Ladies in Waiting*; this will
make you smile again and maybe even laugh *with*, not *at*, yourself.
Having a baby isn't exactly a laughing matter. When it gets tough,
grit your teeth and hang on. Eventually you can look back and smile
—for babies do have a way of getting born.

GOVERNMENT HOSPITAL CARE

Today a Navy wife is assured of the best prenatal care, complete obstetrical care with excellent medical follow-up and postpartum care of the baby and herself if she can arrange to reside near an Army, Navy or Air Force hospital during pregnancy and from six weeks to six months afterwards. This wonderful service means everything to the man at sea, who knows that his wife and baby will get the best that medical science has to offer.

Prospective mothers are briefed at most hospitals in a group on their first visit to the clinic. Fears are allayed, questions may be asked, the young matrons get to know each other and the doctor in charge, in whom they should have implicit faith.

As a Navy wife you should never hesitate to go to an Army or Air Force hospital provided there are accommodations. At any one of these you should be able to have your baby for a minimum, often less than $10.00.

Another thing, the Service nurses are wonderful. They are understanding and kind, especially when they know you are on your own with your first baby.

THE CHRISTENING

The parents may wish to send out engraved announcements, which consist of a joint calling card at the top of which is a smaller one reading

Anne Marie Pye
May first

Invitations to christenings are informal and may be extended verbally, or by telephone, since only intimate friends are invited.

The first step in the plans for a christening is the selection of a name for the baby. This is something about which an outsider should not even make a suggestion or venture an opinion. Next comes the matter of godparents, who should be chosen from among one's intimate friends. Should they live at a distance, proxies may take their place during the ceremony. The idea of godparents is that, if the child should be left alone in the world, the godparents would become its protectors. In Europe, godparents assume great responsibility, but somehow in this country they take their obligations more lightly and consider their duty accomplished if they give the infant a silver porringer, a christening cup, a lovely Bible, or a substantial check.

In the Catholic Church, the christening takes place usually before the infant is two weeks old and is always performed in church, if possible. The average christening in the Protestant churches takes place between the ages of six months and one year and may be performed at home or in the church.

Arrangements with the post chaplain, if he is to perform the ceremony, should be made in advance; he will probably suggest Sunday morning or afternoon as an appropriate time. If the ceremony is held at the chapel, the nurse or someone else will take charge of the infant until time to hand it over to the godmother, who holds it during the baptism. It is very necessary that the godmother pronounce the baby's name distinctly; otherwise the child may carry through life a name not intended for it. A common practice is for her to hand to the minister a card on which the baby's full name is typed or clearly written. At a Catholic christening a certificate of baptism is given to the parents. The chaplain also forwards the original certificate to the Military Ordinariat, 451 Madison Avenue, New York City. Parents of the child should keep their copy of the certificate with other important papers in their personal file or lockbox, since it is necessary for a Catholic to have proof of baptism before entering into a marriage covenant. Should the baptismal certificate be lost, a copy can always be obtained at the Ordinariat.

As soon as the ceremony is over, the godmother hands the baby back to the nurse, who carries it immediately to the waiting car, and she and the baby return home. If no nurse is in attendance, the godmother or a member of the family carries the infant. The baby is dressed all in white. Exquisitely dainty christening robes are sometimes handed down in families, a lovely custom; however, the long christening robe is now almost entirely out of fashion and babies wear any kind of pretty, simple white dress.

It is far easier to have the christening at home. The baby can be brought into the room at the last moment, which is safer because he is not so likely to catch cold. The quarters may be decorated with flowers—pale pink rosebuds and baby's-breath are pretty as a center-piece on the tea table.

The font is always a bowl of gold, silver, or crystal. It is placed on a small, high table. The table should be covered with a dainty cloth and everything placed in readiness for the chaplain. In Hawaii, the baptismal water might be taken from historic Pearl Harbor, later blessed by the chaplain, of course. In Panama, it might be obtained from both the Atlantic and the Pacific or the Panama Canal.

After the ceremony, which is usually held about four or five o'clock, the party resembles an afternoon tea. The mother or the nurse may hold the baby for everyone to admire, but the poor little dear should not be tired out or forced to endure too much. Before the first whimper, he should be returned to the nursery!

Christening "caudle," which is hot eggnog punch, or even champagne, may be served, as this is an occasion which rates something special. An old-fashioned custom is to pass around a loving cup from which everyone drinks as he makes a wish for the baby.

If gifts are brought, they may include a silver knife, fork, and spoon set, a silver cup or mug, silver porringer or, for a tiny girl, a wee string of dainty pearls. Gold rings and bracelets are no longer considered fashionable for infants. One of the most acceptable gifts is a savings bond, baby or larger, depending upon your purse! Gifts are not expected, and whether you bring one or not depends upon how much you love babies in general and this baby in particular.

Your First Baby's Nursery

Linoleum is the ideal floor covering, but that is seldom practicable. Small washable rugs are better than a large rug. Frequent launderings will be in order, and they can go right into the washing machine.

The essentials are: a clothes chest of drawers (if you buy it new, select one with a hanging compartment so that the child can get his own clothes when he is old enough); a low, comfortable chair or rocker to use while feeding the baby; a portable bath-dressing table; a disposal unit for diapers; a fitted wicker basket or tray for bottles to hold cotton, oil, and such necessities. A weighing scale may or may not be a necessity—certainly it is a comfort. A clothes tree is convenient and a bottle warmer is useful but neither is an essential.

"His Majesty's" bed is important; however, it can be a deep dresser drawer or a sturdy clothes or market basket mounted on wheels, so long as it has a firm pillow as a mattress. Lacy, beribboned bassinets are lovely but frightful dust catches, and the baby grows out of them in a wink. It is more practicable to buy a full-sized baby bed at the start, in which he will be able to sleep until he is four or five years old. The screened folding variety of Kiddie-Coop remains popular.

Washable walls of cream color or white with one or two simple pictures make a good starter. Of course, there are inexpensive nursery prints galore, which charm the adult but have little or no meaning for a child. Keep in mind that it is your cherub's room, not yours!

When he learns to toddle, gradually you will remove all of the little-baby signs from the room—the diaper-disposal unit, bathinet, bottle warmer, bottles, and jars. This makes him feel quite grown up, and it has a marked psychological effect on acquiring good toilet habits.

For a while there may be a play pen; then he progresses to the creeping stage, when he will be ready for low shelves which you will provide for his toys and big blocks. Large blocks, even if home-made, are very important in these early years of muscle building.

I should advise you never, never to install one of those fiendish inventions called a "toy box" as nursery equipment. They only teach a child to keep his toys and possessions in the utmost disorder. A little child easily acquires a love of order, and if you have patience you can teach him to have a place for each toy. Believe it or not, he will enjoy putting each toy in its proper spot. It gives him a pleasant sense of achievement!

Standard nursery-school furniture is a good investment as it stands up well under the punishment inflicted by its little user. As soon as your prodigy shows an interest in creative decoration, it will be wise to provide him with a blackboard or, if space permits, a pin-board installed at a convenient height on an unbroken wall. A broad piece of wood-bound cork, on which can be thumbtacked or stapled cheap newsprint paper, will be a joy to him and to you and your landlord, too! He can use chalks, crayolas, or paints and give his creative instinct ample scope. If the scene isn't set for such activities, don't be surprised if energy turns into what you term naughtiness. With patience, if not with ease, you can teach him that this room is his, that his decorative talents belong only here, and in no other room in the house.

EDUCATIONAL INSURANCE

This is a type of insurance that is becoming increasingly popular, because all parents are interested in a college education for their children. It is also a means of saving, and a convenient way to meet the real educational needs of your children. If taken out when the child is very young, the policies involve only small premiums. The plan is that the policy matures when Junior is sixteen, seventeen, or eighteen, and there will be ready cash to send him to either a good preparatory school, if he plans to enter the Military, Naval, or Air Academy, or a standard college.

NURSERY SCHOOLS

So little is really known of the wonders accomplished by a good nursery school! However, a poor school with inefficient and inexperienced teachers is worse than no school at all. If you can possibly afford it, by all means send your child to a good one. Two years of age is not too young for him to enter nursery school although some parents prefer to wait until he is three or even four.

The young child is learning constantly, and what he learns may be desirable or undesirable. Character is taking shape, habits are being formed, skills and attitudes are being developed for better or for worse.

A few of the advantages of training in a modern nursery school are as follows:

1. Companionship with children near the same age
2. The development of proper attitudes—so very important
3. The forming of good health habits—eating, sleeping, toilet
4. The sharing of possessions with other children—toys, books
5. Learning to follow directions, take orders, obey
6. Learning to live and to play in a group

After all, one of the most important lessons in life is getting along with our fellow man, and the age of two years is the best time to start developing the proper attitudes and traits of character.

Preparatory Schools

Many Navy parents place their children in boarding schools when they are old enough, so as to avoid the frequent moves, school transfers, loss of time and credits, and above all the emotional upsets that are bound to occur when young lives are uprooted so often. To me this is one of the sad features and disadvantages of Service life; children should somehow take root like plants. They should have a stable home, childhood friends, an organized home and community life.

On the other hand, the average Navy junior is at home any place; he never meets a stranger. If they don't play handball by the same rules he learned in Hong Kong, then he learns the rules by which they play in San Diego. He has many little shipmates like himself, and when a chance meeting occurs with a former little friend of years ago, it is like old home week.

Scholarships

The Bureau of Naval Personnel, Navy Department, Washington, D.C., publishes a list, "Schools and Colleges Granting Concessions to Sons and Daughters of Officer and Enlisted Personnel—U.S. Navy." Concessions and scholarships are offered by schools, colleges, universities, and summer camps. "Determination of the classes of persons who are included as 'naval personnel' rests with the authorities of the individual schools."

Scholarship assistance for sons and daughters and, in some cases, widows of deceased Service persons is provided by many schools, colleges, special scholarship funds, and, in some cases, by state laws. While such assistance is usually provided only for selected persons needing financial assistance, in some cases the aid is furnished regardless of need. This is particularly true of the state benefits. For additional information on this subject one may contact the Bureau of Naval Personnel, Pers-G212, setting forth the particular geographical area of schools concerning which there is interest. Information on the special state benefits may be obtained from the various State Veterans Commissions.

Similar assistance is available for dependents of active-duty personnel.

Appointments to the Naval Academy

Scholarships may be one thing to win, but an appointment to the Naval Academy is another. It is becomingly increasingly hard for sons of naval officers to obtain appointments. There are six kinds of appointments:

1. "Appointment by Senators, Representatives and Delegates in Congress and by the Vice President."

   Applications for Congressional appointments should be addressed personally to the two Senators from the State in which the applicant lives, or to the Representatives from the applicant's Congressional District, or to all three. Even Representatives-at-large should be approached. They all have appointments.

2. Appointments at large and appointments from the District of Columbia by the President.

   Applications for such appointments should be addressed to the Secretary of the Navy, Washington, D.C., and should give the full name of the candidate, his address, the date of his birth, and the name, rank, or rating of his father. There are 75 Presidential appointments for sons of officers and enlisted personnel and five appointments from the District of Columbia.

3. Appointments by competitive examination from the enlisted men of the Regular Navy and Marine Corps.

   There are 160 appointments open to enlisted men of the Navy and the Marine Corps who have served one year.

4. Appointments by competitive examination from the enlisted men of the Naval Reserve and the Marine Corps Reserve.

   There are 160 appointments open to the Naval Reserve and Marine Corps Reserve each year.

5. Appointments by the President from among the sons of deceased officers, soldiers, sailors and marines of World War I.

   There are 40 of these appointments made each year. Applications for appointments should be addressed to the Bureau of Naval Personnel, Navy Department, Washington, D.C.

6. Appointments from the honor graduates of educational institutions designated as "Honor Schools" by the Department of the Army, and from the members of the Naval Reserve Officers' Training Corps.

   There are 20 of these appointments each year.

There are some very stiff requirements that a prospective applicant for an appointment should know. He must be a citizen of the United

States and have good moral character. He must be not younger than seventeen on April 1 of the calendar year in which he expects to enter the Naval Academy, and not older than twenty-one.

The physical requirements are more than exacting. Eyes seem to come in for the most critical examination. Each must have a normal vision of 20/20.

AIR TRAVEL WITH CHILDREN

Travel by air is commonplace today in the Service. When orders come in, your husband may have to precede you. You are left to pack, give up the quarters or house, and follow with the children. You really have a bit of planning to do, regardless of how green the grass may appear to be at your next station. Let us assume that you are an experienced hand at surface travel, which includes train, boat and motor. Flying, however, is something new to you and especially so with a baby or babies.

If you are traveling on a commercial air line and not by MATS

1. Be sure to let the air line know the ages of your youngsters even though you do not buy a ticket for children under two years of age. If possible, the stewardess will let your nonpaying baby have the spare seat if one is available. (Of course, you can't count on this; you must be prepared to hold your baby all the way, even if he does weigh twenty-five pounds and resembles a wiggle worm in his acrobatics.)

2. Change planes only if absolutely necessary and make plane connections as close as recommended safe (as to time allowance) because stopovers in public air terminals are difficult with children.

3. When making your reservations, choose the fastest trip with the fewest stops, and if possible select a large pressurized cabin plane. The latter is easier on the babies' ears, and the fewer landings and take-offs, the less trouble you have on this score.

Air Travel by MATS

Briefing comes first: All immunization charts for adults and children must be checked; then about two hours before take-off time all baggage must be weighed in, and a regular MATS briefing for overseas travel is given. A movie is shown which is important as it outlines the procedure employed in ditching a C-54 or large passenger transport. A short lecture is given, and remember all of this is for no one's good but your own!

On dependents' flights there are two or more flight nurses, and everything possible is done for the comfort of the passengers. Families are usually seated together in a plane, particularly those with babies (as far as possible removed from VIP's).

MATS service continues to improve all the time, and dependents who have traveled recently have nothing but good things to say about it. Like commercial air lines, MATS even gives passengers a blank form to fill in suggested improvements in the service and your impression of the flight.

Wear a tailored suit, of crease- and spot-resistant material, if possible (unless you wear slacks), and remove the jacket and your hat when you get on the plane. Black is a poor choice since it shows all lint from blankets and paper diapers! Let what may happen to your blouse because you can either change it or cover it later with your jacket. Tuck an extra sleeveless silk jersey blouse in just in case. Wear good-looking but comfortable shoes so you can carry your baby and walk too. Appearance is a great morale factor, and if you keep yourself as neat as possible you will not only look but feel better. If traveling by MATS you will be requested to wear slacks. Take a warm jacket or coat—it's cold at ten thousand feet and the heater may go out. Clothing carried over the arm is not counted against your baggage allowance.

Get a good night's rest the night before leaving because you will need all of your energy to devote to the children; always plan to be rested before you embark on a trip with children. If you have any fear of being airsick be sure to take the new drug, dramamine. The tablets are now an item of issue on all MATS transports. A sick mother is pathetic and the children of a sick mother are more pathetic! Try to keep cheerful and calm because your children's attitude and behavior will be dependent upon yours. Your pediatrician may give you a light sedative for the children, but if they don't relax and sleep don't let it worry you. Just be prepared to amuse them all night long! This takes long-range planning but here are some of the tricks:

1. Take plenty of little toys; you won't want to load your luggage with heavy wooden toys or dolls. Small plastic cars, a matchbox full of buttons and a blunt threaded needle will amuse a three-year-old

for an hour or more. You can tuck in little jars filled with red and white dried beans, fill and refill the bottles and screw on the tops. What harm if a few are spilled?

2. If your child is old enough to cut, put a pair of blunt-end scissors in your purse and a small roll of Scotch tape. Magazines afford lovely pictures, and Scotch tape is never messy to stick up an art gallery on the window or the next seat. A small note pad and pencil come in handy for drawing pictures, but for obvious reasons beware of crayolas, clay, or paint. Crayons might be taken for coloring books for the child old enough to be trusted with them.

3. All ten-cent stores have a fund of tracing and cutout books as well as tiny books that can be read and pack easily, using up little space. Little fellows love to unwind a spool of thread or one of those crepe-paper "Surprise Balls" that have little favors all wound up in them.

4. Do take candy, gum, and cookies but buy wisely. Take only candy that can be eaten in one bite like jelly beans or gumdrops. Avoid gooey, messy candy bars. Hold back on the candy; dole it out as a reward or a surprise for good behavior. As for fruit, leave all juicy fruit like oranges, plums, peaches at home and instead select what can be sliced with a penknife and fed to the child bite by bite. Never give a child a whole apple to wipe all over himself, you, the plane, and fellow passengers. For an older child take a few sandwiches because often meals aloft are strange or the child is too fascinated to eat at an air terminal; his favorite peanut-butter sandwich will be the answer when he announces that he is hungry at 3 A.M.

5. Nature calls: Would that this problem could be eliminated on the trip, but it cannot! On any long trip, "piddling" or "pot-potting" for babies just out of diapers is very difficult. If the child is young enough, put it back into diapers for the trip. However, if you can't do this, take a little plastic "piddling pot" for boys and a regular little "pot" for girls (a small cardboard hatbox is a good disguise for the latter).

6. Whether you like to fly or not, it is a good idea to appear enthusiastic about the trip, so that your children will not be frightened and will enjoy flying. Hold small ones on your lap during the take-off and landing so they will not be frightened. It is a good plan to talk

to them as the engines are revved up prior to take-off, and point out the windows at objects to keep their interest stimulated.

7. Teach them to yawn or open their mouths and swallow on taking off, and when the plane is coming in to land to blow their noses. This helps relieve the pressure on their ears. For older children chewing gum, of course, is in order.

A Motor Trip with Children

1. Have AAA or one of the oil companies plan your trip with reference to shortest routes, best roads, preferred lodging and eating places.

2. Motels are easier than hotels: the car is at the door, many tips are saved; only the luggage you need as you need it is unpacked. No one likes to drag or carry three or four tired little children through the lobby of a hotel. Even the family dog or cat is welcome at most motels, if it sleeps in the car.

3. Don't overload the car.

Another convenience: Take your shoe bag, hanging on your closet door, and fasten it over the back of the front seat, so the compartments will be handy to the back-seat travelers. Fill the compartments with the things the family needs from time to time—road maps, magazines, toys, paper cups, napkins, fruit, and a thermos bottle filled with your favorite beverage.

4. For yourself choose packables for traveling—suits or sweaters and skirts with extra blouses.

5. Include Lux, a collapsible ironing board which fits into your suitcase and a Pak-away electric iron as part of your laundry gear. For the more difficult laundry, stop at a Laundromat and have it washed and dried one day while you and the family have lunch. It can be done and is just that easy.

6. Light diets for children while traveling are recommended, although there is usually one passenger who can't get enough to eat. If possible, eat only at recommended restaurants. Always insist upon pasteurized milk for children.

7. Never use restaurant silver for small children. Paper spoons and cups are preferred; each child should have his own plastic bib to save clothes from spots and for easy cleaning.

8. After several days of restaurant dining, stop at a delicatessen,

select food for a picnic lunch, then stop at a roadside park or an inviting picnic ground.

9. Give the youngsters as much exercise as time permits. They will love sightseeing from five on, and it is amazing how much little ones remember about the historic spots they have visited. This all adds to the pleasure of the trip, and automobile trips can be very educational as well as fun.

10. Plan the children's clothing with care. Be sure not to burden them with heavy clothes or long coats. Short jackets or sweaters worn with corduroy or seersucker slacks and washable T-shirts, depending upon the weather, will prove satisfactory. Remember that children become ill more easily from being overdressed than they do from being lightly dressed while traveling. Dress them as you yourself feel comfortable. Three or four changes for a week's trip should be adequate if you do a bit of laundry as you go along.

Luggage

Suitcases which will not be needed en route can be packed between the front and back seats, and with the baby's crib mattress placed on top will give additional sleeping space. Children tire easily and frequent cat naps improve their dispositions. Sleeping children while traveling in the car depends, of course, upon their ages. Small canvas car beds, convertible to car seats, are on the market, but a bed made of blankets and pillows will also prove satisfactory for children over two years.

Baby rates a zippered bag of his own which will contain only his changes and clothes. This will probably go on the floor in the front of the car. A bottle warmer attachable to the dashboard is a real convenience. A small bag or box containing a one-burner hot plate, and utensils for formula-making placed in the trunk of the car will enable you to make the baby's formula in any motel or hotel room. You'll be glad you took this along!

A "Fort-niter Bag" will hold enough for a family of six if you pack just those things needed at night and for two or three day changes. Pack it in the trunk in the most accessible space so that the car does not have to be unpacked every night.

There will be another bag or perhaps a basket for sheets, disposable diapers, rubber pants, socks, Kleenex, baby oil, cream, soap, socks, extra overalls, towels, washcloths, and in one compartment a can opener, bottle opener, paper cups, spoons, straws, and bibs.

No experienced mother will start on a motor trip without the little sprout's toidy seat, if he is used to it. It can be camouflaged with a plastic cover, and baby's routine need not be disturbed. Many mothers find it easier to feed the baby in the car before taking the family into a restaurant to eat. The car seat serves as a high chair and you have your formula or baby food, cups, and spoons at hand. This type of planning often prevents restaurant scenes. A baby does not like changes of environment at feeding time; if fed in the car first, he will go along and keep happy in a high chair with his favorite toy or perhaps a cookie while the family enjoy their meals.

To keep the older children occupied is important too. Take along crayons, coloring books, push-out puzzles, beads to be strung. When they become restless, bring out a new trinket. The whole family can enjoy guessing games or favorite stories.

CHILDREN ON A NAVAL STATION

Each station has its own regulations in regard to the deportment of children but here are a few general rules:

1. Don't fail to acquaint your child with local rules in regard to the swimming pool, golf course, tennis courts, the Officers' Club.

2. Don't permit your child to impose upon neighbors; discourage frequent calls, picking flowers, teasing pets, playing in driveways and garages.

3. Don't allow vandalism, such as defacing, destroying, or injuring government property or private property.

4. Don't permit a child to deface quarters, write on walls, break windows, dig holes in lawns.

5. Don't allow impertinence to guards, or tolerate misconduct on school bus.

6. Teach obedience to traffic rules in regard to crossing busy intersections, proper riding of bicycles, scooters, etc.

7. Children or their pets should not be allowed near hangar lines, docks, gun sheds, firing ranges.

8. Try to control unnecessary noise, crying, or any play that is annoying to neighbors.

9. Teach respect, consideration, and courtesy for older people.

10. Remember the old saying that "little pitchers have big ears." Be careful not to discuss anything of an official nature before children; they may not get the true meaning and repeat something very different from what was said. What is sometimes worse, they repeat all too accurately what was said, and to the wrong person.

11. A positive effort should be made by parents to explain to their children that rank should never be mentioned, even casually. For instance, never say, no matter how it is meant, "Oh, she's a Captain's daughter!" "His father is a CPO."

12. Don't feel that an invitation includes your children, unless they are specifically mentioned in it. Never take your children with you on a formal call, even if they remain in the car. Stretch a point and hire a baby-sitter if the call is a must. Arrange for your children not to be in the living room when you are receiving formal callers or having dinner guests.

13. Wise parents ignore children's quarrels; you should be too adult to let your children's quarrels become quarrels between parents, even if *your* child is *right*.

14. Neither is it wise for parents to criticize the behavior of other children. Have a care! Yours may be guilty of the same conduct tomorrow.

15. In general, impress upon your children the fact that their misbehavior can cause their father to suffer official humiliation.

Most people love a well-mannered, courteous child, but no one enjoys a rude, spoiled "little monster"! Navy children on the whole are usually well disciplined, orderly, and courteous, but always remember they reflect you and their home training.

Chapter XIV

NAVY LIFE IN WASHINGTON

APPROXIMATELY five thousand naval officers are now on duty in Washington and vicinity, and the number of the enlisted personnel also is much greater than in any previous period of peace. Besides the personnel assigned to the Navy Department, which now is divided between the Pentagon, the old Navy Department building on Constitution Avenue, and various other buildings such as the Bureau of Yards and Docks and the Navy Department Annex in Arlington, many officers and enlisted personnel are attached to activities of the Potomac River Naval Command, such as the Naval Air Station in Anacostia and the Receiving Barracks and Naval Reserve Training Center at the Washington Navy Yard, to various experimental and research activities, and to the Naval Gun Factory.

Satisfactory housing accommodations for naval personnel in the city of Washington are hard to find, rents are high, and the situation with regard to schools is most difficult. Because of these conditions, a great majority of Navy families reside in the suburban areas adjacent to Washington—Chevy Chase, Bethesda, Kensington, Wheaton, and Silver Springs in Maryland, and Alexandria, Arlington, Fairfax, and Falls Church in Virginia.

To assist officer personnel to obtain suitable and convenient living accommodations, there has been established in the Pentagon, under the control of the General commanding the Military District of Washington, an Armed Forces Service Center, which has as one branch the Armed Forces Housing Office with a Housing Counselor. In order to give efficient service it is necessary for the Counselor to have specific data such as: Where will the applicant be stationed? How many, if any, children are in the family; what is the age and sex of each? Will the children desire to attend public or parochial schools,

and if so, at grammar or high-school level? Are furnished or unfurnished accommodations required? What is the maximum rental
that can be paid? Does the applicant prefer an apartment or a house?
Has the family any pets? Will the applicant drive to and from his
office or depend upon public transportation? Would he like to share
a car-pool arrangement?

For naval personnel employed in the Pentagon or the Navy Department Annex in Arlington, living accommodations in Arlington
County or in Alexandria are most convenient. There are in this area
many large apartments of the garden style, mostly two-story multiple-
unit dwellings. Probably the best known of these is Parkfairfax;
another is the Presidential Gardens. Convenient to the Gun Factory
are the Naylor Gardens Apartments on 31st Street, S.E., which are
popular and attractive.

For personnel who desire to buy or to rent a small home, there are
many large building projects. Homes in these projects differ in size
and desirability, but by careful reading of the advertisements in the
daily papers it is possible to determine the suitability for one's needs.
Many have found it profitable to buy and retain a home here since
it can often be rented on leaving.

Because of the difficulty in rapidly obtaining suitable living accommodations one of two plans should be followed: (1) The family
should delay arrival in Washington until the husband has found
accommodations; or (2) if the family is to arrive with the husband,
he should be sure that advance reservations have been made at some
hotel where they can stay until a satisfactory home has been
located.

There is another organization, the Armed Forces Hostess Association, whose primary objective is to assist all Service personnel of the
armed forces on duty in the vicinity of Washington. This Association
of volunteer workers, composed entirely of Service officers' wives, was
formed in 1949 and maintains an office in the Pentagon, where
someone is always available to aid those in need. Recently the First
Lady saw unification at its best when she was honor guest at the
Fifth Anniversary Luncheon and Musicale of the Armed Forces
Hostess Association at the Army and Navy Country Club. The Association maintains a card file of late information on transportation,
schools, camps, shopping facilities, nurses, cleaning women, and baby-

sitters. It also has much information on living conditions abroad in areas where armed forces personnel are likely to be stationed.

LIFE IN WASHINGTON

Navy life in the nation's capital is totally different from life in a navy yard or at some station in or near a small town. If you live in the suburbs your most intimate friend through propinquity may be the wife of a civilian, a diplomat, an Army officer, or a Congressman. You will contact your Navy friends at some general gathering, but it may take time. You will be busy in your new home, possibly driving your husband to work in order to have the use of the car during the day, or you may be driving your children to school.

Despite high rents, servantless lives, and costly living conditions, most naval personnel welcome assignment to duty in Washington. The Navy wife considers that these disadvantages are outweighed by the cultural advantages afforded (concerts, musicales, art galleries, and lecture courses) and the thrill of being an integral part of the life of the capital of the United States.

If this is your first visit to Washington or residence in Washington, there are certain national shrines and definite beauty spots you should see in your first enthusiasm. Buy a thirty-five-cent map of the city and get oriented. The site for the nation's capital was selected by President Washington, and the plan for the city's streets and circles was made by a young French engineer, Major Pierre Charles L'Enfant. You will be charmed by the physical beauty of the city of Washington with its wide tree-lined streets, its famous Rock Creek Park extending for miles through the northwest section of the city, and the boulevards along the bank of the beautiful Potomac River.

Probably the building in Washington having the most interest for women is the White House, the official residence of the President of the United States and family. The White House, except the private living quarters, is open to visitors forenoons except Saturdays, Sundays, and holidays. Regular tours are conducted under experienced guides. Because of knowledge and familiarity with their subject, such guides are worth their cost.

Diagonally across from the White House stands Blair House, a home with historic memories which in the last few years has taken on a new interest since it serves as the official guesthouse for the nation. As a caravansary it has had an imposing guest list of visiting notables, and during the period of repairing the White House, President Truman and his family lived there.

Since Blair House was acquired by the government, it has been refurbished and now houses a priceless collection of Americana. Chiefs of state and sometimes prime ministers visiting the United States officially are normally entertained for one night in the White House, after which they transfer to Blair House or the embassy of their native country.

It is best to plan so that the sights you wish to see fall into groups. If you start with the Capitol building, along with the pages, other tourists, and politicians who crowd the corridors you will want to see the House of Representatives, which usually is in an uproar, though most of the members seem to be chatting or reading the newspapers. It appears that most of the business is done in committees.

Also, you will want to see the Senate chamber before taking a walk through the tunnel or riding the little electric subterranean railway to the Senate Office Building, where you might be lucky enough to have an appointment with your home-state Senator. Having started your walkathon, you might as well step over to the Library of Congress. Here are preserved the originals of many rare documents. The Declaration of Independence and the Constitution of the United States used to be kept here until recently but are now permanently housed in the Archives Building. Upon leaving the Library, you might end your sightseeing day with a visit to the Supreme Court, which is within easy walking distance.

On another day you might plan to visit the Washington Monument and see the splendid view of the city from the windows near its top. Don't make the mistake of trying to climb up the steps! Take the elevator. If you must have more exercise, you can walk down, but remember, there are no elevator stops to pick up exhausted pedestrians.

On this same day it will be convenient to circle the Tidal Basin, especially if the cherry trees are in bloom, thus obtaining many different views of the Washington Monument, the Jefferson Memorial, and the Lincoln Memorial. You may also include in this trip a visit to the Smithsonian Institution, which has been called "Mother America's Attic." There you will find some of the early airplanes designed by the Wright brothers, Lindbergh's "Spirit of St. Louis," and Wiley Post's dapper "Winnie May."

At the end of a trip to the National Gallery of Art, otherwise known as the Mellon Art Gallery, the Freer, the Corcoran, and the Phillips Art Galleries, you will realize that Washington now has art galleries and museums not excelled in Europe. There are frequent lectures on art in the National Gallery of Art during the winter months. You will also wish to visit the Red Cross Headquarters, the Auditorium of Constitution Hall, and the Pan American Building.

Another day should be taken to visit George Washington's home, Mount Vernon; old Christ Church in Alexandia, which George Washington attended, and Robert E. Lee's home in Arlington. Also, in the Arlington National Cemetery is the tomb of the Unknown Soldier and the Amphitheater built as a memorial to those who lost their lives in war in defense of their country.

You will enjoy seeing the modern hospital at the Naval Medical Center at Bethesda, second after San Diego, California, in size of naval hospitals. Entrance to the hospital for treatment must be by recommendation of some doctor attached to a naval dispensary.

Naval personnel may use the Army Commissaries. A Commissary privilege card may be obtained by application to the Commandant, Potomac River Naval Command. Such card will designate the Commissary to be used by you.

You undoubtedly will wish to make the thirty-three-mile trip to Annapolis to visit the United States Naval Academy. Try to go in the spring on the day that there is a dress parade of the Brigade of Midshipmen; this will give you the thrill of your life. Failing this, make your visit on the day of a home football game. If your husband is a Naval Academy graduate, don't fail to visit Alumni House, and if at all possible attend the Annual Reunion of Naval Academy graduates held each fall, usually in October. Besides the Naval Academy, there are many beautiful old homes open to visitors, and the Maryland State House where George Washington resigned his commission as Commanding General of the Continental Army.

CALLING

There is very little official or duty calling in Washington today. The number of naval officers on duty in this vicinity makes any idea of a general exchange of calls impracticable. Customs with regard to calling differ in the various bureaus, offices, and divisions. An officer upon reporting for duty should inquire as to the custom within the unit to which he is attached. Often the head of a unit upon his reporting for duty will hold a reception, stating on the invitation that acceptance will be considered an exchange of calls. In some units calls are exchanged between all officers attached to that unit. At the Naval Gun Factory all calls are made on Mondays.

In pre-World War II days it was customary for officers of the grade of Commander and above to leave cards at the White House as a form of respect, by driving to the Pennsylvania Avenue entrance and leaving the cards with the doorman, who usually came to the car to receive them. Though leaving cards at the White House is not required, many officers still do leave them. Such calls are not returned, but later the President may invite the higher-ranking officers and their wives to a reception.

Most Presidents have held annual receptions for the officers in the upper grades of the armed forces. Should you be fortunate enough to receive a formal invitation to the White House, it must be answered within twenty-four hours. Good form decrees that replies to such invitations should not be mailed, but delivered in person or by messenger. If you receive an invitation to lunch or to dine at the White House it amounts to a command, and takes precedence over any other engagement. The President is addressed as "Mr. President"; the First Lady, as "Mrs. ————." On an invitation to an informal dinner, "Black Tie" is written in the lower left-hand corner to indicate that the lady is to wear a dinner gown and the gentleman a dinner coat (tuxedo) or uniform. Men invited to dinner with the President and First Lady have the impulse to wear white tie and tails, but usually a dinner coat is in order. Presidents are men too, and they find "Black Tie" more comfortable and quite correct. The Chief of Naval Operations gives a series of dinners and receptions in the beautiful home assigned to him. Naturally it would be impossible for him to entertain all Naval officers in Washington on duty.

NAVY WIFE ACTIVITIES

Since the calling is so limited today, a young Navy wife coming to Washington for the first time often is lonesome. Distances are great, traffic is a problem, and the lack of a central meeting place tends to isolate her. The best and most practical way of meeting Service wives is to offer her services to one of the many volunteer organizations, such as the Navy Relief; the Red Cross; the Soldiers, Sailors, Marines and Airmen's Club; the Jango, or the Armed Forces Hostess Association. Another excellent way to make friends is to engage actively in the work of some church or charitable organization.

Wives of noncommissioned personnel will find it interesting and advantageous to join the Navy Wives' Club. There is an active chapter of this club located in the Bellevue Housing Project adjacent to the Navy's Bellevue Research and Experimental Station.

Entertaining in Washington

Most of the entertaining by officers and their wives in Washington consists of group cocktail parties in a club, often when a senior officer is arriving or leaving, and informal buffet suppers in their homes. The latter are usually managed without a maid. Owing to the high cost of living, the average Navy wife does her own cooking. Sometimes a Dutch treat dinner will take place at one of the clubs. A cleaning woman may sometimes be on tap to help in a little gathering for a few guests at dinner time, and a cocktail party at home or in a club takes care of most of the usual social obligations.

Among the clubs most often used by Service personnel are the so-called "open messes" at the Naval Gun Factory and at the Naval Medical Research Center at Bethesda, Maryland. Officers of all branches of the armed forces, including the Coast Guard, may obtain membership cards to these clubs simply by showing their Service ID cards. There are several other clubs available to officers of all our military Services at a nominal monthly membership charge. These are located at Bolling Air Force Base, Fort Myer, Fort McNair, Andrews Air Force Base, and Fort Belvoir.

Two popular private clubs for officers are the Army and Navy Club, located at the corner of 17th and I (Eye) Streets, N.W., in Washington, and the Army and Navy Country Club, located in Arlington, Virginia. The town club is used primarily for dinners and luncheons, though there are quite a few permanent guests, mostly retired officers. The Country Club has several swimming pools, many tennis courts, and a twenty-seven-hole golf course. It holds weekly dances and popular Sunday-night buffet suppers.

There are many other private country clubs in the vicinity of Washington. Most of them are expensive and have waiting lists for membership, such as the Washington Club, the Sulgrave Club, and the Chevy Chase Country Club, which has an excellent golf course. There are also several smaller country clubs, such as the Belle Haven Country Club and the Fairfax Court House Club, which are good family clubs for personnel living in the vicinity.

For those who enjoy golf but feel they cannot afford the more expensive country clubs there are municipal golf courses in Washington at Hains Point and in Rock Creek Park. Bethesda and Prince George County, Maryland, near Bladensburg, have public golf courses. The greens fee at these courses, while higher than at the municipal courses, is reasonable. At most of these golf courses there are tennis courts also.

Swimming pools are available at several of the clubs located on government property, and most of them may be used a portion of the day by dependents of enlisted personnel.

Small yacht sailing, motor boating, and canoeing are favorite summer sports in this area. There are several yacht clubs, and sailing races are held frequently. Although there is some fishing in the upper Potomac, most of it is done from the shore.

There are many picnic grounds in Rock Creek Park, on Hains Point, at Belle Haven and Fort Hunt, in Virginia, and along many of the roads in Maryland not far from Washington.

For the musically inclined, frequent summer concerts are given free by Service bands at the Water Gate near the Memorial Bridge and on the steps of the Capitol. During the winter concerts are given by the Boston and Philadelphia Symphony orchestras, and Washington is proud of having its own National Symphony Orchestra, which is becoming more and more popular.

In order to take advantage of all the opportunities in the way of the theater (some of the Broadway hits have their tryouts before critical Washington audiences), interesting lectures, and concerts of all kinds, it probably will be necessary to simplify your style of living. This will be easy, with usually only breakfast and dinner to prepare, since practically all naval personnel lunch near their offices. Many of the apartment houses have dining rooms, and a great majority of Navy families dine out several times a week in preference to having a servant.

Washington has many good restaurants and hotels that are popular for dining and dancing. At present, the Shoreham is probably the most popular with Navy personnel. In the summer there is dancing on the terrace. The Mayflower has an attractive cocktail lounge. Tea dances there are meeting places for pretty debutantes and handsome diplomats. The Carlton and the Statler also have inviting cocktail lounges.

Pierre's is generally considered the best French restaurant. It is popular for luncheons, and there one sees the best-dressed women in Washington. It is also an excellent place for dinner, but there is no music.

It is interesting to go down to the water front on Maine Avenue for some of the best sea food you ever tasted. Among the famous restaurants are Herzog's, Hogate's, and O'Donnell's. The Occidental on Pennsylvania Avenue, one of the oldest in Washington, is well known for its sea food and steaks. An excellent place for roast beef and steaks is Fan and Bill's on Connecticut Avenue. In the more distant suburbs, Normandy Farms and Mrs. K's Toll House Tavern in Montgomery County, Maryland, and Collingwood and the Little Tea House in Virginia, are excellent places to dine on a warm summer evening.

Throughout the city there are many Hot Shoppes which are good places for family meals. The Allies' Inn, opposite the old State, War, and Navy Building, has an excellent cafeteria. And in Georgetown are two comparatively new restaurants, the Town House, very good but expensive, and the Carriage House, less expensive, but good. The Greenway Inn on Connecticut Avenue and Cathedral Avenue serves only dinner. One of the good times to go there is shortly after twelve noon on Sundays before it becomes crowded. The fried chicken dinner—which seems hard to find any more—with home-made rolls— still harder—is one dollar and fifty cents.

A popular place in which to spend a few hot summer days is "Big Meadows Lodge" on the Skyline Drive, about three hours' motor trip from Washington. A double room and bath is $8.00 per day. Meals are moderate in price and good.

Washington is the national headquarters for many patriotic societies. Continental Hall, the headquarters of the Daughters of the American Revolution, in addition to the necessary administrative offices has an excellent historical and genealogical library, and an auditorium which seats more than four thousand. The annual Continental Congress of the

DAR is held in this auditorium. The Army and Navy Chapter of the DAR in Washington, with 650 members, is the largest chapter in that organization. It has much Service spirit.

The beautiful national headquarters of the National Society of Colonial Dames of America, Dumbarton House, is located in Georgetown. The National Society of the Daughters of Founders and Patriots of America holds its annual General Court in Washington, usually at the Shoreham Hotel. The National Society of Sponsors of the United States Navy, composed of ladies who have christened combatant ships of the Navy, holds its Annual Meeting in Washington, ending with a luncheon at the Mayflower Hotel. This Society, with 800 members, offers scholarships to sons of deceased and retired Naval and Marine Corps personnel to a preparatory school for the Naval Academy, if possible of their own choosing. Three wives of Presidents are members. A reception at the White House by the First Lady is usually held for the Society during the month of May.

Navy wives whose husbands are on duty in Washington and vicinity have organized many social clubs, most of them limited in membership to wives of officers in the same type of work, for example, the Bureau of Aeronautics Wives' Club, the Supply Officers Wives' Club, the Submarine Officers Wives' Club, the Doctors Wives' Club, and many others. All of these clubs are engaged in volunteer work such as the Navy Relief. Except in summer, they usually meet once a month. Upon reporting for duty, an officer should inquire if there is any such club to which his wife is eligible.

The Navy Relief Ball in the Sail Loft in the Navy Yard is a big event in Washington. The chairman is usually the wife of a naval official or of a high-ranking naval officer. The program and decorations are elaborate, and many thousands of dollars are made. The following night at the same place another ball is held for enlisted personnel, with the same program and decorations.

Many officers' wives take an active interest in the support and management of the Soldiers, Sailors, Marines and Airmen's Club. This is operated by the Army and Navy League, a club composed of five thousand women, for the benefit of enlisted personnel in the vicinity of Washington who have no homes here. Rooms are furnished these men for one dollar a night, and meals at minimum prices. To operate this Club requires about $65,000 per year, which is far in excess of the amount taken in from rooms and meals. Membership dues are $1.00 or $5.00 or $10.00, or $100.00 for life. Donations also are made by other clubs. This is a "home away from home" for enlisted men of all branches of our armed forces. Its doors have never been closed since its founding in 1898. In one year as many as 24,000 men have been lodged for the night. It is the only club of its kind in the United States owned and operated by Service women. It has, in addition to dining-room facilities, an attractive lounge with radio and television, a well-stocked library, a recreation room with pool tables, and a lovely patio. Also, there is an information desk to provide data in regard to sightseeing, movies, sports, and other forms of entertainment. It provides a much needed club for the enlisted personnel and is worthy of the support of every officer's wife.

Navy life in Washington will probably include attendance at many weddings at the Naval Chapel, Naval Security Station, 3801 Nebraska Avenue, N.W. Many are elaborate and beautiful, and many are quite simple. There will also be a number of naval funerals. The services will most probably be held in the Chapel at Fort Myer, with interment following in Arlington National Cemetery.

PROTOCOL

Even experienced Washington hostesses who know most of the answers in social and official realms are often hard put to it when it comes to "precedence" and "who ranks whom." In entertaining Service people the Army, Navy, and Air Force *Registers* may be consulted to obtain the dates of commissions of officers of corresponding ranks. Since the unification of the armed forces under the Secretary of Defense (a cabinet officer), the Secretaries of the Army, of the Navy, and of the Air Force have lost their former cabinet rank. Because of the order in which the respective departments were created, these Secretaries rank in the following order: Secretary of the Army, Secretary of the Navy, and Secretary of the Air Force. The Chief of the Joint Staff takes precedence over all other officers of the armed forces; the Chief of Staff of the Army is senior to all other Army officers, the Chief of Naval Operations to all other naval officers. Among all other officers in the Army, Navy, Air Force, Marine Corps, and Coast Guard precedence goes with grade, and if of the same grade, then by date of respective commissions. An exception to this is the

Staff Corps officers, whose precedence is given in a so-called "list of running mates" in the *Navy Register*.

If by chance you are entertaining diplomatic representatives or civilians holding high positions in the government, we suggest that you consult the Chief of Protocol at the State Department.

SEATING ARRANGEMENTS

It is customary to seat the guest of honor at the right of the host, but at large official parties when toasts are to be given or speeches made, the guest of honor is seated opposite the host. On such occasions, if the table is long and narrow, the host and guest of honor are seated in the center of the length of the table, not at the two ends.

The second and third ranking guests, counting the guest of honor first, are seated on the right of the host and of the guest of honor respectively, the fourth and fifth ranking guests on the left of the host and guest of honor respectively.

Where civilians are concerned, account must be taken of prominence and public office held. Among those having no public office, age and local prominence are the best guides, but Navy guests, irrespective of age, should be interspersed among civilians, especially if the dinner is on board ship.

Many times throughout this book we have stressed the fact that there is no rank among women; yet when officers are accompanied by their wives at a formal dinner they are seated according to their husbands' rank.

At a ladies' luncheon, opinions differ on this point! However, the senior officer's wife present is usually placed at the right of the hostess if there is no guest of honor. The seat on the right of the hostess, the seat on her left, and the seat opposite her are all places of honor.

RETIRED NAVAL OFFICERS

When they retire, many naval officers and their families choose Washington as their permanent home. Wives of retired officers enjoy life in the capital. They often keep busy with welfare and social activities, and are stimulated by contacts with many different types of people. For those who have served several tours of duty in Washington, the desire to remain near the center of government is strong, and in no other place are there so many opportunities to enjoy reunions with old friends, as many of them will visit the capital. My advice is: Keep in touch with your Navy friends after you retire. There is no group who know you so well or who will give you such an understanding affection.

Once having known the capital city, most people realize that "There's no place like Washington."

Chapter XV

ILLNESS, HOSPITALIZATION, AND EMERGENCIES

THE Navy is like one large devoted family. In times of illness or death no intimate circle of friends of long standing can be closer or more deeply stirred. There is no limit to their true understanding and genuine symphathy because many of them have experienced sudden tragedy in their own lives, and all of them know that on any day they may suffer a similar loss.

GENERAL-TYPE HOSPITALS

One of the economy measures of unification of the Services was the closing of many large Army and Navy hospitals.

The larger U.S. naval hospitals now open in this area are located at:

Beaufort, South Carolina
Bethesda, Maryland
Bremerton, Washington
Camp Lejeune, North Carolina
Charleston, South Carolina
Chelsea, Massachusetts
Corpus Christi, Texas
Great Lakes, Illinois
Jacksonville, Florida
Key West, Florida

Memphis, Tennessee
Newport, Rhode Island
Oakland, California
Oceanside, California
Pensacola, Florida
Philadelphia, Pennsylvania
Portsmouth, Virginia
San Diego, California
St. Albans, New York

The Army general hospitals now open in the continental United States are:

Army and Navy .... Hot Springs, Arkansas
Brooke .... San Antonio, Texas
Fitzsimmons .... Denver, Colorado
Letterman .... San Francisco, California
Madigan .... Tacoma, Washington
Walter Reed .... Washington, D.C.
William Beaumont .... El Paso, Texas

Unless your illness is serious enough to require isolation or a private room you will probably be placed in a women's ward where privacy is an unknown quantity.

Should you not be a bed patient, you may be asked to make your own bed and to go to the patients' dining room for your meals. Hospital meals for bed patients are always served at the most unusual hours, and after a week's sojourn you will find yourself losing all track of time. Breakfast varies, but it is early enough to remind you of your boarding-school days; dinner follows the natural hour of midday, and you will receive the light collation called "supper" any time between four and the usual cocktail or tea hour. General hospitals have expert dietitians. The cost, at present, is $1.75 per day; so naturally, on this limited amount a patient cannot expect anything very individual, fancy, or special to tempt his appetite. The food is wholesome, well cooked, and nicely served, though inclined to be on the heavy side.

With obstetrical or surgical cases, each patient should provide her own special nurse if she can possibly afford it. In obstetrical cases, the special nurses should be engaged in advance, and many young mothers arrange to take the nurse home with them from the hospital. This is wise, because if the hospital is crowded, obstetrical patients are often sent home at the end of three or five days, and certainly the services of a qualified nurse are needed at this time.

Patients who receive an abundance of flowers usually ask that some be sent to other patients or to the various wards, and this is often done when a patient is leaving the hospital.

Tips on Being a Visitor at a General Hospital or Other Military Hospital

1. Be careful to observe the visiting hours, usually from two to four o'clock in the afternoon and from seven to eight o'clock in the evening. Morning visits are seldom allowed.

2. Observe signs in corridors requesting "Quiet . . . No Loud Talking."

3. Either send in your name or ask the nurse if it is convenient for you to call on a patient. Never enter a patient's room unannounced.

4. Doctors prefer that the visitor do most of the talking, but keep the conversation in a light, cheery vein. If the patient is bent on talking about her operation, give in gracefully and listen. Avoid launch-

ing into a long dissertation on an operation *you* once had; the patient will not be interested. After all, it is her moment; let her enjoy it.

5. It is unwise to ask the patient, "How do you feel?" If she looks well, she will resent being told so, and if she looks ghastly, you should be too tactful to tell her so.

6. Common sense should warn you never to visit anyone who is ill if you have a cold or are recovering from one.

MEDICAL CARE FOR DEPENDENTS

Medical and dental care and, when required, hospitalization are provided for all naval personnel. Dependents of such personnel may receive medical care at an Armed Forces Medical Facility (Navy, Army, and Air Force dispensary and hospital) providing that certain elegibility requirements are met. As one can never tell when medical care may be needed, all naval personnel having dependents should take immediate steps to obtain authorization for their dependents to receive such attention. Dependents must necessarily be cared for only after the needs of officers and enlisted personnel have been met. During an emergency, it may be impossible for the dispensaries to administer to other than the active Service personnel, except in cases demanding immediate attention.

Medical care for dependents comprises services and treatment for acute medical and surgical conditions, *excluding* nervous, mental, or contagious diseases or those requiring a long period of specialized care. The funds available to the Department of Defense do not permit the payment for civilian or private hospital care. Dental treatment for dependents is available as an adjunct to in-patient hospital or dispensary treatment.

A Dependent's Card for Medical Care is issued upon application by the officer or enlisted man to the personnel officer who has his service record. (On some stations only the dependent's identification card is required.) If such record is not available at his duty station, he may apply directly to the Personal Affairs Division, Bureau of Naval Personnel. Should he be unable to obtain such card, owing to the exigencies of the Service, the dependent may apply directly to the Personal Affairs Division.

Fully appreciating the fact that adequate medical care for dependents of Service personnel is a great aid to morale, the Navy has expanded this service to a size considerably greater than originally contemplated. An extensive dispensary service staffed with medical officers specially trained in the diseases of women and children is available at all of the larger naval stations and at many of the smaller. At the larger stations these specially designated doctors devote practically their entire time to the medical care of Service personnel. In general the dispensaries are equipped and operated practically the same as are offices of civilian medical practitioners. Regular office hours are provided for outpatients. Eye, ear, nose and throat specialists are in attendance at the larger dispensaries and are available at all naval hospitals. The important prenatal care for expectant mothers and after-care for both mothers and babies is provided, and parents are urged to take advantage of them. Mothers are requested to bring in their babies at regular intervals during the important first year in order that diets, weights, etc., may be checked and corrective measures promptly instituted if necessary. Accurate records are kept of all patients.

Varying in detail at different stations, especially as regards distances covered, medical attendance for dependents sick at home is provided at all naval stations. The naval family practitioner is available at all hours for sickness and does not keep office hours. Patients requiring hospitalization are taken to civilian or naval hospitals, as the case may be, and cared for there by the naval doctor in attendance. As in civil practice, the same doctor usually attends patients sick at home or in hospital until the case is completed, though others may be called in consultation. While all naval medical officers have to take their tours of sea duty, the naval family practitioners are rotated in such duty ashore so far as practicable.

NAVAL HOSPITALS

Naval hospitals equipped to care for dependents have wards with private, two-, and four-bed rooms available for dependents. All facilities obtainable in the better civilian hospitals are provided, including delivery rooms for obstetrical patients and nurseries for newborn babies. At stations where such hospitals are located the outpatient dispensaries for dependents are situated near these wards, the whole forming a family practice department. This greatly facilitates the work of the doctors detailed to this duty.

Dependents are charged a flat rate of $1.75 a day for hospitalization. Of this sum, 75 cents per diem is credited to the Naval Hospital Fund, a trust fund for the maintenance of naval hospitals which derives its revenues from within the naval service and is administered by the Secretary of the Navy, the trustee of the fund, subject to the control of Congress. The remaining amount is deposited to the credit of the naval Exchange store of the hospital, accounted for separately from all other monies, and expended by direction of the Commanding Officer to defray those costs of hospitalization not provided by the law.

The Naval Hospital Fund provides subsistence, the more usual medicines, X-ray films, surgical dressings, laboratory services, and incidentals. The hospitalization costs of dependents borne from sums deposited with the Naval Exchange store officer include the wages and subsistence for additional employees required for the care of dependents, such as civilian nurses, maids, and culinary employees; the service of civilian specialists when required; blood transfusions; and the cost of special medicines and drugs not regularly stocked by the naval medical department.

Flowers and Gifts

Flowers are always a welcome gift. Since government hospitals have a very limited supply of vases and flower receptacles, it is well, if you take flowers, to have the florist arrange them in inexpensive containers. Small blooming potted plants are quite practical, since they last longer and do not require much care from the busy nurse.

An amusing book, a best seller, or several of the small, inexpensive, paper-bound pocket editions make welcome gifts. Book stores make up charming packets of six or more current magazines directed toward the interest of the patient. These arrive in bright cellophane wrappings and add a cheery note to the sickroom. A box of mints or candies or a basket of tempting fruit resembling a small "bon voyage" basket, in which are placed small jars of jam, marmalade, or jelly, often appeal to a convalescent. But always think twice before your selection is made. Don't send books to a person recovering from an eye operation, and don't send fruit—especially sour fruit—to a friend who is still gagging and groaning from a tonsillectomy.

For children, any little novelty or a "surprise basket" will help pass the long, tedious days of recovery. Gift departments in the large stores make a specialty of these novelty baskets and boxes. They can be made as individual as you like. For instance, there may be a surprise planned for each day in the "week basket." A note explaining the system and clever little verses accompanying each gift make it "sort of a treasure hunt idea," so that the child will enjoy today and look forward to tomorrow. The basket may contain inexpensive books, games, puzzles, and a limited amount of sweets (if they are permitted). What children, especially little boys between the ages of six and twelve, really adore is a large bundle of those horribly stupid books of comics. Why is not for me to question. The tastes of little boys have always been a puzzle to me. They like comics, and if you want to please them, you'll take them comics.

Navy Doctors

While all medical and dental officers of the Navy have the official title of the corresponding line rank, those below the grade of Captain are commonly addressed as "Doctor." Admirals and Captains of the Medical Corps are usually called by their line title. "After all, many men can be officers in the Navy," as someone explained, "but not all naval officers can be Doctors, and for that reason many prefer to be called 'Doctor.' "

Navy Nurses

The Navy Nurse Corps (female) is under the jurisdiction of the Bureau of Medicine and Surgery, which in turn is under the direction of the Secretary of the Navy. Established May 13, 1908, the Nurse Corps consists of a superintendent and an assistant superintendent, appointed by the Secretary of the Navy, whose terms of office may be terminated at his discretion, and of as many chief nurses, nurses, and reserve nurses as may be needed in time of emergency.

Navy nurses are eligible for duty at naval hospitals and on board hospital and ambulance ships and transport planes. All nurses in the Corps are appointed or removed by the Surgeon General, with the approval of the Secretary of the Navy. They must be graduate nurses of an accredited school and registered three-year course, and their promotion is subject to an examination as to their professional, moral, mental, and physical fitness.

Nurses are *not* allowed to receive gifts from patients or from relatives or friends of patients for services rendered when on duty. Also, according to *Navy Regulations* (Article 1649), the authority of a nurse, necessary for the performance of duty to which she may be assigned, shall be duly recognized and enforced.

MOURNING

In time of mourning an intimate friend or a servant should be at the door of the home to receive callers, to take messages, and to receive cards. No one should ask to see the bereaved person unless either the person receiving or some member of the family suggests it. Navy wives are schooled in being practical. Often they purposely busy themselves with their personal affairs as soon as possible. There are certain immediate adjustments to be made, and they are wise in not wishing to be alone with their thoughts. Unless prostration or illness from the shock prevents, to keep as busy as possible is the best course. A morbid preoccupation with one's own tragedy is as distressing to others as callous flippancy. Dignified, honest sorrow is no discredit to any person, man or woman, and is never out of place.

Mourning apparel does not receive the formality and regard it did in former years. A Navy widow looks through her wardrobe and usually finds appropriate black dress, coat, or suit. Stores and all dressmaking establishments give precedence to mourning orders, and will often open shop after hours and on holidays to accommodate a customer. Often friends or acquaintances offer to lend veils and wraps.

MILITARY FUNERALS

Military funerals for naval officers are divided into six classes as follows:

1. With chapel service
2. Without chapel service
3. With graveside service only
4. With ceremony prior to shipment of remains
5. Burial at sea
6. Memorial services

The selection of honorary pallbearers, if they are desired, is made by the family of the deceased or its representatives.

The pallbearers march at the side of the hearse, the junior to the left and leading, the next junior to the right and leading, and so on. Depending upon their age and the distance to the place of interment, they may ride in advance of the hearse. Eight men are selected as body bearers, and march immediately behind the body.

If the deceased was a flag officer, a unit commander or captain of a ship, his flag or pennant or the commission pennant is draped in mourning and displayed at halfmast in the bow of the boat carrying the body. The flag or pennant is also carried immediately in advance of the body in the funeral cortege to the grave, but not upon the return from the grave.

FUNERAL PROCESSION ON SHORE

A funeral procession on shore shall be formed as follows (Article 342, *Navy Regulations*):

Escort commander and staff
Band
Escort
Clergy
Pallbearers (when riding)
Bearer of personal flag or pennant, or the commission pennant of the
   deceased
Body and pallbearers (when marching)
Family of deceased
Mourners in inverse of rank:
   a. enlisted men
   b. officers from ship of deceased
   c. other officers
   d. foreign officers
   e. distinguished persons
   f. delegations
   g. societies
   h. citizens

It is said that at the funeral of George Washington the troops came first, then the clergy, and next the General's horse with the two grooms. After the body came the mourners with Lord Fairfax as the last mourner. Rear Admiral Leland P. Lovette describes the recent funeral of a distinguished and greatly beloved Admiral in which two old colored retainers preceded the honorary pallbearers, all of whom were high-ranking officers of the Navy. Death is a great leveler, and as Rear Admiral Lovette explains, "the reversal of rank at funerals is an acknowledgment that at death all men are equal. Seniors take their proper precedence in the procession after burial. This form of the 'last shall be first and first shall be last' is carried out in the recessional and processional of churches."

On the march to the place of interment the procession moves in slow time, the music being an appropriate funeral march; the ensign and the ship's battalion colors, the latter draped in mourning, are carried in the center of the escort; the drums are draped in mourning and muffled.

Upon returning from the place of interment, the column moves in quick time, and the mourners march in order of rank. When clear of the cemetery, the mourning and muffling is removed from the battalion colors, and the drums and music play a march.

An officer or pallbearer wears a mourning badge on the left arm and sword hilt. Regardless of the grade or rate, the coffin is covered with the national flag, which, upon request, is presented to the relatives of the deceased, or to a school, patriotic order, or society to which the deceased belonged.

FUNERAL ESCORT

Navy Regulations states that an escort not to exceed one person may be provided to accompany to place of burial the bodies of officers, enlisted men, or nurses who have lost their lives in the naval service. The escort furnished under this authority may be a relative or friend (not in the Service) of the deceased.

With an unmarried officer, a brother officer is usually asked to escort the remains to the home of the deceased, but in the case of a married officer, it is customary for the widow and children to act as escort to the place of burial.

BURIAL AT SEA

In this day it will seldom be necessary to commit a body to the deep; nevertheless the ceremony of time-honored tradition should be known by all. If for any reason the deceased is buried at sea, the body is placed in canvas or coffin with weights to insure its sinking. An American flag is placed over the body and gently pulled off as the body is released over the side.

It has ever been customary for all officers and men not on duty to attend the services of a late shipmate. The chaplain, or in his absence, the captain or an officer detailed by the captain, reads the burial service at sea. In most cases the Episcopal prayer-book service is used. The ritual ends with the very beautiful and time-honored words, "we therefore commit this body to the deep, to be turned into corruption, looking for the resurrection of the body, when the sea shall give up her dead, and the life of the world to come . . ."

At this point of the service, "we commit the body to the deep," a seaman tilts the grating or wooden platform, slips off the flag and the body is projected into the ocean.*

Origin of Certain Customs at Military Funerals

Firing three volleys at military funerals dates back to old Roman days, when these ancient people cast earth upon the coffin *three times.* It was also customary for the Romans to call the dead *three times* by name, which ended the funeral ceremony, after which the relatives and friends of the deceased pronounced the word *"vale"* (farewell) *three times* as they departed from the tomb. Another, less pretty, version is that three volleys are fired into the air at imaginary devils which might get into men's hearts at such a moment as the burial of a comrade-at-arms (pure superstition).

The more comforting thought is that when the firing squad discharges three volleys over a grave, they are, in accordance with the old Roman custom, bidding their dead comrade "farewell, three times!"

Taps or Nunc Dimittis

The sounding of taps immediately following the firing of the three volleys as the last act of the burial ceremony involves a deep-felt sentiment: "Rest in peace." There is no other call so beautiful, no other call that arouses so many emotions in the souls of military personnel as the sounding of taps.

> Fades the light;
> And afar
> Goeth day,
> Cometh night;

* Leland P. Lovette, *Naval Customs, Traditions and Usage,* United States Naval Institute, Annapolis, 1939.

And a star
Leadeth all
To their rest.

MEMORIAL SERVICES

In the case of death and burial on foreign shores, or loss of life at sea or in any disaster when no military burial services have been held, it is customary to hold memorial services in honor of the deceased. The services are conducted according to the denomination that has been requested. The Navy Department generally announces the wishes of the widow if a memorial service is to be held; and while it is a painful ordeal for the bereaved to undergo, it often brings consolation and helps to assuage their grief to a small extent by honoring the memory of a dear one.

The following account of a memorial service was taken from *The Army and Navy Register* (names, dates, and places have been changed):

The Navy Department announced on March 20, that in compliance with the wishes of his widow, the ashes of the late Lieutenant Commander Scott Kenner, U.S. Navy, killed March 5, in the crash of an R.A.F. Ferry Command plane, are to be scattered from a naval plane on Pensacola Bay, Florida.

Simple non-military memorial services, conducted by Chaplain James Raphael, U.S.N., will be held in the Chapel-by-the-Sea, near the Air Station.

The ashes were sent from England on March 15, after funeral services in Edinburgh, Scotland, on March 8, and memorial services at St. Martin-in-the-Fields Church, Trafalgar Square, March 10.

FLOWERS

If the family prefers to avoid the added complication of flowers, the following notice is added to the funeral notice which appears in the daily papers: "Friends are requested not to send flowers," rather than the phrase "Please omit flowers," which is often seen but is rather abrupt.

If flowers are sent, the officer in charge or someone designated by him should remove the cards and record a brief description of each offering. The list is turned over to the family of the deceased after the funeral.

EXPENSES OF BURIAL—MONUMENT OR MARKER

The necessary and proper funeral expenses of officers and enlisted men of the Navy and Marine Corps are allowed only when death occurs while in active service and shall in no instance exceed $200.00.

If the widow or family does not provide a monument in a national cemetery, the Government erects a white marker headstone of regulation pattern inscribed with the rank, name and branch of service of the deceased. The widow or family should not contract for a private monument until both the design, material and inscription have been submitted to and approved by the Navy Department.

LETTERS OF CONDOLENCE

Many find a letter of condolence difficult to write, yet a truly sincere note at a time of sorrow is always appreciated. The letter should not be long, nor should it be filled with biblical quotations, platitudes, or affected sentiment. A person in grief, whose eyes are dimmed with tears and whose heart is aching, does not feel up to reading a long philosophical dissertation.

The letter of condolence should show admiration of character or fine traits of the deceased, and express genuine affection. If you cannot honestly say anything of this nature, don't give false praise to the dead, but write a sincere word of sympathy to the bereaved ones. Avoid harrowing the feelings by too-familiar allusions to the deceased.

A simple letter of friendship or a telegram expressing genuine sentiment, showing admiration for the one who has passed to the great beyond, is about the greatest solace that we can offer. A sincere handclasp without a spoken word, a note conveying three lines of sincere sympathy, or often just the presence of a quiet friend will speak volumes to a broken heart.

Letter of sympathy to a close friend whose husband was killed in a submarine disaster or airplane crash:

Dearest Mary,

I know the shock of this has been very great. It's useless to try to say all the things I want to say. If there is anything I can do, let me know immediately. In any case, I will be over to see you. May I come soon?

Yours devotedly,

Letter of condolence to a young mother who has lost a beloved child:

My dear, dear Margaret,

Even a devoted friend feels helpless at such a time, knowing that so little can be said or done that really brings comfort, but your friends are with you in understanding and love. Perhaps later on the memory of this may bring some of the consolation that I so long to give you now.

Devotedly,

Type of letter or note to a friend whose husband was a shipmate of your husband:

Dear Betty,

If there is anything that Bill and I can do, I really hope that you will let me know. We, like everyone else, are terribly shocked, and our thoughts and love are with you.

Most sincerely,

Answers to Letters of Condolence

There is no necessity for haste in answering letters of condolence, telegrams, or floral tributes; however, they should always be answered with a personal note of appreciation unless the grief-stricken person is prostrated or for some reason is unable to write. In that case, some member of the family should perform this service.

One may simply write, "Thank you so much for your kind sympathy" on a visiting card. Engraved cards of thanks for letters of condolence are not regarded as good form except in the case of some very prominent person, when hundreds of such expressions of sympathy would have to be answered by some simple method. Most persons are so touched by the love and tenderness shown them by their friends in a recent sorrow that they really want to write a sincere and genuine note of thanks.

Record of Emergency Data

The emergency data contained in DD Form 93 should be meticulously filled out and kept current by all naval personnel. This form is filed as part of the service record and is the means by which naval authorities know whom to notify in the event of injury or death of an officer or enlisted man. It also constitutes the deceased's instructions as to the disposition of death benefits. This form shows: the person or persons to be informed in case of emergency; to whom are to be paid the death benefits and Serviceman's Indemnity; the life insurance companies to be informed automatically in the event of the Serviceman's death; and the persons (including commercial life insurance companies and banks) to receive special allotments in the event the Serviceman is missing, interned, or otherwise detained outside of naval jurisdiction. *Care and completeness are essential* in making out this form.

The form should be prepared upon initial entry into service and upon re-enlistment or call to active duty, upon promotion to officer rank, and whenever there is a change in status of the Serviceman, such as marriage or divorce, or a change in beneficiaries or in their addresses.

ILLNESS OR DEATH OF DEPENDENT

In case of serious illness or injury of a dependent of a Navy man the nearest naval dispensary or naval hospital—or if there are no naval medical facilities in the vicinity, Army or Air Force facilities, or private facilities—should be notified immediately. A message should be sent to the Serviceman; if he is on a ship anchored in the port, contact should be made with the Shore Patrol, requesting them to send the message to the ship. If the Serviceman is employed at some near-by shore activity the Officer of the Day at that station should be contacted. If the Serviceman's ship is at sea, the call should be to the nearest Navy communication station, or the Communication Office of the Naval District, requesting that the Serviceman be informed by radio and being sure to give his full name, service number, rank or rating, and the name of the ship to which he is attached. If the crisis occurs in or near a naval activity to which a chaplain is attached, he will be happy to be of assistance. In case financial help is needed, the Navy Relief or the Red Cross is the agency to call.

IN CASE OF DEATH OF SERVICEMAN

In case of critical illness, injury, or death of a naval Serviceman, his dependents will be notified promptly. Where possible, such information will be given orally by the Commanding Officer, or other officer, in person, who will usually be accompanied by the chaplain and a close friend of the dependent. In case the Serviceman is on board a ship at sea, or at a distant station, the original notification and progress reports will be made by radio or telegram. Under war conditions there may be some delay, but every effort will be made to keep the next of kin informed. The next of kin is responsible for informing other relatives.

The death of a Serviceman creates a most serious situation for his dependents. His pay, allotments, and his dependents' right to occupy government quarters or to receive an allowance for quarters stop immediately. In the case of government quarters, however, his dependents usually are allowed a reasonable period for packing and other preparations for moving.

The chaplain will call at the home of an officer or enlisted man in case of serious illness, death, or other emergency. He is prepared to give advice in regard to funeral arrangements, and in case of financial need will contact the Navy Relief Society or the National Red Cross to obtain the required assistance.

The Supply Officer will advise the dependents and help them prepare the required forms of application for the benefits provided for widows and dependents, for packing and transportation of household effects, and for the transportation of these and of the family to the place they have chosen to reside. He will arrange for such packing and transportation.

Again may I caution you that all bank accounts, stocks, and bonds, real estate, and automobiles should be registered or titled, "Joint ownership, with right of survivorship." Otherwise action to draw money from such account or to dispose of such property cannot be taken until after the decedent's will has been probated.

Sources of Emergency Aid for Dependents

The Navy Relief Society is a private organization conducted by naval personnel for the purpose of aiding dependents in financial need and in procuring government benefits. It has forty-two auxiliaries widely distributed in all naval districts and all major outlying bases. It is supported almost entirely by naval personnel.

The Navy Relief Society is kept informed by the Bureau of Naval Personnel and Commandant of the Marine Corps of all deaths occurring in the Navy and Marine Corps; in each case the name, address, and relationship of the nearest of kin as given in the Serviceman's record is furnished. If the relationship is that of wife, mother, or child, the Society immediately investigates the circumstances of the dependent survivor. The investigation is systematic, expeditious, and confidential. Assistance is rendered whenever an urgent need exists and is in the form of lump sums or of monthly allotments. In case of urgent need, financial aid may be granted even if the Serviceman is living.

The American Red Cross also is prepared to aid dependents of deceased naval personnel through its Home Service Program. When there is no Navy Relief Society activity in the vicinity, the dependents of deceased naval personnel who are in need should apply to the Red Cross. The Red Cross may give financial aid and certainly will assist in the preparation of application for federal and state benefits.

SOURCES OF INCOME FOR A BEREAVED FAMILY

All families must face the realities of life to the extent that they give some thought to the matter of a plan in the event of the death of the family provider. A young widow without children is not in a very difficult position, but the widow with small children definitely is. Any Navy wife whose husband dies while he is on active duty usually can look to four sources for future income:

1. The husband's accrued pay. Application must be made for this; a Supply Officer will provide the forms.
2. Benefits provided by the United States Government:
   a. A gratuity of six months' pay of the deceased.
   b. Personal pension to widows and children (and in certain cases other dependents).
3. Life insurance:
   a. Serviceman's indemnity: payable to a Serviceman's survivors only if death occurred on or after 27 June 1950, or within 120 days following separation from the Service. This indemnity is $10,000, except that in the case of personnel carrying United States Government Life Insurance or National Service Life Insurance the indemnity will be the difference between $10,000 and the face value of policies carried in the agencies mentioned above.
   b. United States Government Life Insurance, or National Service Life Insurance, if carried.
   c. Commercial life insurance, if carried.
4. Personal savings and investments.

Six Months' Gratuity Pay

The six months' gratuity is paid only if the deceased is of the regular Service and on active duty at time of death. It is not paid to Naval Reserve personnel. The pay includes longevity, and all additional extra-hazardous-duty pay, and pay for small arms qualifications. It is paid to widows, children under legal age, or to designated dependents, as determined by the Secretary of the Navy. There usually is several months' delay in obtaining this payment.

Personal Pensions

Application for pension must be sent to the Director, Dependents' Claims Service, Veterans Administration, Washington, D.C. Forms will be supplied by the Supply Officer. Payments do not begin until after all necessary papers to substantiate claims are filed and approved. The following should be sent with application: certified copy of public or church record of marriage; in event of prior marriage, certificate of custodian of public record or other acceptable proof of death of, or certified copy of decree of divorce from, the former husband or wife; birth or baptismal certificates of widow and each child under eighteen years of age.

The Veterans Administration is authorized under existing laws to provide compensation to dependents of enlisted men who die while on active duty providing the enlisted man's death is *in line of duty* and not the result of willful misconduct. Widows and children become eligible for compensation regardless of their income.

Eligibility is as follows:

1. Widow must have been married to the officer or enlisted man at the time of his death and must have lived with him from the date of their marriage until death. Compensation ceases if the widow remarries.

2. Child or children must be unmarried and under the age of eighteen.

3. Child: legitimate, legally adopted, stepchild providing he was a member of the deceased Serviceman's household, or an illegitimate child of an officer or enlisted personnel (male or female), providing the required evidence is submitted to the Veterans Administration.

If death occurs in line of duty during wartime service, the following amounts are awarded:

1. Widow .... $ 75.00
2. Widow and one child 121.00
3. Each additional child 29.00
4. No widow, one child 67.00
5. No widow, two children.. 94.00 (equally divided)
6. No widow, three children. 122.00 (equally divided)
7. Each additional child .... 23.00 (total to be divided equally)
8. One dependent parent ... 60.00
9. Two dependent parents ... 35.00 each

The Veterans Administration has ruled that dependents of Servicemen who die in flight during peacetime if flight simulates combat conditions or is of an extra-hazardous nature are entitled to wartime rates.

If death occurs in line of duty during peacetime, amounts are:

1. Widow $60.00
2. Widow, one child 96.80
3. Each additional child 23.20
4. No widow, one child 53.60
5. No widow, two children.. 75.20 (equally divided)
6. No widow, three children. 97.60 (equally divided)
7. Each additional child .... 18.40 (total to be divided equally)
8. One dependent parent ... 48.00
9. Two dependent parents... 28.00 each

LIFE INSURANCE

The Servicemen's Indemnity Act of 1951 prohibits the further issuance of United States Government Life Insurance and National Service Life Insurance, and instead provides for a gratuitous indemnity in the maximum amount of $10,000, payable to the Service member's survivors in the event of death while in active service on or after 27 June 1950, or within 120 days following separation from the Service. If, however, the Service member was insured under USGLI or NSLI (mentioned above) the value of the indemnity will be $10,000 less the face value of such other government policies. Members who hold these policies, if they so desire, may surrender them and thus become eligible for the full indemnity. Full consideration should be given to the fact that life insurance may be continued in force after leaving the Service by the payment of the premiums, whereas the indemnity ceases 120 days after separation from the Service.

Owning life insurance in adequate amounts and of proper types is as much a necessity for naval personnel as for any other thinking individuals. The important point is to fit the amount and type to your specific needs.

The types of government life insurance mentioned above are not now available to naval personnel, but those who now hold such insurance may continue it in force. Those whose dependents now are protected only by the Servicemen's indemnity should consider the taking out of additional commerical insurance before they leave the Service.

Officers should give serious consideration to joining the Navy Mutual Aid Association, which provides $7,500 insurance on favorable terms. Upon notification of the death of a member, $1,000 will be sent to the decedent's dependent by telegraph. This sum will help to tide the dependent over the period before the receipt of death benefits.

Commercial Life Insurance

A family can estimate its life insurance needs by setting down its best estimate of the family's minimum income requirement in the event of a fatality to the husband. The idea, of course, is to keep the family unit intact during the children's dependency period without requiring the mother to be off earning a living. Knowing the income needed, one may arrive at requirements with respect to commercial insurance by subtracting such income as is already guaranteed from Government benefits, government life insurance, and Servicemen's indemnity. This income deficiency is then translated into the policy amount required to make up the difference in monthly installments. Most officers carry some commercial insurance, but total life insurance premiums (government and commercial) normally should not exceed 10 per cent of the husband's monthly income.

Educational endowments written upon the life of the father for the benefit of the children constitute an excellent method of guaranteeing funds for the children's education. These policies normally deliver the full face amount to the father if living at the maturity date, and to the children's mother or guardian if the father dies prior to that time.

Normally speaking, so-called "retirement income policies" are a mistake for the younger officers because the protection afforded for the high premium involved is entirely too small to cover the family's needs.

As with all technical subjects the advice of a well-informed person is valuable. Older brother officers can sometimes give this advice or can recommend a competent, trustworthy insurance man who has served them in the past. In addition to the monthly payment your commercial life insurance is designed to produce, keep the following in mind: Deal only with a long-established, reliable company; the younger you are when the policy is taken out, the lower the premium; be sure the policy is valid in wartime; and do not strap yourself unduly in order to carry excessive life insurance.

LEGAL EMERGENCIES

Attached to nearly every large naval shipyard or naval activity is a legal officer who will be glad to help Navy dependents in legal matters. If contact can be made with any such legal officer, Navy Supply Officer or chaplain, or with the Navy Relief, Red Cross, or a veterans' organization, a Navy wife should not employ an attorney in private practice to assist her in making claims for any death benefits. The required forms for such applications may be obtained from the sources mentioned above, and they will be happy to forward them to the proper authorities.

EMERGENCIES WHEN TRAVELING BY CAR

If while traveling by car with your husband an accident should result in his serious injury or death, telegraph the Commanding Officer of his ship or station, or if in the process of changing stations the Commanding Officer of the ship or station to which he has been ordered, giving your husband's name *in full*, his service number, his grade or rating, and a short but accurate statement of the situation. If your husband has been taken to a hospital, give the name of the hospital and of the doctor attending. Be sure to include an address at which you can receive a reply to your message. Get in touch with the nearest armed forces activity (preferably Navy) and request assistance. If not near any Service facility, apply to the Red Cross, Travelers Aid, or veterans' organization. Inform the nearest agency of your automobile insurance company, and if possible obtain a copy of the police report of the accident absolving your husband of blame.

Should you be traveling without your husband, send a telegram or radio to him including in the address his full name, grade or rating, Service number, and the name of the ship or station to which he is attached. Be sure to include your return address. Steps as described above should be taken to obtain assistance, to inform the automobile insurance company, and to get a copy of the police report of the accident.

WARTIME EMERGENCIES

During wartime a Serviceman may be reported missing, missing in action, interned in a neutral country, captured by an enemy, or beleaguered or besieged. For any period during which he is carried in such status he is entitled to receive, or to have credited, the same pay and allowances to which he was entitled at the beginning of such condition, and his allotments will be paid. His right to such pay and allowances terminates upon proof of his death, or upon the date of death as determined under the Missing Persons Act, in most cases about one year from the date he was reported missing or captured.

By the Geneva Convention of 1929 sixty nations agreed to treat prisoners of war humanely, and to insure their being adequately housed, clothed, and fed. In each civilized nation the Red Cross attempts to inform their dependents as to the physical condition and manner of treatment of such prisoners of war. Thus, through the efforts of the Red Cross of enemy or neutral nations the American Red Cross may be as well informed as the Bureau of Naval Personnel, if not better. Also, if it is positively known that a certain Serviceman is a prisoner of war, the Red Cross, through international agreement, may be able to send him packages containing food or other comforts.

Consequently, dependents of Servicemen reported missing, or presumably captured, should maintain close touch with the local Red Cross chapter, and inform it of any change in address.

How to Make Emergencies Easier to Bear

Most of us put off doing the things which would, if done, make easier to bear the emergency of death. Failure to record the decedent's desires as to place of burial; his or her failure to make a will; to place all possessions in "joint tenancy with right of survivorship"; to obtain required birth and marriage certificates; to record the location of wills and insurance policies; to provide the wife with a general power of attorney; and to keep up to date form DD 93 are some of the causes of distress which can be avoided by proper timely action.

Chapter XVI

BEYOND THE CONTINENTAL LIMITS

N AVY wives should learn early in the game not to complain about conditions they cannot change. Should you be stationed in the tropics, don't sit around and grumble about the rain or moan about the heat. It won't do one particle of good, and if you keep busy you will forget about the weather. Bridge won't be enough to fill your time, and you will find yourself counting boats pretty soon. Take up the study of Spanish, or some other language, start collecting something, even if it is only sea shells. Go sightseeing in spite of the rain and learn everything you can about the customs of the place. Do something to keep yourself interested. Cultivate any worth-while civilian contacts that may come your way and, above all, don't be so provincial that you fail to appreciate and recognize the fine qualities of the natives. Make social contacts outside of Navy circles when you can. It is broadening.

Running water—a spray in full play on the garden just outside your window—will give a cool sound, and if you have a fountain in your garden, turn it on in the morning and evening even if the charges are extra for the water.

In the tropics government quarters are usually designed for comfort. Some are equipped with ceiling fans, and almost all include a dry closet. An electric light must be kept burning in a dry closet, but even so, the efficient housewife has the servants air all woolens on sunny days. Mold, moths, and mildew are a constant source of annoyance and ruin. Leather goods should be kept polished and aired often.

What to Take to the Tropics

Any reed or wicker furniture you may have
A sewing machine
A washing machine (nonautomatic) (In many places water is ra-

tioned, or the pressure is not strong enough to operate the automatic kind.) An automatic is good in Puerto Rico.

Kitchen utensils (Iron rusts on Guam and Okinawa.)
Flat silver and china, inexpensive crystal or glassware
Inexpensive lamps (both floor and table)
Rain gear and umbrellas
Plastic raincoats and hats for each member of family
Baby cribs and children's beds
Electric iron, toaster, mixer, waffle iron, radio, lamps with new extension cords
Electric roaster

Before packing any electrical equipment it is best to consider the current system. Electric current varies. In some places 110-volt, 25-cycle alternating current (A.C.) is in contrast to 60-cycle current usually available in the United States. Electrical appliances containing motors or transformers wired for 60-cycle current cannot be operated in the Canal Zone and therefore should not be shipped to the area. Heat-generating electrical appliances (irons, toasters, vibrator-type razors, etc.) are not affected by the differences in cycles and should be brought to the area.

Some Things Not to Take to the Tropics

Overstuffed furniture
Antiques (meat for the termites)
Expensive lamps, curtains, or hangings
Fine rugs
Pictures and valuable books
Furs, woolen clothing, or blankets
Pianos and string instruments
Veneered furniture, expensive mirrors
Leather equipment
Iron utensils (rust)

Take your entire wardrobe to Hawaii, although today you can buy real island clothes in Honolulu. Many of the island prints are featured in sun-back dresses, pake-mus and holo-mus. A pake-mu is a combination of the Chinese straight dress and the old Hawaiian muu-muu. It is tight fitting with a stiff inch-high collar, like the Chinese dress, then has the loose, flowing, lined sleeve of the muu-muu.

Holo-mu is the modern version of the holoku and muu-muu; usually low necked and often sleeveless, it does not have the long train of the holoku, but hangs just to the ankles. Hats are seldom worn, even in church; most of the women go bareheaded except in the Catholic Church. There are lots of good dressmakers in the islands, where you can have clothes made at a reasonable price.

Ten to one, you will wear a larger size in shoes after a tour of duty in the tropics. Anyway, take plenty of shoes, and don't depend upon the shoes that the native shoemakers produce.

HAWAII

There's the perfume of a million flowers
Clinging to the heart of old Hawaii.
There's a rainbow following the showers
Bringing me a part of old Hawaii.
There's a silver moon, a symphony of stars
There's a Hula tune and the hum of soft guitars
There's the Trade Wind, sighing in the heavens
Singing me a song of old Hawaii!

Service in Hawaii should not be included with other tropical duty, chiefly because of its climate. You can use here anything you can use in the States. It is a land of sunshine, and the climate is as nearly perfect as at any spot yet discovered by man. The ancient Hawaiian vocabulary includes no word for weather. It was so even, with no changes, in those days, that there was no need to mention it. Rain is spoken of as "liquid sunshine," and the double rainbows and lunar rainbows are a sight to delight the aesthetic soul of man. Rainbows are so common that the university football team is known as the "Roaring Rainbows." Mothers never think of calling in their children, who slide around on the lawns, frolicking in the refreshing drizzle that blows down from the cloud-wrapped peaks of Mount Tantalus. The normal temperature in Honolulu is 72 degrees, with an all-time low of 58 degrees. On the hottest day on record in Honolulu the mercury soared to 87 degrees; but at a time like that, the best thing to do is to hie yourself over to the Rest Camp at Kilauea in the mountains and relax. It isn't the heat, but the humidity can be terrific if the trade winds stop blowing for a few hours.

An automobile is a necessity, since Pearl Harbor is ten miles from Honolulu, and the city itself covers a vast area. The increasingly heavy traffic is one of its greatest problems. It seems as if everyone in Honolulu is on wheels of some kind, with the cars varying from the latest model Packard to ramshackle Fords of ancient vintage. Walter Winchell says, "Filipinos always buy a car together; instead of all owning the machine, each claims a part, one a horn, another a hub cap, still another a wheel." There are strict parking laws and efficient traffic officers always on the alert for minor violations, although speed demons seem often to go unnoticed. The motor trips are beautiful and the roads are excellent. Taxis are high.

Honolulu is proud of the fact that it has never had a case of rabies, so if you plan to take your favorite wire-haired or your beautiful Persian cat along, you should know beforehand that your pet will have to remain in the Territorial Government Quarantine Station for 120 days at a cost of 25 cents a day. There is no way of getting around the law, so you will only waste your time trying!

Food is necessarily higher in Honolulu than on the mainland, and prices continue to increase. The native markets are interesting with their tempting arrays of Hawaiian fruits and vegetables. June, July, and August are the months for the delicious sun-kissed pineapples. Mango, breadfruit, avocado—each has its season, though papaya seems to ripen the year round. Meat from the mainland is expensive, but native beef from the ranches of Hawaii and Maui is good.

GUAM

Guam is the largest and most beautiful island of the Marianas, and the general information given here is also applicable to Navy life on Saipan, Okinawa, Kwajalein, and Johnston islands, where small groups of naval personnel may be based.

Postwar Guam has a new civilian look. After more than fifty years under naval government rule, the island's administration was transferred fully to the Interior Department July 1, 1950.

Agaña, the war-demolished capital, is slowly rebuilding along modern lines. Sheds, prefabs, and Quonsets can be seen near typhoon-proof buildings. Guam today has fairly modern commercial stores and markets, a bus line, a full-scale school system, the Bank of Guam housed in a Quonset, a cathedral, and many churches.

The island is only 25 miles long and 6 miles wide, and covers an area of 150 square miles. It averages 90 inches of rainfall a year, and if that means little to you, I can explain it better by saying that mildew will cover everything in the way of leather, shoes, boots, boxes, and pictures with long, long gray whiskers. Further evidence will be the deterioration of all electric appliances and the wicked way your sewing machine will rust. It really gets damp on Guam.

Despite the wetness and humidity, the climate is agreeable and healthy. When the monsoon winds blow, typhoons often follow. There are three conditions in naval parlance. No. 1 is a directive which means make preparations for a bad blow or storm. No. 2 is the signal to secure everything. No. 3 is the signal to take shelter in a cave or whatever security has been previously arranged.

A million-dollar breakwater has been built. The beaches are not good because of the coral reefs, but swimming holes are made by blasting into the coral formation. Nimitz Beach, Tumon Bay, and Camp Dealy are the popular beaches.

The public school is located one mile from Agaña. Army and Navy wives with previous experience, also professional teachers, staff this consolidated school. The PX or Ships' Service and Commissaries are well stocked. Frozen and canned milk only is available.

Quonset huts serve as quarters, and ingenious young couples have made them quite attractive and livable, but in a hot climate, believe me, they are still Quonsets! They are equipped only with showers. The first bathtub to make its appearance on Guam was in 1946. An automobile is a necessity on Guam and the few roads are good. Another necessity is a cat to keep the fruit rats away from the quarters. Ants are plentiful but there are no snakes on the island. Many Navy families raise chickens so as to have fresh eggs.

The Ships' Service and the Exchanges carry children's clothes and toys; however, it is a good idea to take sturdy shoes for both yourself and the children as the coral cuts the soles badly. Shipments of handmade bags and shoes arrive from time to time from Manila; no duty is charged.

For amusement there are good movies and tennis, but at present no golf course. The fishing should be good by now. The Japanese dynamited most of the surrounding waters and beach during their occupation. Cocktail parties, buffet suppers, and picnics contribute to the social life. Formal evening dresses of washable material are worn, and everyone dresses . . . like the Britisher who lived in the Malayan jungle and dressed every evening for dinner to remind himself that he was still a gentleman.

Helpful Hints

1. Hats are rarely worn on Guam; though bandannas or scarves are a necessity because of the wind.
2. Hosiery is seldom worn, though a few pairs of nylons for trips are fine.
3. Take plenty of low-heeled shoes to last for the entire tour.
4. Cotton underwear outlasts silk, nylon, and rayon. Nylon is hot.
5. Lightweight plastic raincoats for the rainy season are in high favor.
6. Take *cotton* clothes of all kinds: sun suits, playsuits, bathing suits, sports dresses, afternoon dresses of organdy, voile, swiss, and formal evening dresses of cotton or washable materials.
7. Leave all overstuffed furniture in storage in the States. Take baby cribs and young children's beds.
8. If you use a sewing machine take it along and include all types and plenty of findings for your sewing.
9. If you have a washing machine be sure to take it, also a mangle, electric iron, toaster, mixer, waffle iron, radio, clock, lamps with new extension cords.
10. Take all of your kitchen utensils. Rust and mildew pose two problems on Guam, so Pyrex ware, aluminum, and stainless steel are recommended in preference to iron utensils.

Okinawa

The trip by air to Okinawa from the States takes thirty-odd hours with various stopovers; by ship, with good weather, it takes about sixteen days.

The climate and scenery of Okinawa are similar to those of Florida. The lovely cool nights are comparable to nights in San Francisco, and it stays cool as long as the sun is hidden. The summers are very hot but pleasant with the near-by beaches. The rainy season is similar to that of the Philippines.

Hookworm in the soil makes it dangerous to eat anything grown underground, and most native children have the disease from going barefooted.

The Okinawans have two kinds of homes, the Japanese type and the more affluent home with a red-tiled roof. The wooden, Japanese type of home usually has a thatched roof. The interior is furnished with grass mats on the floor, low tables with tea and sake or wine sets, shrine niches for religious moments, and sliding bamboo screens which can be opened to the outdoors or closed against the typhoons and cold weather. Everyone has a small garden, perhaps on the side of the mountain, terraced to retain the water.

Shopping will be limited to the Commissary and Exchange. In general, the "Helpful Hints" given for Guam will hold for Okinawa with a few added suggestions:

1. Visit a dime store and stock up on essentials like thumbtacks, curtain rods, picture wire, clothespins, and the hundred and one things you need in settling a house.
2. Include your spice cabinet, herbs and condiments that will give zest to your cooking.
3. Take a good supply of your favorite soaps, powders, and perfumes.
4. Include a bolt or so of cretonne or chintz.
5. Take sturdy walking shoes and plenty of cotton play clothes plus as many cotton evening dresses as you can manage.

The University of Okinawa is run by the Army.

The Thrift Shop is really a Woman's Exchange because here articles one doesn't use are sold to someone else who needs them. Okinawan maids are available, and though untrained they are eager to learn and anxious to please.

Each month brings new dependents to "Okie," and it is a gala day when a ship docks. Everyone turns out to meet the ship in gaiety and celebration.

The daily arrival and departure of MATS planes give one a nice feeling of keeping in touch!

Midway Island

Midway is 3,200 miles west of San Francisco. Its climate is semi-tropical. The vegetation and bird life usually afford a very pleasant surprise for new arrivals. Instead of the desolate island they pictured, they will discover a luxuriant growth of trees, shrubs, flowers, and grass, and a remarkable variety of birds.

Only government quarters are available, and of course quarters must be certified by the Commanding Officer as being available before dependents are allowed. A waiting list is maintained at the present time. Government quarters are adequately furnished with special tropical-type furniture. However, you must bring your own linens, dishes, cooking utensils, and small electrical appliances. A washing machine is desirable and a good iron is a must. The chaplain will furnish "hospitality kits" for those whose household effects have not arrived. These consist of basic kitchen utensils including dishes, pots, and pans. Most Stateside furniture such as upholstered chairs, studio couches, and other large and expensive pieces deteriorate very rapidly in tropical climates and should not be brought to Midway. Woolen or expensive rugs should be left at home, but bring ample throw rugs and summer rugs. A record player with sufficient records and a good radio will provide relaxation.

You should take only washable clothes and a few woolen clothes for the winter months when the temperatures sometimes drop to the middle fifties. Bathing suits, shorts, halters, rompers, dungarees, and sweaters are the thing. In general, dress is informal. Gloves, hats, and stockings are usually omitted. A good raincoat for every member of the family, with accessories such as rubbers and galoshes, is important. An item not to be overlooked is shoes for the children. Bring a good year's supply of clothes and shoes for yourself and them. The Officers' Club has approximately four formal dances a year, for which long dresses will be required. Families with children of school age will find that casual clothing will best fill the need. For the most part, boys wear slacks and sport or Aloha shirts. Girls prefer skirts and blouses.

Midway is very fortunate in having an excellent Commissary store. Ample quantities of all types of food are available at reasonable prices. Packaged frozen foods are in supply and fresh vegetables and fruits are flown in twice a week on the "Logistic" plane. Butter, cheese, eggs, and fresh milk are at hand.

Midway boasts a fine amateur radio station which is available to you for contacting friends or relatives back in the States.

Midway is one of the most beautiful islands in the Pacific Ocean and provides a healthful environment for both children and adults. The bathing beach far excels the beach at Waikiki. The station has an excellent gymnasium. There is also a miniature golf course.

SAIPAN, KWAJALEIN, AND JOHNSTON ISLANDS

Health and sanitation conditions are excellent, generally speaking. There are no wild animals or poisonous snakes of any kind on Saipan. Johnston Island lacks servants; the same is true of Kwajalein. On many of these islands there are no school facilities, so the Calvert System is recommended.

Children should wear shoes at all times outside the area directly around the quarters as there is a high incidence of transmissible intestinal parasites among the natives.

Store facilities are very limited. The Navy Commissary and the Navy Ship's Store (centrally located in the supply area) are about the only shopping sources available. Certain native shops, such as the cobbler's, jeweler's, and handicrafter's, draw a fair trade.

A policy has been established whereby dependents of Service personnel are authorized to travel via government transportation (not including air) on a revenue, space-available basis or commercial transportation between Saipan and Guam for the purpose of visiting and shopping trips, providing the necessary housing accommodations are prearranged, i.e., confirmation from friends on Guam that housing space is available to visitors.

THE PHILIPPINES

Before World War II Manila was called "The Pearl of the Orient." Today it is a heartbreaking sight. Next to Warsaw, it was said to be the most completely devastated city in the world. Living in Manila today is said to come under the heading of pioneering; however, morale is high and enthusiastic reports pour back on the progress that is being made in the rehabilitation program.

Only artesian, distilled, or boiled water should be used for drinking or cleansing the teeth. One of the luxuries of service in the Philippines in prewar days was the ease of obtaining well-trained servants, but no more; times have changed. Inflation has been ruinous.

A private car is a great convenience; a bicycle or scooter will prove its worth. Army jeeps have replaced the small horse-drawn *carromatas*. The Filipinos have gone to great length to paint their jeeps every color of the rainbow. Pink, blue, orange, and green are the favorite colors. They also have given their mechanized horses fancy names such

as "Mae West," "The Manila Bombshell," and "Mary Nell." Jeeps
are quite commonly used as taxis, but a ride in one is not good even
for a person with low blood pressure.

What to Take to Manila

Shoes (white)	China, silver, and	Play suits, slacks
Shoe polish	glassware	6 cotton evening
Hats . . . large garden	Sports clothes	dresses
variety!	Shorts	Rain gear
		Bathing suits

Take all kinds of shoes, plenty of the play or sport shoe variety.
Serviceable white linen, duck, or gabardine shoes that will clean well
are preferable to suedes and leather. You want nothing that will
mildew, because if it will mildew anywhere, it will in the tropics,
I assure you. Include a generous stock of white shoe polish, your
favorite kind.

For the Philippines you will want the same kind of sports clothes
as would be good in Florida or California. Sunback dresses, if you
like them, lots of play suits, shorts, slacks, and all the cotton evening
dresses you can manage. Six will see you through a season if you
take a good stock of material along for replenishing.

Take a variety of rain gear; the rainy season lasts from two to six
months of the year sometimes. Be sure to have several colored plastic
umbrellas, raincoats or capes of bright shades, light in weight and
color, but the serviceable kind that won't stick together. Of course
you will want several bathing suits, caps, and a beach coat or so.

Not too many naval dependents are sent to the Philippines; the
ones who are stationed there live mostly at Sangley Point and Subic
Bay.

THE NAVY WIFE IN JAPAN

The four seasons in Japan are as clear cut as their names, and each
season has its peculiar attractions. In January comes the New Year
with all its gaiety, the greatest holiday in the Japanese calendar. In
January and February skiing and skating are in full swing at many
mountain and hot-spring resorts in the north.

In February, with the blossoming of the plum trees, the annual
cycle of blossoms begins, the peach and the pear in March, the world-

famous cherry blossoms in April. In May the azaleas, wisterias, tree peonies, and irises complete the cycle with the various other blooms.

In early and middle summer, Japan is almost covered with rich velvety green foliage, while in the fall the country presents a colorful picture of beautiful tinted leaves, which thousands of people make a special visit to see. No other season in any country has such an ideal climate in the autumn as Japan. It is the chrysanthemum season. Japan's long seacoasts provide innumerable bathing resorts where the heat is allayed by cool sea breezes.

Cabin baggage, regardless of the season, should include some winter clothing, since most ships travel the great-circle route to Japan through cold northern waters.

Japan's climate includes a variety of weather and temperature changes with hot, humid summers and long, pleasant falls with some rain as fall is the typhoon season. Spring is rather foggy and hazy though beautiful days are interspersed, and winters are sunny and clear, with frequent snows in the northern part but snow only once or twice during the season in central and southern Japan.

As a result, winter as well as summer clothing is needed, plus an adequate supply of rain gear. The PX stocks a good supply of clothing, including adult wear, children's and infants' clothing, and layettes. However, stocks are limited as to sizes and variety of items, and it is not always possible to obtain particular articles of clothing when they are needed, especially for children. Shoes that fit are the biggest problem along the clothing line for Americans in Japan. Well-known brands of shoes, such as I. Miller and British Walkers, are among those stocked but it is hard to get one's size. Most of the clothes are labeled "Californians" and the prices compare with Stateside prices.

Navy families sometimes rent Japanese residences, which are often large, rambling structures, complete with picture windows and secluded rock gardens. However, few Japanese houses have central heating systems, and in most the American occupants must rely entirely on electric heaters during the winter. In some cases the Navy family occupies the entire house; in others the Japanese owners live in one wing or section. In Tokyo a few families get permanent housing in apartments, which come in one-, two-, and three-bedroom sizes. The housing situation in the Tokyo-Yokohama area is serious.

Japanese native houses are of flimsy structure with no solid foundations. The partitions are of paper screens with the usual sliding windows, sliding doors, sliding screens, and sliding planks to cover the windows in case of typhoons. Storage space is in the most remarkable places—over the windows, under the windows, in closets in every room and small ones above them. Most of the houses have delightful gardens with tiny dwarfed crooked trees. If you wish to get on with your Japanese gardener, include many ten-cent packages of vegetable and flower seeds, which will delight his horticultural soul and guarantee you flowers the year round.

Various developments have been built for military personnel. Notable among them are Washington Heights and Grant Heights in Tokyo, which are in effect United States communities.

What to Take to Japan

Electric coffeepot	Steam iron
Electric fans	Iron skillet (essential)
Electric iron	Strainers, sifters, pans
Electric heaters	Sharp kitchen knives
Electric toaster	One good can opener (a must!)
Electric vacuum	Rotary egg beater
Radio, converted	Wash cloths
(and tubes)	Cotton material
Phonograph, converted	Zippers, findings
(and records)	Shoes (to last for tour)
Electric roaster	Mattress and pillows

The electric current in Japan is 100 volt, 60 cycle. Most electric appliances operate slower than in the States, so electric clocks and television sets do not work properly. Radios in Japan must be converted unless you live in one of the United States housing developments.

General Information

1. For travel to Japan a passport is necessary.
2. Embarkation port by boat for Yokohama is San Francisco or Seattle.
3. Embarkation port by air for Tokyo is Travis Air Force Base. Baggage accompanying dependents by air must not weigh more than a hundred pounds.

4. All personnel must have a series of immunization shots.

5. Dogs and cats are the only pets which may be taken to Japan.

6. Normal full medical care is available to Navy dependents. All emergency cases beyond the capacity of medical facilities in the theater are flown to the United States unless the patient specifically refuses to fly. General health and diet of dependents are closely watched in the Far East.

7. Dependents are under military law from the time they sail from the United States until they return. Air police, military police, and Japanese police protect American families during their stay in Japan.

8. If possible, an automobile in first-class condition should be taken to Japan with some extra parts. Speed limits are lower than in the United States and are strictly enforced. Driving is on the left side of the road. Gasoline is rationed, but the ration is more than adequate for normal use.

9. Walking in Japan differs from walking in the United States. Sturdy shoes with low heels prove more serviceable than open-toed, high-heeled footgear for shopping tours and walking. Japanese etiquette requires shoes to be removed before entering houses. One pair of walking shoes that can be slipped on and off readily will find many uses.

It is suggested that dependents bring bottles for children, seasick tablets, plenty of children's clothing, especially shoes, cosmetics, your own tailored clothing and millinery, ladies' underclothing and plenty of teen-age clothing, and baby medicine (baby aspirin, etc.). And make sure that your Serviceman files stoppage of allotment or change of address form with his disbursing office before you travel.

Many servants speak some English, as they have been employed by Americans before, but their comprehension is limited. Many speak excellent English; some speak and understand just enough either to infuriate you or to make you laugh. They work slowly and are very kind, especially to children. If they like you, they give you presents, and if you treat them with consideration, they are more than grateful and go to far extremes to show it. As a race, the Japanese are extremely emotional. They cry very easily and, if embarrassed, will laugh to hide it.

The most important rules to follow when supervising Japanese servants are: (1) Be patient. (2) Speak slowly and distinctly. (3) Use pantomime. (4) Demonstrate how things are to be done. (5) Don't shout or display exaggeration. (6) Treat the servants courteously.

The schools are strictly Stateside, with imported books and teachers. Schools ranging from kindergarten through high school are located in every military area.

Entertainment is on a high level in Japan; there is always something of interest going on in the cities and at military installations. All types of athletic contests take place on the bases, while the Japanese also entertain with judo matches, sumo wrestling, and kendo, an ancient type of fencing which uses long bamboo poles.

Within easy motor or train distance there are mountain, lake, and seashore resorts where the military operates hotels. There are also golf courses and tennis courts, and fishing (both salt and fresh water), boating, mountain climbing, and skiing are popular.

Army movies and stage shows are scheduled, and Japan's leading symphony orchestra and opera company occasionally make appearances at base theaters. Every village has its own festival, and all Japan turns out in gay kimonos and holiday attire for New Year's Day, the cherry-blossom festival in April, and a long list of traditional and religious holidays.

Famed Mount Fujiyama is sixty miles west of Tokyo and rises to 12,425 feet above sea level.

Try to visit *Nikko,* famous for its shrines, located in the mountainous Honshu lands of Japan; *Kyoto,* the center of fine arts, where the annual cherry-blossom festival is held; *Nagoya,* where headquarters of the Fifth Air Force is located, and also the center of the porcelain industry; *Osaka,* the most modern industrial city of Japan; and *Kobe,* the main seaport of central Japan.

Foreign visitors regard the Tokyo Ginza as one of the most interesting spots in all Japan.

SERVICE IN THE CANAL ZONE

The Headquarters of the 15th Naval District is located on the *Pacific side* of the Isthmus of Panama. The naval activities at this terminal include the Radio Station, Balboa, the Radio Station Summit, and the Naval Ammunition Depot. Panama City, the capital of the Republic of Panama with Balboa and Ancon, are the principal cities on the Pacific side.

On the Atlantic side are located the Naval Air Station at Coco Solo, the Gatun Radio Station, the Naval Magazine, and the Navy Radio direction finder station at Toro Point near Fort Sherman. Cristobal and Colón are the leading cities on the Atlantic end of the Canal.

Living Conditions at Coco Solo

Government quarters of concrete construction (a few of frame) are provided for officers on duty at the submarine base and at the air station. When any are not occupied, they are assigned on a temporary status to the Inshore Patrol, Naval Intelligence, and Section Base personnel. Most of these quarters are very comfortable with three bedrooms, two baths, large combination porch-living room, dining room, kitchen, and servants' quarters.

There are practically no suitable furnished or unfurnished houses for rent near by, and the inferior accommodations that are to be had are very high in price.

Panama isn't what it used to be when it comes to servants; in fact they are scarce and of a very indifferent type. The Panamanians and Negroes find working in restaurants preferable to domestic service, and many have government work.

The Washington Hotel, fronting the sea, in a parklike enclosure, is expensive, but it is always crowded with Navy people. It is government owned and is the only place on the Atlantic side to stay. A cosmopolitan group of travelers congregates at the Washington. It is filled, too, with Servicemen and pretty young girls and Navy wives who are following the ship.

Living Conditions on the Pacific Side

In the 15th Naval District located in Balboa there are eighteen sets of quarters, including those of the Commandant. Those not occupied by heads of departments are assigned according to rank. The quarters are rather high concrete bungalows on stilts, excepting those of the Commandant, who resides in state in a large two-story house.

For the many officers and enlisted men who have to live in Panama City, finding a suitable home is quite a problem. Furnished houses for rent are almost unheard of; and the unfurnished ones have very high rentals. There are a few modern apartments, but all have long waiting lists. Before the construction of a new apartment house is even nearly completed, all the apartments are rented.

The Tivoli Hotel is always crowded with Navy people, though it is quite expensive. The food is good.

Markets

On the Atlantic side food is obtained through the Army, Navy, and Panama Canal Commissaries. There is also a native market in Colón.

On the Pacific side there is no Navy Commissary, but necessary provisions may be obtained from the Panama Canal Commissary and the Army Commissary at Corozal. There is a native market in the city of Panama where fowl, fruits, vegetables, and fish can be bought reasonably. The fish is excellent. The milk from the Commissary is good, and cold-storage eggs are plentiful. The meats are reasonable, but vegetables, although of fair quality and variety, are expensive.

Recreation

Officers and their families enjoy a variety of sports in Panama, including golf, tennis, bowling, badminton, sailing, fishing, and swimming (if a place can be found where the water is clean and free of sharks). Despite the rain, golf is played all year! The following clubs are available: Panama Golf Club, an eighteen-hole course about six miles from Panama; Fort Amador Golf Club; and Pedro Miguel Golf Club at the Mira Flores Locks.

The Stranger's Club in Colón and the Union Club in Panama City give reciprocal privileges. The dues are nominal for Service personnel.

Cities and Shopping

On the Pacific side of the Isthmus is old Panama City; on the Atlantic side is modern Cristobal. They represent two different worlds, two civilizations, two religions, and two races. Panama sells crucifixes and Cristobal sells Frigidaires; Panama smokes black tobacco, Cristobal smokes yellow; Cristobal sleeps on Beauty Rest mattresses, Panama in feather beds. It is a country of anachronisms.

Colón's streets are lined with Hindu shops, shops with wonderful displays of Oriental goods, French perfume, Panama hats, and fascinating goods that are tempting to the feminine shopper. English and French china are real bargains today. They are less than half United States prices. Silver may also be ordered at a discount, but linens have advanced in price with each shipment. French perfumes are excellent buys—way below Stateside prices. Swedish crystal, teakwood, ivory, and wonderful linens are available. Remember to pay only half the asking price in the Hindu shops since bargaining is part of the fun of shopping.

LIFE AT GUANTÁNAMO

Guantánamo, Cuba, is one of the principal Naval training bases. You will travel by MSTS ships direct to Guantánamo.

When you arrive you will be welcomed on this more or less isolated base with open arms. The women will be avid for States news and the sight of the last word in clothes; therefore, look your best. The Officers' Club is the rendezvous for social activities, and because of lack of outside entertainment facilities, it is utilized to a great extent.

The climate is tropical, averaging during the day in summer months 87 degrees, but the nights are usually cool. During the winter months, light blankets are welcomed at night. The atmosphere is dry, and medical officers state it is one of the most healthful of tropical stations.

The married officers' quarters are limited in number (as usual) although it is expected that sufficient quarters will be available for all officers ordered to the station. Married officers should by all means find out if quarters will be available prior to the departure of the family from the United States.

The new quarters for officers are of tropical frame construction, consisting of a large living and dining room, entrance hall and porch, kitchen, three bedrooms, two baths. All the floors are tiled, and a garage and servants' quarters are in a building detached from the house. Electricity is used for cooking and heating.

All public quarters are furnished throughout except for mattresses, pillows, bed and table linen, hangings, china, silverware, glassware, and kitchen utensils. It is wise to bring silverware as it is expensive in Cuba.

Some Things to Take to Guantánamo

Curtain material—cretonne or otherwise	Flat silver
	Visiting cards
Floor lamps	Inexpensive crystal ware
Table lamps	Linens
Utility tables	Blankets
Card tables	

Drapery material for curtains should have body to it, as the constant wind tends to make light materials stringy in appearance.

Marketing

On the station a Commissary store is in operation which carries a comprehensive stock of well-known brands of canned groceries, cold-storage meats, fruits, and vegetables. Once in a while it is impossible to get celery or lettuce, but on the whole the marketing situation is satisfactory.

Local meat, fowl, and vegetables are obtainable but are of an inferior quality. In season, local oranges, grapefruits, papaya, pineapples, bananas, and mangoes are available and of good quality. During dry seasons the milk supply is limited. A new milk plant has been established on the station, which will produce a better grade of milk at slightly lower prices.

Recreational Facilities

Swimming, tennis, baseball and softball, sailing, motor boating, hiking, hunting, shooting, fishing, picnics, horseback riding, band concerts, club dances, nightly open-air movies, a good library and reading room comprise the recreational facilities.

Radios: Long-wave sets are suitable only after dark and during the winter months. Short-wave sets can be used any time. Radio sets can be purchased at the Navy Exchange at a greatly reduced price.

Riding: The mountain and beach trails are picturesque and beautiful.

Hunting and shooting: Game in Cuba consists of deer, ducks, large blue pigeons, doves, and wild guinea. Trap shooting and skeet are available.

Clubs: A well-appointed Officers' Club is in operation, also a Club for Chief Petty Officers which is available for married Petty Officers. There are no hotels, restaurants, or like accommodations available. There is an active Officers' Wives' Club, a CPO's Wives' Club and White-hats' Wives' Club.

Puerto Rico

Puerto Rico means "Rich Port." The islands lie in the path of the trade winds, and the climate is like that of Hawaii, except that the nights are not so cool. The highest recorded temperature is 92 degrees. Living conditions are excellent and the quarters are considered the most desirable in the Navy. They are built for the climate—hurricane-proof concrete houses, quite spacious and nicely furnished. Since there are plenty of quarters, you will probably be able to accompany your husband when he reports. The Navy provides a household kit with linens, dishes, and essentials for your use until your own things arrive.

If for any reason you should want to live off the station, charming Spanish houses and ultramodern apartments are available, but rents are quite high.

Servants are available—good and bad, trained and untrained. The Navy pass office runs an employment service. You may hire Spanish-speaking Puerto Rican maids or English-speaking maids from the Virgin Islands. Sometimes you have to hire and fire two or three to find a good one, but it's worth the effort. Normal wages are $7.50 per week, and since the quarters are large the maids are well worth the price. Most quarters have maids' rooms and baths. Laundresses are available to work by the day.

Excellent schools are maintained by the Navy and Army jointly. From nursery school and kindergarten through the eighth grade, children attend the Antilles Consolidated School. Standards are high, equipment is good, classes are small, and the teachers are hired from the States. High-school students attend private schools in town, through special arrangements made by the Navy. Classes in the public schools are taught in Spanish, with English a compulsory subject.

The 10th Naval District headquarters maintains seven separate housing areas scattered throughout San Juan, so plenty of housing is available. On the main station, the quarters are spacious, attractive, and well furnished, with rattan living room furniture and beautiful mahogany for the dining room. The stoves are electric, the refrigerators are roomy, and all ranks above Lieutenant Commander have deep-freezes. No washing machines are furnished, so be sure to take one, preferably automatic. Again, remember that the climate causes rust and corrosion.

Food is always a lively topic of conversation, probably because most of it is imported. Prices in the Navy and Army Commissaries are about the same as in chain stores in the States. In the city, food prices are quite high.

The native markets are fascinating and fruits are inexpensive and delightful. Oranges are a hundred for a dollar, there are twenty-eight varieties of bananas, and papayas, mangoes, and avocados are a real treat. Don't buy any vegetables (especially leafy ones) on the native market that can't be peeled and cooked, since intestinal diseases are prevalent in the island.

Cotton and rayon washables are comfortable for everyday wear through the entire year.

Cleaning facilities are not good in Puerto Rico. Short evening dresses are most popular and it is a good idea to bring several from the States. Foreign ships visit San Juan often and formal parties are exchanged by the ships and the station. Bring cotton cocktail dresses also and daytime dresses that are sleeveless and low necked. Attractive clothes are available in San Juan, but it takes time to locate the shops selling them. If you wear a narrow shoe size, take enough shoes for two years.

Remember San Juan is a Spanish city and Spanish customs are intermingled with American ones. Ladies never appear downtown in shorts or in strapless dresses.

Puerto Rico has no rainy season, so raincoats are unnecessary but an umbrella is needed, since there are frequent showers. Nylon dresses are much too hot, and so is nylon lingerie.

A private car is needed in Puerto Rico—especially if you are going to Roosevelt Roads. A Puerto Rican license is necessary to drive in Puerto Rico, but it is issued as a courtesy to military personnel if you have a license from the States. The same applies to automobile license tags.

Three excellent highways ring the island, and the intersecting roads are well paved and well marked. Be prepared to find the mountain roads narrow and full of curves, but the scenery is beautiful.

Do not buy a new car to take to Puerto Rico, as the climate and the salt air cause rust and corrosion.

San Juan

San Juan, the largest city on the island, is a wide-awake capital, not the siesta-inclined, tropical town featured in the movies. Its White House or Casa Blanca is now occupied by the Commanding General of the Puerto Rican Department.

The official residence of Puerto Rico's Governor-General is La Fortaleza, and it is reputed to be the oldest building under the American flag. A tremendous old battle-scarred Spanish Fort, El Morro, stands guard at the entrance of the harbor.

Night life in San Juan is interesting, with three casinos strictly controlled by the Puerto Rican government. They are located in the new Caribe Hilton Hotel, the Condado Hotel, and Jack's Club. Drinks are expensive in the night clubs, but Latin music and mambo dancers make an occasional tour diverting. Many excellent restaurants are available, serving Puerto Rican, American, and Continental food. The Navy keeps a list of those approved by the Department of Health.

San Juan is a historic city with old churches and forts and narrow, colorful streets. You can sightsee for days. Be sure to tour the island. The mountains are spectacular, and beautiful beaches ring the whole island.

The Puerto Rican people are friendly, hospitable, and courteous. Remember they are American citizens and are insulted if you call them natives.

"Puerto Rico reeks of romance and tragedy! Its charm and mystery are intangible, yet beauty and sadness are there." There is also plenty of sunshine and pleasant living.

TRINIDAD

Because of its location in relation to the equator, Trinidad enjoys the nearly constant climate of a tropical island. Its weather in general is somewhat more pleasant than that in many of the West Indian Islands. Dependents are advised to bring lightweight clothing suitable for tropical climates and preferably washable. However, since evenings are noticeably cooler, lightweight woolens, sweaters, and

light coats and jackets may be worn comfortably. There is no trend
to formality in the daytime, but evening clothes may be worn as the
occasion warrants. Raincoats are a necessity and should be of the
plastic variety.

Housing facilities are very limited. Government-furnished quarters
provide housing for approximately 50 per cent of the dependents
of enlisted personnel, and 75 per cent of the dependents of officer
personnel. Government quarters have stoves, refrigerators, beds with
mattresses, and other furniture adequate for basic needs. The following articles should be shipped or brought along:

Table and floor lamps	Cotton or straw scatter rugs
Silverware	Linens, lightweight blankets
Dishes	Washing machine, sewing machine
Cooking utensils	Refrigerator dishes
Electrical appliances	Water or fruit-juice bottles

Domestic servants are available and wages run approximately $3.00
to $4.50 in U.S. currency per week.

One of the most interesting places to be visited from a historical
point of view is Port-of-Spain. With nearly 93,000 inhabitants it is
the capital city of the island and the chief city of Britain's Trinidad
and Tobago Colony. Visitors seem delightfully attracted to the
Botanic Gardens located on an abandoned sugar plantation.

A religious event of primary importance in the lives of Trini-
dadians is the beginning of the Lenten season. Queen's Park Savannah
in Port-of-Spain is the center of the festival's carnival activity, which
resembles the general scheme of New Orleans' Mardi gras. Prior
to the carnival itself, the Calypsonians, composers and singers of
Trinidad's famous folk songs, receive their share of public applause.
Programs are sung nightly in calypso "tents."

Pitch Lake, located near the Brighton section, is sooner or later
seen by almost every tourist in Trinidad. It has a surface area of
nearly 200 acres and is a seepage of natural asphalt; in fact, the
world's largest source and formation of asphalt is centered here. At
the center it is always liquid, but elsewhere it is solidified or semi-
solid. This "lake" is located on the edge of the oil fields and the
"Pool" of pure asphalt has a depth of 200 feet at some points.

Scotland Bay, a recreation area for enlisted personnel, their dependents, and guests, has an excellent swimming beach, ball diamonds, tennis courts, picnic pavilions, and a canteen center where ship and station parties and dances are held from time to time.

THE BAHAMAS . . . BERMUDA

Bermuda has an oceanic climate which is mild and healthful, but rather damp. Rain is frequent and considerable wind is present during the winter months.

Be sure to take a good supply of cool *washable* clothing, raincoats, and some woolen suits or dresses for the cooler months. No extremely heavy clothes are needed. You are urged to bring sufficient clothing as it is expensive and hard to obtain locally. Many of the parties given in Bermuda are formal, requiring long dinner or evening dresses with short evening or summer coats or wraps for winter.

Shorts are worn for bicycling, boating, and golfing and on the beach. Wearing shorts on the streets is permitted, but the majority of Bermudians frown upon it. A "Police Order" limits the length of shorts to two inches above the knee, and this means when riding a bicycle. Items which are very practicable, and expensive here, are bathing suits, good play clothes, and play shoes. Shetland and cashmere sweaters may be purchased, as well as doeskin French suede and leather gloves, far cheaper than in the United States.

Public quarters are available on a limited basis. The majority of houses off the base are rented furnished. Desirable cottages rent from $80.00 and up. Utilities range from $14.00 to $22.00 per month depending on the number of electrical and gas appliances in the cottage.

Bermuda Oddities

It is necessary to use water sparingly at all times since rain water is virtually the only supply. It is collected in well-kept cisterns.

There are no public schools in Bermuda suitable for American children. Private schools range from $50.00 to $150.00 per year, depending on the age and grade of the child and the school attended. There are no educational facilities for college students. There is a nursery school at the naval station.

The Bermuda government operates a bus system with scheduled runs to all parts of the island. The Navy operates boats, weather permitting, between the naval base and the city of Hamilton. When weather does not permit the operating of boats, Navy busses are operated instead. There are plenty of taxis, which are not too expensive. The Bermuda government limits the size and horsepower of all private automobiles. The only American car that meets the specifications is the Crosley. As there are no Crosley agencies located on the island, there are no spare parts. English cars can be purchased for $1,000 and up with immediate delivery. Repair facilities for English cars are adequate, but expensive. Naval personnel without cars depend upon naval transportation, island transportation, bicycles, and motor bikes. A popular motor bike is the American-made "Whizzer," which can be purchased on the naval base through the Navy Exchange. Fuel for cars, bikes, and boats can be purchased on the naval base.

As Bermuda is a British Colony any English money in a traveler's possession will be retained by the Bermuda authorities upon entering the island. Navy personnel are urged to bring funds in American dollars (no English money).

THE AZORES

The strategic geographical value of the Azores makes this a vital spot for the defense of the United States and of western Europe. The climate is generally considered semi-tropical.

Lajes Field, home of the Azores Air Transport Station, is situated at the northeastern tip of the island of Terceira—third largest of the nine islands in the Azores archipelago. This archipelago is a part of Portugal and occupies an area equal to three-fourths the size of Rhode Island. United States personnel stationed on Terceira are guests of the Portuguese, rather than tenants. Since approximately 99 per cent of the population is Catholic, religion dominates the political, economic, and social aspects of their lives. The natives of Terceira are extremely polite, sincere, friendly, and hospitable. They are hard-working, fun-loving people who usually marry young and dedicate themselves to a full family life.

Limited government housing of one-, two-, three-, and four-bedroom type is available for officers and enlisted men of this station. All bachelor personnel, or married personnel stationed at Lajes Field without their families, are assigned temporary-type government quarters. BOQ's are available to officers and civilians, while both open bay and partitioned barracks are provided for enlisted men. Generally, the BOQ's are divided into two- to four-man rooms. Living conditions are becoming increasingly crowded, and a number of Quonset huts have been erected to house the overflow. New BOQ's and airmen's barracks are in various stages of construction.

There is a cottage park on this station and another one adjacent to the station. Cottages can be locally constructed or bought from rotating personnel at prices ranging from approximately $1,400 to $2,500. Houses are available in the small villages near Lajes Field at a maximum rent of $35.00 per month. Usually, it is necessary for the tenant to spend from $350.00 to $750.00 to install a refrigerator, hot-water heater, hot-water system, screens, wood floors, and a transformer to cut the island electricity to 110 volts. There are no hotel accommodations except for temporary family rooms on the station.

The tenant must furnish all furniture in off-station housing. Cottages, when purchased from other personnel, sometimes are sold with all basic furniture, including stoves and refrigerators. The only electrical appliance now authorized for personnel residing in cottages is a hot-water heater.

Domestic help is normally available, although the number of maids, gardeners, etc., who speak good English is limited. Most domestics speak a bit of English and are adept at picking up the more important phrases used in daily work. The cost of a maid is 13 escudos (46 cents) per working day.

The Dependents School offers a complete curriculum for elementary- and secondary-school-age children.

There is a completely equipped and staffed USAF hospital and dental clinic on the station.

TRIPOLI

U.S. naval Communication Unit FOUR is located on Wheelus Air Force Base, an installation of the United States Air Force. The Unit operates a major relay station and has ship-shore and air-ground positions. Wheelus Air Force Base is located in Port Lyautey, French Morocco, seven miles from the port city of Tripoli. This is the city made famous by the Marines Hymn. Tripoli is both the capital city of the province of Tripolitania and one of the two seats of the federal government of the federated provinces of Libya. Libya was granted independence on 24 December, 1951, by a resolution of the United Nations.

The climate of Tripoli compares with southern California or southern Florida. At the present time government housing is unavailable to Navy personnel, owing to the USAF point system. However, commercial (off-base) housing is available in Tripoli. Prices vary considerably, depending on the date of construction. The average rent paid during 1953 was approximately $67.00 monthly. Concurrent travel is not presently authorized.

Automobiles may be shipped to the Port of Tripoli from the NYPOE (New York Port of Embarkation). The USAF operates a Commissary open to all married personnel. All types of American foodstuffs are for sale there. In addition, a good supply of fresh local vegetables is available. The USAF hospital located on base ministers to all Navy personnel. Dependents' schooling is offered through the high-school level. The medium of exchange in Libya is the Libyan pound, based on the English pound system. One pound equals roughly $2.80 in U.S. currency.

At this writing BuPers (Bureau of Personnel) is being asked to raise the tour of duty for married people from one to two years. This would seem desirable inasmuch as the original investment for furnishing can be expensive, and at least a month normally elapses before dependents can join their sponsor. It is highly recommended that the senior Petty Officers be married. The key men would then be stationed here over a longer period and make for a stability which is presently obtainable only by continued extensions. The duty here is a hundredfold more satisfying to married people. With a corps of happily married people attached, the single men have a place to get together.

ALASKA

There are three distinct climates in Alaska. Along the south coast the winters are generally mild and the summers cool, with considerable annual rainfall. This region includes Anchorage, Juneau, Ketchikan, Seward, and a few other cities, but in this climatic zone most of the Navy people are in the Anchorage area. There the average January temperature is 20 degrees above zero, although there may be a few days and nights of 20 degrees or more below. The snow is rarely more than a foot deep. During the summer the nights are cool, the days in the 70's and 80's.

The second climatic region is the interior, where both summer and winter temperatures are more extreme. At Fairbanks, Eielson, and Big Delta, all Army stations, the thermometer drops to 50 degrees or more below zero every winter, although usually not for very long at a time. There are protracted periods of zero- to 20-degrees-below weather during January and February at both places. In the summer, on the other hand, temperatures often rise into the 90's.

The third region is the true Arctic, north of the Brooks Mountain Range on the coast of the Arctic Sea, but you won't be stationed there. This region, populated almost exclusively by Eskimos, has an average year-round temperature of only 10 degrees and only fifteen frost-free days a year, between the first and the fifteenth of July.

Kodiak

The 17th Naval District Headquarters and the Naval Operating Base including a medium-sized air station are located on the large island of Kodiak within sight of the mainland of Alaska on a clear day.

The city of Kodiak is seven miles from the naval station and the population is about 3,000. The climate in Kodiak is comparable to that of the Puget Sound area in northwestern Washington. The temperature ranges from a winter low of about 7 degrees Fahrenheit to a summer high of about 75 degrees. Average winter temperature is 31 degrees and summer 52 degrees. The most difficult feature is not cold weather but lack of sunlight—clouds, fog, and rain. The four-month summer brings greenness to the hills, and flowers are profuse. In winter, occasional storms and williwaws produce high winds.

Some of the roads in the immediate area of the naval station are paved and the others are gravel. An automobile is a basic necessity since government transportation is limited and of necessity strictly controlled.

Children living in Navy housing go to the station schools while those living in the city of Kodiak attend the city schools.

Housing

Alaska is not a perennial deep-freeze and you will not live in an igloo! All married officers and all married enlisted men in pay grades 5, 6, and 7 are eligible for government quarters. Housing on the naval station is limited, and waiting periods vary from eight to ten months for enlisted personnel and ten to eleven months for officers. From time to time housing is available in the city of Kodiak, but it must be inspected and approved by the Off-Station Housing Officer before the Commandant will authorize entry of dependents. Most housing in Kodiak, however, is considerably below Stateside standards. Government quarters at Kodiak are adequately furnished with all basic furniture, including kitchen range and refrigerator. Sufficient floor lamps and rugs are also included in the furnishings.

Your present wardrobe, with some additions, should prove adequate. A warm overcoat is a must item, as are heavy-soled walking shoes, raincoat, and galoshes. Heavy clothing is not needed for daily routine living, but sessions at the Ski Chalet or overnight camping trips make it advisable to bring woolen suits, sweaters, woolen socks, warm gloves, woolen scarves, and ear muffs. For a child a ski suit is ideal. Generally speaking, the accent is on informal dress. However, evening gowns and dinner jackets are desirable for occasional formal parties.

Bring along a radio too. All radios will pick up WVCQ, the local AFRS station, and many Stateside stations may be heard over short-wave radios, with the reception especially good in winter.

Clothes

In the cities of Juneau, Sitka, Fairbanks, and Anchorage one sees fashionably dressed women. The cities are very cosmopolitan, and anything can be bought, but luxuries come high. Inflation hit Alaska during the gold rush and prices have soared ever since. A fur coat is not a necessity, but if you have one, take it along. A warm cloth topcoat with a removable parka and inner lining will prove sufficient. Wonderful bargains are to be had in furs, such as reindeer, fawn, sealskin, silver fox, and ermine, but the cost of making up the furs is something else. A fur coat will be less expensive if bought in the States. It is suggested that lightweight woolens be included in your wardrobe, over which you can wear a very warm coat. Take a good supply of sweaters and skirts, woolen dresses, afternoon dresses, and evening dresses. A pair of lined overshoes or galoshes and a pair of fur-lined carriage boots for evening should be included. The sportswoman should take along a ski suit with a windbreaker, and ice skates.

Equip yourself with plenty of warm slacks and warm underclothing. Be sure to include rain gear, a trench coat with hood. You may take a trip into the interior by dog sled or go up to Fairbanks to attend the winter Ice Carnival; so be prepared by taking warm but not heavy apparel.

Recreation

If you like to fish or hunt or ski or take pictures, you will find Alaska made to order for you. If you don't, chances are you will learn before you leave. Moose, caribou, mountain sheep and goats, bear, game birds, and rabbits have long provided some of the best hunting on the continent, as well as being a major source of food for the native population. Salmon and trout abound in the streams away from the major cities. However, game laws are strictly enforced as a conservation measure, and for the first year of your stay, when you are classed as a nonresident, you will find big-game hunting expensive. Winter sports are excellent in most parts of Alaska from about December to April, and you will find as many skiers on the slopes near the larger cities as you will in the major ski resorts in New England and the Rockies. Ski tows, lighted slopes, and good access roads with frequent bus service make skiing a pleasant sport for a winter Saturday or Sunday afternoon. Ice skating, snowshoeing, and tobogganing are also popular, as is sledding for the younger set. There are the usual facilities for indoor sports, including "Alaska's favorite game," bingo, weekly dances at the Officers', CPO, and Service clubs, bridge, and many more.

Just about every Alaskan, and every visitor and Serviceman, has a camera and uses it constantly. Alaska's mountains and lakes remind one of Switzerland, and the southern coastline, with its deep fjords and towering glaciers, resembles the coast of Norway. At many points in Alaska the sun is visible at midnight on the longest day of the year, in June, and in the long, dark winter nights the northern lights brighten the sky with their indescribable beauty. Film is available in all sizes and types, and photofinishing facilities compare with those in the States.

Tourist attractions are everywhere, and there are several trips you can take to see the Alaska of the Eskimos and the gold-rush days. In the summer, you might take a steamer trip through the famous Inside Passage, where you will see dazzling white glaciers, huge mountains, and valleys filled with exquisite flowers. Visit Sitka, the old Russian capital, and Skagway, where you can follow the gold-rush trail of '98 through Dead Horse Gulch, past Inspiration Point and Pitchfork Falls. At Ketchikan and Wrangell you will find Indian tribes, many of whose homes are decorated with totem poles. The Tlingit and Chilkoot tribes still hold their potlatches, or big feasts and dances, right in town. If you have the opportunity, you should also see Juneau, the capital. From Anchorage you can drive to the village of Hope, site of the first gold strike in Alaska, where there is still gold to be panned in the streams, and to the ghost towns of Ernestine and Copper Center.

Anchorage and Fairbanks have two outstanding social events in the winter, the Anchorage Fur Rendezvous and the Fairbanks Ice Carnival. Eskimos, Indians, miners, hunters, and just plain people crowd the cities for the big festival week, with native dances, dog-sled contests, and other reminders of the past.

While you are in Alaska, you may want to visit Nome, Kotzebue, St. Lawrence Island, or some of the coastal villages, but few Navy families do, because of the time and expense involved.

Adak

Adak is one of the Andreanof Islands and is located in the southernmost part of the Aleutian chain. The terrain is mountainous and rugged; the island is covered with tundra and is treeless. Fresh-water lakes and streams are abundant. There is no native population or any civilian community on the island. Adak is favored by the Japanese current, the mean winter temperature being 32 degrees Fahrenheit.

You are allowed to ship 500 pounds of household effects express to Adak at government expense from your last duty station. This shipment should include necessary essentials such as linens, silverware, chinaware, kitchen utensils, and other light furnishings. The Navy will provide storage for nonessential effects at government expense. Application to the nearest Supply activity is all that needs to be done. The Navy will do the rest. Your effects may be stored as long as one year beyond completion of your overseas tour of duty.

Recreational facilities at Adak are widespread and varied. The Village Gymnasium has athletic gear available for issue to Service personnel, dependents, and civilians for the following sports: basketball, softball, badminton, boxing, wrestling, track, skiing, riflery, ice skating, and fencing. Bowling alleys and the Rollerdrome are located in the Village Gymnasium. The Polar Plunge, located in the Bering Recreation Center, is for year-around swimming. The Enlisted Men's Club, known as Hammerhead Lodge, is available to all military personnel and their guests. Package store privileges exist at all three clubs. Another popular recreational activity goes on in the Idle Hour Shop, where hobbies are pursued. A ski lift and ski lodge are located on Mount Moffett some five miles distant.

Adak from a Navy Wife's Point of View

I would like to give you a Navy wife's view on Adak. If your husband comes home and says "Honey, we're going to Adak," don't be alarmed; be happy. To me, Adak was a most wonderful experience and a beautiful place to see. The Navy has outdone itself to make it a worth-while tour of duty. The housing is lovely; completely furnished houses except for linens and dishes. There is a fine theatre, a bowling alley, roller rink and swimming pool for everyone's use and also many organizations. There is never a dull moment on windy Adak!

Adak is located 943 miles west of Kodiak and 421 miles from Attu. It is a distance of 1032 miles to Anchorage on the mainland, and 2383 miles from Seattle. This is a region of active and dormant volcanoes. Looking some twenty miles due east of Adak's Kuluk Bay, one can see the still active volcano Mt. Sitka rising 5740 feet on Great Sitkin Island.

The weather on Adak is quite changeable with strong winds coming up without a warning, but there are many days that are very pleasant too.

The Chief's Club welcomes White-hats and their families and has inexpensive family-style meals and very good music in full swing much of the time.

Although there are only 90 miles of roads on Adak, an automobile is a basic necessity. If you like to hike, Adak is a most interesting place to do so. There are more than 450 species of seed plants and ferns on the island. Wild flowers grow everywhere and are really beautiful in the summer. In the winter there is a ski-lodge with all kinds of skis and toboggans for your use.

The school is modern and very fine, with Alaskan teachers or possibly Service wives.

Last but not least is the Navy Wives' Club #94. Believe me, when you walk into a meeting there, you really feel you are welcome and wanted. Everyone has a smile and a cheery "hello" and it is not hard to get coöperation when you are made to feel that you are a part of a happy family.

Sincerely,
MARY FULLER
NWCA, Club #37

ARGENTIA, NEWFOUNDLAND

Naval Station Argentia is located on the site of what was formerly a small Newfoundland fishing village. It is approximately ninety miles southwest of St. John's, the capital city.

Summers in this latitude are retarded; spring may be said to arrive in June. Winter is generally mild until January, and the worst months for storms, snow, ice, and high winds are from January to April. Weather at Argentia may be classed as uncertain, subject to bitter squalls and blizzards of short duration. Flat terrain and surrounding water expose Argentia to excessive winds.

Servants of average ability are available, and the wages are reasonable. The Commissary and Exchanges are well stocked, and the base supports its own dairy. Of course, all prices are higher than in the States.

As to clothes: Tailored suits are practical and are much worn by the British women in St. John's. Excellent British woolens are available. A full-length fur coat is almost a must, or a warm coat such as an alpaca pile or one lined with alpaca. An adequate supply of shoes should be included in your wardrobe, but all types of overshoes can be bought in St. John's.

There are many interesting motor trips, and the Newfoundland Railway connects all the principal towns. The roads are poor, but beautiful scenery is at your finger tips. In the summer, with the boat trips available, one is reminded of the fjords and scenery of Norway.

Your wardrobe should be adequate for the tour and it should include a complete shoe wardrobe, overshoes, stadium boots, and rain apparel for each member of the family. Hats and gloves are important items. Casual clothing should include sweaters, skirts, and slacks. Cotton dresses are appropriate for summertime wear.

Each child should have snow suits—several pairs of snow pants and a jacket with hood. Children's caps with ear muffs are recommended for protection against the wind. In general, heavy clothing, including woolen socks, is desirable.

The Exchanges carry children's necessities, and an excellent special order department is operated by the Air Force Exchanges at the following air bases: Pepperell, McAndrew, Ernest Harmon, Goose, and Narsarssuak.

Be sure to take personal kits for the care of your hair—curlers, shampoo, and permanent supplies. There are a few beauty shops on or near installations in Newfoundland but dependents going to Argentia will have to be prepared to "roll their own." Include plenty of creams, lotions, toilet soaps of all kinds.

The Ship's Store of the naval station stocks some toiletries, magazines, newspapers, tobacco, electrical devices, photographic supplies, and limited items of clothing, kitchenware, and infants' clothing. Patent medicines and products for self-medication are not stocked, other than simple remedies such as vaseline, vitamins, aspirin. Bring your own favorite medicines to stock your medicine cabinet.

Quarters for dependents on-station are limited. Waiting lists are maintained, and no arrangements may be made for moving dependents to Argentia without prior permission of the Commanding Officer. (Information received from Naval Station Argentia advises that quarters for dependents are not at present available. The average wait is from eight to ten months. The entry of dependents is not approved at this time.) Quarters on the station are equipped with furniture, electric stoves, and refrigerators, but no blankets and linens. It must be borne in mind that pictures, curtains, dishes, and luxury items cannot be obtained in Newfoundland as reasonably as in the United States and should be brought. Washing machines and vacuum cleaners are not furnished in quarters. Deep-freeze units, for those who own them, are practical for storing game, fish, and berries in season. No facilities exist for storage of household effects, and only such articles as actually can be used should be shipped.

Radio reception in this area is not particularly good. A short-wave set is desirable if you have one.

Private autos are permitted and encouraged, subject to certain controls and customs regulations. You should know that no car may be sold to U.S. nationals or Canadians without *prior consent of the Commanding Officer and preparation of the required documents by the Legal Officer.*

The climate at Argentia is conducive to rust. Particular trouble is encountered with the chrome trim and bright work on automobiles. Purchase of a new car specifically for use during the tour of duty at Argentia is not recommended. Of course, the high winds and driving snow of winter and the cool summer temperatures make convertibles impractical.

Trout and salmon fishing is popular, and fishing gear, artificial flies, etc., are suggested for those interested in this sport. A sled and toys for the children may be purchased more economically in the United States, and ice skates can be used if the winter is unusually severe.

On the naval station are located an Officers' Club, Chief Petty Officers' Club, Enlisted Men's Club, and an American Civilian Club with the corresponding Wives' Clubs.

Chapter XVII

SERVICE IN EUROPE
AND SOUTH AMERICA

NATO

(North Atlantic Treaty Organization)

NATO is an organization consisting of fourteen sovereign nations, each retaining full independence of decision and action. The Treaty was signed in Washington on April 4, 1949, by the United States, Canada, and ten nations of western Europe—Belgium, Denmark, France, Iceland, Italy, Luxembourg, the Netherlands, Norway, Portugal, and the United Kingdom. Greece and Turkey also acceded to the treaty in 1952.

At the head of NATO is the North Atlantic Council, made up ot top cabinet officers from each NATO country plus a permanent representative from each country. At the top of NATO's military organization is the Military Committee, which is responsible to the Council. The Supreme Headquarters, Allied Powers, Europe (SHAPE) is the best known of NATO's military commands. SHAPE directs the integrated NATO forces in western Europe. It is a true international command, with a British Field Marshal as Deputy Supreme Allied Commander, a French naval deputy, and a British air deputy.

SHAPE is broken down into three subordinate commands: the Central Europe Command, the Northern Europe Command, and the Southern Europe Command. There are also two special NATO commands: the Channel Committee, with headquarters in London, and the Canada-U.S. Regional Planning Group.

SHAPE

(Supreme Headquarters, Allied Powers of Europe)

The organization of SHAPE is much like any other U.S. Joint Headquarters. Naval officers and enlisted men are assigned to the various divisions throughout the entire organization. All divisions are multi-service and multi-national.

Naval personnel assigned to SHAPE in many instances are promptly engaged in work which is entirely non-naval. In addition to the naval officers attached to SHAPE at Fontainebleau, there are numerous naval officers assigned to NATO in Paris, to the Military Aid Group, to the NATO Defense College, to the Embassy, and to other activities located on the Continent.

THE NAVY WIFE IN FRANCE

Should your husband be ordered to France, you will find an entirely different kind of living. It is necessary to arrive with an attitude that you will accept things as you find them. The French are just as proud of their country and its traditions as we are of ours, and they have no intention of changing. You can make yourself miserable chafing over the many inconveniences, or you can take them in your stride and enjoy to the full the many, many wonderful opportunities offered you. Enjoyment of your stay in France will be largely up to you.

There are many tricks to selecting a house or an apartment in Paris, and it is wise to take your time. Desirable quarters are scarce and rents are high. Heating is very expensive and most houses are very hard to heat. In apartments a charge is made for heating over and above the monthly rental. It is helpful to rent a place previously occupied by Americans because not only can they better explain the advantages and disadvantages of living conditions but in most cases they have improved the comfort of the quarters.

Whether to live in Paris or the suburbs depends largely upon your own taste. Families with small children or teen-age boys usually prefer the suburbs. Make sure that you locate near to transportation; life can be very complicated if you are not reasonably near the train, bus, or *Métro* (subway). You can estimate the average rent to be around $200, and this does not include utilities.

Regardless of what you have heard about Paris shops, unless you can afford the *haute couture* fashions, you will find clothes very expensive. Lingerie and nylons are good at the Exchange. Be sure to include plenty of *warm clothing*. Except for a short period in the summer, Paris is damp and cold. Many women find winter-weight cotton underwear practical. Take sufficient pairs of shoes for your entire stay, as French lasts are different from ours, and also French shoes are expensive. Walking shoes, preferably those with crepe-rubber soles, to ward off the dampness, will be useful. You are advised to take suits, a warm coat, sweaters, wool dresses, raincoat, galoshes, umbrella, cocktail dresses (black and dark colors should dominate), dinner dresses, and evening clothes. Naturally the number of evening clothes you will need will depend largely on the nature of your husband's assignment. For your children take plenty of warm clothes. It is well to open an account with a U.S. children's shoe store, so that shoes may be reordered as needed.

Household Effects

Articles that will make life more comfortable:

Lamps—a must
Rugs—small scatter variety
Furniture—no, but small tables, perhaps your favorite bed and chair
Refrigerator—yes, even if you have to put it in the living room
Washing machine—nonautomatic
Vacuum cleaner—very useful
Stove—yes, gas is preferable
Radio—yes
Television set—no
Dishes—yes
Blankets—definitely
Pillows—yes, French pillows are larger than ours and do not fit our pillow slips
Electric appliances, such as an iron and toaster—yes

Medical Attention

There is a U.S. Army Dispensary in the American Hospital in Paris, with a Dental Branch attached. The services are not adequate for most difficulties and the staff is small. In the case of serious illness or accident, patients are sent to a large Army hospital in Germany, of which there are several. Serious emergency treatment for patients who cannot be transferred to Germany is provided by the civilian staff of the American Hospital, most of whom are French doctors and nurses.

Money

SHAPE personnel are paid in military occupation currency, which may be converted to U.S. Government checks or to French francs at the Pay Office. It may *not* be converted to green U.S. dollars except when leaving France for the United States.

Servants

You will find it necessary to employ one or more servants. Finding good help is one of the keys to an enjoyable stay in Paris. Again, if you are lucky enough to find servants who have previously worked for Americans, you will have a head start.

Here are some of the headaches: Finding accommodations requires diligent searching; living in hotels is very expensive; Commissaries carry a restricted variety of stock; and sometimes it is necessary to travel for a distance of 55 miles (110 miles round trip) to make Commissary purchases. Coal is expensive (approximately $35.00 per ton). Bathroom facilities are antiquated but passable. Public transportation is nonexistent between some housing areas and duty stations. Travel by private automobile is expensive.

However, just walking through Paris is an exciting experience, not to mention living there. Somebody once said that "To study Paris is to gain a window that opens out onto the history of Europe." Nostalgically my mind runs back over past days there . . . to the gay, painted shutters . . . lilacs in bloom in the Bois de Boulogne . . . the lacelike shaft of the Eiffel Tower . . . the bookstalls along the Seine . . . crêpes suzette at the Café de la Paix . . . Mass at Notre Dame . . . an afternoon at Versailles. There is no city in the world like it.

Bon voyage, et bonne chance!

NATO HEADQUARTERS IN OSLO, NORWAY

The city of Oslo is the capital and the largest city in Norway, having all of the advantages of a resort town. The offices of the Military Assistance Advisory Group (MAAG) and the Service attachés are in the former Hotel Terminus (American Embassy Annex) located at Nedre Vollgate 18, about six blocks from the Chancery.

The Norum Hotel, Bygdoy Alle 53, the Nobel Hotel, Karl Johans Gate 33, the Stefan Hotel, Rosenkranz Gate 1 and the Slemdal Hotel, Stasjonsv 4 (catering especially to personnel with children) have proved most satisfactory to those MAAG members who have found it necessary to remain in hotel quarters for an indefinite period.

Norway as a whole enjoys a very favorable climate. The weather is generally brisk and stimulating except in November and December when there is considerable rain. The climate is considered healthful for all ages except those afflicted with sinus ailments.

Housing

Desirable houses and apartments are not easily obtained in Oslo. The usual waiting period for new arrivals is from two weeks to three months depending upon the standard of their requirements.

Unfurnished apartments are almost impossible to find. "Furnished" apartments are usually only partially furnished, and rarely include an electric refrigerator or adequate linen, silverware, china, and kitchen utensils.

There is a wide variety of furniture available in Oslo, but it is rarely up to American standards. Norwegian beds in particular are considered inferior, and it is recommended that all such basic items of household furniture be brought from the United States. Electric refrigerators, electric irons, vacuum cleaners, kitchen utensils, electrical appliances, and washing machines are expensive and difficult to obtain. Completely automatic washing machines require transformers and do not operate satisfactorily as a general rule. Further, technicians in Oslo are unfamiliar with this type of equipment and are often unable to make necessary repairs.

Food

The Norwegian diet of meat, fish, bread, boiled potatoes, and milk is standard in Oslo. There is unlimited good milk, cheese, and eggs. Most personnel find it desirable to regularly import supplies of shortening, canned and fresh fruits, canned vegetables and meats, and luxury specialties to suit individual tastes. An ample supply of unusual condiments and spices should be brought.

MAAG personnel are able to procure groceries in case lots from the Army Commissary in Bremerhaven, Germany, approximately every two months.

Clothing

With the exception of woolen knitwear (ski sweaters, scarves, socks, mittens, etc.) and winter coats, an adequate supply of clothing and household textiles should be brought. Shoes offer little variety, and narrow widths and particular sizes are next to impossible to find. It is recommended that all customary items of haberdashery be brought or purchased later from the United States; they are expensive and of relatively poor quality in Oslo.

Women should bring a complete wardrobe, as the local women's apparel is inferior and expensive. All luggage should be brought, and a large leather shoulderbag is particularly recommended.

Since the climate is chilly or cold for eight months of the year, it is advisable to concentrate on warm clothing. The most practical coat, which can be worn rain or shine from October until April, is the alpaca-lined gabardine trench coat. So much the better if there is a hood and the lining zips out, because a raincoat is essential the year around. Wool hoods, ear muffs, and scarves are likely to replace hats on winter days. Stadium boots are an absolute necessity, as well as rubbers and high rubber boots that fit over shoes. Since many of the streets are paved with cobblestone, bring along some sturdy thick-soled walking shoes in addition to as many dress shoes as you can manage. A long wool housecoat and warm pajamas are desirable, as are woolies and a few pairs of sporty cotton or wool gold stockings. The Norwegians look their smartest on the ski slopes, and ski clothing of fine quality, style, and reasonable price can be purchased in Oslo. Ski boots are especially excellent here and in comparison to U.S. prices a remarkable buy. Norwegian skis are among the finest in the world and again are relatively inexpensive. Complete ski equipment (clothing, skis, poles, etc.) for an adult can be bought for about N.Kr. 447 ($62.50).

There is a considerable amount of formal entertainment, for the diplomatic corps primarily, so at least two or three evening dresses are necessary. (The Chief of MAAG, chiefs of Service sections, and their deputies appear on the Diplomatic List.)

The stock of children's clothes is extremely limited and expensive.

Dry cleaning is only fair, quite expensive, and slow. One should bring a supply of cleaning fluids or a powder to take out small stains. Good reliable servants are available but difficult to find.

Schools

The American School in Oslo, organized by Embassy personnel, provides elementary education to the eighth grade. It uses the instruction system of the Calvert School of Baltimore, Maryland. Norwegian schools can, as a whole, be considered the equal of American schools.

Sports

The Norwegians are an outdoor, sports-loving people, and the country offers excellent opportunities for skiing and skating in the winter and tennis, golf, sailing, and bathing in the summer.

There is some ice skating during the winter on the lakes and fjords. As soon as the snow melts the hiking season begins, and every Sunday until the next snowfall many Norwegian people take to the mountains with packs on their backs. Tennis is very popular and Oslo has several good clubs.

To best enjoy the Norwegian countryside it is preferable to travel by car, motorcycle, or bicycle.

Social Life

Diplomatic corps parties are numerous, mostly receptions, cocktail parties, and informal dinners. The same is true of the nondiplomatic group but in a much more informal way. Norwegian parties are usually dinners and are only rarely followed by bridge as the Norwegians prefer conversation. It is not considered polite to leave too early after a Norwegian dinner, and it is customary to send flowers after the first acceptance of a Norwegian's hospitality, or to take them with you on the first visit. However, a basket of fresh fruit (seldom available in the market) is an extremely welcome substitute.

As not many official calls are required, a large supply of calling cards is not necessary. Informal fold-over cards for notes are useful. Invitation cards may be obtained locally.

The Norwegians are very sociable and do much entertaining in their homes, where Americans are quite popular and welcome guests. The normal Norwegian dinner hour is from three to five o'clock, but dinner parties in both Norwegian and foreign homes usually commence at seven to seven-thirty. Cocktail parties, usually confined to diplomatic homes because of the high tax on alcoholic beverages, are generally from six to eight o'clock.

Many private parties are formal and include dinner, coffee, and supper. Following cocktails and dinner—accompanied by much *skaaling* with aquavit, beer, and wine—the guests are offered coffee, cakes, and liqueur and later highballs. Around midnight a supper is usually served, consisting of hot soup, bread and butter, coffee, and cakes. The Norwegians are great conversationalists, so much of the evening is devoted to talking. Self-introduction is the rule; when entering a room full of strangers one shakes hands and exchanges names with each person present. Parties are often extremely late, but one cannot leave early without running the risk of offending the host or hostess.

NATO HEADQUARTERS IN NAPLES, ITALY

Naples is neither as hot in summer nor as cold in winter as Washington. You dress very much as you do there. Warm clothes for winter (remember, it rains a lot), cottons, linens, silks for summer. Black is always good for winter. Woolen underwear has been very popular too. You will use lots of cocktail dresses, short dinner dresses, and one or two long evening dresses (an evening gown is a must for gala nights at the opera and frequently at the Allied Officers' Club). You will wear hats more often than at home but they are inexpensive and easily acquired here. Be sure and bring a large supply of shoes (even the ones made to order don't fit comfortably). Walking shoes are a necessity, at least one pair with crepe or rubber soles. Gloves are a specialty in Naples and inexpensive.

Children's clothing is as at home but remember extra shoes. Boys wear "levis"; girls wear woolen skirts and sweaters.

Dressmakers and tailors are reasonable. Dressmakers really don't need patterns; all you need is a picture and they do wonders. Materials can be obtained here but bring patterns and *sewing notions* (zippers, thread).

Be prepared to stay at a hotel or *pension* (boardinghouse) for some time—maybe two or three weeks, maybe a month or two. It is not easy to locate an apartment or a house.

When they say unfurnished here, it is the truth—four walls.

Closets or even shelves are usually lacking. Bring all your household gear but do have a big trunk or box with you containing coffeepot, sheets, blankets, towels, and a few cooking utensils so you can camp out in your rented apartment or house. Often household goods takes two or three or more months to arrive.

Try to limit the number of electrical gadgets you bring. The electricity is not dependable. Have flashlights. If you have an oil lamp or an alcohol stove, bring it along. Candlesticks too, so that candles are ready to be lighted when the fuses blow out. Candles are available.

Bring everything you have in household things and clothing but *don't* buy to bring.

BE SURE TO HAVE WITH YOU

Plenty of *shoes*
If you wear glasses, two pairs, and bring your prescription. It can be filled here.
Your own brands of cosmetics
A good can opener
Hot-water bottles
Warm sleeping clothes
Overshoes, raincoat

RECREATION AND SOCIAL LIFE

Naples offers ample opportunities for sports and outdoor recreation during the summer months. The beautiful bay is ideal for sailing and fishing. Within easy driving distance are several miles of beautiful beaches. The Isle of Capri offers many other fine bathing places.

The nearest golf course is in Rome.

The city of Naples is famous throughout the world for its museums. The Naples area is ideal for sightseeing. It is world famous for its many places of scenic or historic interest. Tourists come in thousands from dozens of countries to visit Pompeii, Capri, Ischia, Sorrento, Amalfi, Ravello, and Vesuvius. These are easily accessible to all personnel stationed here.

The outstanding custom is shaking hands. You shake hands meeting and saying good-by to everyone. Be prepared to have your hand kissed when meeting French or Italian men.

ATHENS, GREECE

Greece is in approximately the same latitude as the state of Ohio. The climate varies from sub-zero winters in the mountainous regions to hot summers in the Athens area, with cool nights. Snowfall is light.

The country of Greece is about 80 per cent mountains. Generally speaking, Navy personnel should come prepared for both weather extremes.

A limited number of private houses or apartments are available in Athens and the suburbs. In general, rental rates are inflated, and houses, utilities, and related services do not measure up to American standards. New arrivals to Athens will be wise to investigate thoroughly before making rental commitments. If you finally locate a house within the area covered by the city water system, you very probably will not have water every day. The number of hours the water is available will vary with the season and the annual rainfall. All the houses have electricity but you can never be certain when an extra jolt will blow out your fuses or when the power in the central plant will fail. An adequate supply of candles or other nonelectrical lighting and cooking appliances should be on hand.

Since April, 1951, the Association of American and British Parents has been operating the schools. Considerable and generous assistance has been rendered by the American Mission and State Department in the form of services, transport, and subsidy of children of Mission personnel.

Medical care for dependents is available insofar as medical personnel and facilities will permit. No obstetrical care is offered, but prenatal care can be given. Pregnancy and certain major surgical cases are transferred to a U.S. Army hospital in Germany.

During the winter months you will find most of the homes inadequately heated, so warm clothing is necessary. The dresses worn by the women during the day and evening are similar to those worn at home. Woolen slacks and sport shirts are comfortable for relaxing at home. They further help to counteract the chill of the very cold marble floors. Take flannel nightgowns or pajamas, also a heavy woolen robe. Lightweight cottons and washable silks are extremely popular. Complete your summer wardrobe with as many washable dresses as possible.

It is not customary to wear slacks, shorts, sun suits, or play suits in town or on the streets at any time, but play suits and sun suits are excellent for sun bathing and beach wear. Lightweight slacks can be worn for excursions and on trips to the beach. However, it is usually too warm to wear anything but shorts. At least two formal dresses and two dinner dresses should be added to round out your wardrobe. An adequate supply of all types of shoes is imperative. Closed toes and heels are advisable in winter because of the cold. On account of the long summer season, white shoes are worn extensively.

Materials purchased here are generally more expensive than they are in the States. They are sold in Athens by the pic, which is approximately 25 inches.

The Greek unit of currency is the drachma. At present there is no coin money in circulation. The current exchange rate is 15,000 drachmae per one U.S. dollar.

ANKARA, TURKEY

(NATO Headquarters in the Middle East)

Not many, but a few, Navy wives may have the experience of living in the Middle East. It is hard to describe Turkey; we shall give only a few pointers as related by the wife of an attaché.

First of all, she suggests that you take everything you can within your baggage allowance. Most of the entertaining will be done in your home and you will need all your nicest things from the sofa to the silver service. In addition, everyday china and glassware will be needed because the servants smash it with the greatest of ease. She says, "I personally would never come to Turkey without everything I own." It seems the windows are unscreened and are very wide. Also, there are many French doors. A bolt of window material is a good idea, and another bolt for draw drapes, as there are no window shades and the drapes help keep the cold weather out. A roll of wide-width window screen will prove a joy, and should you find a place previously occupied by Americans, you can easily dispose of the screen at no loss. Other fixtures needed will be curtain rods with extensions, towel racks, and all sorts of things from the dime store, such as picture hooks, picture wire, tacks, etc.

Most startling to Americans is the general lack of closets in Turkish apartments and homes.

An electric refrigerator, a nonautomatic washing machine, and a small bottled-gas cooking stove will make your life happier. Don't bother to take electric heaters; they are too expensive to operate. A 2,000-volt transformer is needed to handle such things as toasters, irons, and waffle irons. A Hallicrafter radio with short-wave band is fine if you want news from home.

Ankara is cold in winter. The houses are poorly heated, so warm clothes and dresses with jackets or sleeves are really essential. Warm slacks are all right for indoors but are not worn on the streets. Include plenty of jerseys, sweaters, and warm house slippers. Again, your entire shoe wardrobe. Most wives order clothes from magazines or a professional shopper.

A school is in progress using the Calvert System, but since Calvert doesn't go farther than the first year of high school your teen-ager may have to be tutored. There is a Teen-Club in Ankara and Boy and Girl Scouts are being organized, plus a newly formed Wives' Club with all the usual activities.

Izmir, Turkey

Izmir is the port city on the Aegean Sea. There is a three- to six-month waiting period for apartments. The Navy has an accredited school in Izmir, grades one through twelve. Trained servants are to be had but they are difficult to find.

The climate is similar to that of Southern California with dry hot summers and cool wet winters. Clothing is about the same as for Washington, D.C., and be sure to take enough for your entire stay.

It is suggested that you take furniture, draperies, screening, curtain rods, electric refrigerator, washing machine, gas stove, and calling cards. Don't take electric heaters. Living conditions are about the same as those described for Ankara.

Navy Dependents in French Morocco

Morocco, to many of us, is associated with the Sahara, but Navy people who have been stationed there describe it as a "cool country with a hot sun," meaning it is hot in the sun and cool in the shade. Morocco is much like California—like living in San Francisco and visiting Death Valley and Palm Springs. There is a critical housing shortage and most of the housing available is below American standards. Officers and enlisted men occupy temporary-type "dallas huts" and tents.

It is almost impossible to obtain hotel accommodations unless reservations are made well in advance. The rates are usually lower than in American hotels, but accommodations are not comparable. Private baths are considered a luxury.

If you wish to be comfortable, you should ship your own household goods and furniture, particularly an ironing board, kitchen cutlery, household linens, and all equipment to take care of infants and small children. You will find rugs useful on the customary tile floors. Of course the stores in French Morocco are well stocked with household goods and furniture (there is no dearth or shortage), but the prices exceed those of the United States by 50 to 300 per cent. Children's toys are very expensive. In the furniture line, beautiful French and Spanish antiques can be purchased; Moroccan rugs are also worth buying. Rabat is a famous rug center. French, Spanish, Jewish, and Arabic servants are available at wages ranging from 55¢ to $1.50 a day. Again, there is the language barrier.

In general, it is suggested that complete summer and winter wardrobes for all members of the family be secured before leaving the United States. Women wear hats for all occasions other than extremely informal or formal affairs. Raincoats are a must, and again, complete your shoe wardrobe before leaving home. Women's low-heeled shoes can be purchased, but high-heeled shoes should be ordered from or purchased in the United States. Yard goods can also be purchased, but at high prices. Cotton goods should be shipped from the U.S., and if you plan to sew, include sewing notions and patterns.

Service-operated schools providing for grades one through eight have been established.

Dependent care in French Morocco is limited to emergency cases. Seriously ill dependents or those requiring care and treatment are evacuated to the nearest adequate Armed Forces Medical Facility.

French Morocco offers swimming and bathing at the beach resorts, skiing at mountain resorts, fishing, and hunting. During the winter months Casablanca and Rabat offer horse racing and dog racing. Two golf courses are available. Also, the intense bright sunlight, plus the unusual scenery and local life, makes Morocco an ideal country for camera enthusiasts.

THE NAVY WIFE IN GERMANY

Germany is a country of quaint, Old World charm—one of the historic spots where ancient customs still prevail. In addition, the region's colorful past is reflected in the beauty of the Black Forest and the sunny vineyards framed by the snow-capped Alps. Throughout Germany, Navy dependents are looked upon as products of democracy. Consequently the individual American's every speech and action makes a direct and lasting impression upon the German people.

If your orders read by boat, you will travel MSTS from New York to Bremerhaven, Germany; if by air, from Westover Air Force Base by MATS to Frankfurt Air Force Base or to one of the air bases in Germany. Sometimes, owing to the scarcity of rail accommodations, dependents are required to pass a night in Bremen after their arrival by transport. Accommodations are provided on the transport or at hotels.

The time of year you arrive in Bremen will determine the type of clothes in which you should land. The winters in Bremen and Berlin are severe, but the year-round climate is similar to that of Pennsylvania.

The Commander, U.S. Naval Forces, Germany, and the major part of his staff are located in Heidelberg.

Quarters for the most part are private homes that were requisitioned by the Army during the early days of occupation, though an increasing number of apartment houses are being constructed. Quarters are usually assigned in accordance with rank seniority among officers and rating seniority in the enlisted grades. However, family size, among the junior grades particularly, is an important determining factor. Enlisted personnel below the grade of second class are not permitted to bring dependents to the European Command.

The type of house will naturally vary in each community. All billets, family or bachelor type, are equipped with adequate sanitary facilities, electricity, and either central or space heating. For the most part the fuel is coal. All family-type quarters when available have as a minimum a living room, dining room, at least one bedroom, kitchen, and bath. Each room is also equipped with the necessary items of basic furniture, but at present there is a serious shortage of rugs, lamps, curtains, draperies, and kitchen equipment.

While it is not advised that fragile or expensive items of furniture and equipment from the United States be shipped to Germany, basic items, loss of or damage to which can be tolerated, can always be used and will make you more comfortable.

The following are recommended to be included in the household goods you ship to Germany:

Linens: table, bath, and bed including bedspreads	Electric appliances including a refrigerator, toaster, iron, heater, mixer, radio, phonograph (and records). German ovens are small and an electric roaster helps.
Silver	
Card tables	
Lamps	
Pictures	
Crystal	Kitchen utensils
China	Small scatter rugs
Vases	Knickknacks
	Nursery furniture

THE NAVY WIFE IN LONDON

The headquarters of the Commander-in-Chief, U.S. Naval Forces, Eastern Atlantic and Mediterranean, is located at 20 Grosvenor Square, London (with entrance on 7 North Audley Street).

England is a small country but the city of London covers 700 square miles. In fact the whole of Great Britain—comprising England, Scotland, and Wales—is scarcely larger than Minnesota. Moreover, no part of England is more than 100 miles from the sea.

The climate compares with that in Seattle or Boston, and cold and dampness prevail three-fourths of the year. Days are long in summer and very short in winter.

Furnished houses and apartments suitable for the average family come high. When you are looking for a house to rent, it is advisable to take along an English friend. Most of the British people make every effort to be friendly to Americans. Again, may I stress: "Every American who goes to England is, in a sense, an ambassador for the United States." Even though the language is the same in Britain, remember that the British have different ways of doing things. This is all by way of prefacing a few don'ts:

1. Don't expect a kitchen like the well-equipped ones in the U.S. An electric refrigerator in England is something of a luxury.

2. Don't look for a place with central heat. Be prepared to provide your own system for heating.

3. Don't expect your electrical household appliances to work without checking the type of electric current before you sign a lease for a house or flat. You may have to buy a transformer.

4. Don't complain about the time it takes the British laundries. It usually takes from one to two weeks for laundry since it is necessary to use some type of chemical in the water. The chemical with the lime in the water tends to shorten the life of clothing about 25 per cent, it is said.

As a Navy wife you may find it necessary to revise your sights downward on housing and your housing expenses upward if you are going to live in London. It is well to consult a legal adviser and officers who have experienced the local customs on leases before making final arrangements on housing. Rent is always payable in advance, and often three months' advance rent is required. Agents' fees and dilapidations deposits frequently add to the high initial cost. You may be surprised to find that leases for five years or more are frequently required.

"English weather is perverse." The cold is penetrating because of high humidity, so this situation can best be met by dressing, as the English do, in woolen underclothing and heavy suits. In summer there is an occasional wave of high temperature, but it does not usually last for more than two or three weeks. Take plenty of warm clothes such as sweaters and stoles to wear around the house. Heat in most cases comes from a small coal grate in each room. One wife suggests including a pressure cooker, since you may find it useful for tenderizing tough cuts of meat. One other tip is this: If you are planning to take your car, you might buy a small British car instead. Cost of maintaining the large American car is very high.

It is suggested that you think twice before you plan on taking household pets to England. There are various restrictions and requirements. The general cost is $400.00 per pet and not less than six months in quarantine.

EUROPEAN DIPLOMATIC POSTS

In every important capital of Europe there is a group of naval officers on duty serving as naval attachés with the American Embassy. In London, Paris, Rome, and Moscow the group is headed by a Rear or Vice Admiral.

Officers selected for this type of duty are usually chosen carefully. A knowledge of languages is important, particularly the ability to speak French fluently, as this is still considered the diplomatic language. Of course, an outside income is always an asset whether it belongs to the officer or his wife. Inflation has swamped Europe, and living is almost prohibitive for a naval officer dependent solely upon his pay.

This is one type of duty in which an officer's wife plays an important public part. She must know how to meet all groups of society, be versatile, have the ability to entertain visiting Congressmen and foreign diplomats, and be able to whip up a dinner for twenty-four persons or so on a few hours' notice. This little story may illustrate the importance of the "unwritten fitness report" of a Navy wife:

A vacancy came up for a naval attaché in Rome. Two officers were being considered for the post. The selection, however, was difficult as there seemed to be no difference at all in their ability according to their official records. Both men were likable, personable, and possessed of equal diplomatic ability. Finally, the Solomon of the Selection Board said, "Well, which one of their wives would fit in better on this detail?" This made the selection easy!

When an officer is selected for attaché duty, he becomes a member of a very distinguished Service with a justifiably high morale. His life is bounded by the discipline of the Service and his obligations to his country. He is on duty twenty-four hours a day; he is the living representation, not of the average American, but of America as a world power.

His conduct is circumscribed by international custom and usage, and he must weigh every act in the light of the effect it will have on the reputation of the country which he represents. Just as in the armed forces, the higher the officer's rank, the more of a public figure he becomes and the more his conduct is scrutinized in all its details. When he commands the highest post in the diplomatic Service he is the personal representative of the President of the United States. The diplomat's wife moves right along with her husband and is just as much in the service of the government as her husband.

It takes time and effort for the diplomat's wife to make things go smoothly; she is expected to make her home a center where government officials and colleagues of the diplomatic corps like to come on easy and friendly terms. She is expected to take an active interest in all sorts of local enterprises, American and foreign, such as hospital, church, and school openings and benefits. At all these affairs she demonstrates a friendly attitude. She is also expected to attend and to take an interest in cultural and sporting events with the idea of winning and keeping friends for America.

There is a constant stream of visitors, both official and unofficial. VIP's arrive in droves. Three or four Congressmen descend for a few days' visit—usually on very short notice. Plans immediately have to be made by the Embassy for a series of dinners and luncheons and perhaps a reception. If you should have any personal plans, as a diplomat's wife you must be prepared to shelve or discard them. The amusing part is that each visitor looks upon his own sojourn as an incident apart, a pleasant interlude for the diplomats, and a breath from home for the exiles. To the diplomats this is no more than a steady stream; however, successful diplomats have notably gracious manners, else they would not be diplomats.

PREPARATION FOR NAVAL ATTACHÉ DUTY

More and more, the State Department recognizes the need for trained career diplomats. Since naval attachés come in this category, special training is now being given naval officers ordered to foreign duty. Provision is also being made for their wives to attend lectures on life in foreign capitals and briefings concerning the countries to which their husbands will be assigned.

Officers are trained from twelve to eighteen months at the Language School at Monterey, California. Since a naval attaché's duty will be of a different type from any you and your husband have previously experienced, you must realize that he will begin an intensive program of study for his assignment in the system.

You will be sent a booklet that will guide you in preparing for your role as a naval attaché's wife. The station and housing reports will give you general pictures of living conditions in the country to which you will travel. From your perusal of the station reports you will get the rosy side, but—"forewarned is forearmed"! Be prepared for the seamy side and a few thorns as well. Later in this chapter I will explain what I mean by the thorns. No doubt you are already wondering exactly what will be expected of you and, in turn, what you may expect from the assignment.

RESPONSIBILITIES AND OBLIGATIONS

It cannot be overemphasized that American official personnel stationed abroad are guests of the people of the countries in which they are stationed. Remember the following; have it printed and framed; hang it beside your mirror and read it out loud every morning of your stay in the country where you are assigned or visiting:

NEVER COMPLAIN ABOUT THE COUNTRY OR THE PEOPLE

Your actions will be scrutinized not only by the people of the country but also by compatriots traveling or residing abroad. The degree of attention given your conduct by compatriots abroad far exceeds that which it would receive in the United States. Acting in a dignified and proper manner will naturally preclude any suggestion of excessive drinking, or of undue familiarity and effusiveness in public.

Today English is the major language of the world. It is understood by countless persons everywhere. Never make disparaging remarks in public, either about the country of residence or about the United States, under the delusion that no one can understand. It is not unusual for an American tourist to cudgel his brain and go to great lengths in explaining directions in his faltering French only to have a Paris taxi driver answer in excellent English!

An attaché's wife must be willing to attend social functions and reciprocate. She must have a real interest in the people and country to which her husband is assigned; above all, she must be considerate of her husband's free time.

A successful wife can assist her husband in the following ways:

1. Remember to be a good mixer. Don't be clannish. Make friends among the foreign groups.

2. Think of the possible consequences of something you are about to say before you say it.

3. Look your best at all times. One never knows when a formal call may be paid.

4. Look ahead and make plans for family get-togethers and for social functions that will not conflict with other parties.

5. Look always at your engagement pad before accepting another engagement. (Carry that extra little black book.)

LANGUAGES

It is impossible to say enough of the importance of knowing the language of the people. To be an accomplished linguist is one of the greatest assets a wife in a position like this can possess. Use the foreign-language records, go to class, have a tutor, and read as much as possible of the history and customs of the people.

Servants are necessary, but they are also a problem. The attaché's wife must be able to talk to them in order to: (1) have a personal understanding of their problems and situations; (2) have harmony in the household; (3) have a smoothly run household; (4) have the ability to make out menus and get what was intended; (5) have her husband's best tux shirt washed and ironed for a certain important night.

Socially, if an attaché's wife cannot converse with the majority of guests at a cocktail party or dance she will find herself alone. She will find it very embarrassing, too, at a dinner party if her partner, after his first pleasantries, devotes the rest of his time to the lady on his other side who speaks his language!

SOME OF THE THORNS!

You will probably find plenty of *real* complaints but always remember *you are a guest,* and in addition recall the American feeling and our typical expression, unspoken or verbal, to foreigners: "If you don't like it here, go back where you came from." It works both ways!

Your big problem may be the electricity. It will go on and off, will dim, then have a surge and blow all your delicate electrical appliances. Or perhaps the plumbing won't work. The plumber and electrician will promise on their sacred word of honor to come tomorrow, but they won't show up for three weeks. When they do show up they will do only half the job, then they won't come back for another month. Perhaps the elevator won't work. You will have dysentery, and at first it will make you sick to go to the native markets, to see the meat hanging in the open with flies swarming over it. Guests will drop their cigarettes on your best rugs instead of on a conveniently placed ash tray.

As for automobiling, at first you will think everyone drives with his horn and often on the left-hand side of the street. Your maids will pull every conceivably silly stunt and you may have to fire and hire dozens of them before you get a good team, and before you learn to handle them. The answer: Relax, grin and bear it! Every time you and your husband start to complain, make a pact between yourselves and remind each other with an understanding smile, "You never had ir so good!" And it will be true.

Keep in mind that the people, your hosts, are as proud of their country as we are of ours and they are quick to resent criticism. However, many of them think all Americans are out to drain their economy dry. A few may resent seeing your shiny, good refrigerator and high scale of living; seeing you drive a new car through their streets. The important thing to remember is that you are more than a guest, you are an official representative of the United States Government and its people. So . . . you never, never criticize, even among yourselves.

PROTOCOL

To the attaché's wife and to most hostesses protocol means "precedence"—who ranks whom, and how to seat dignitaries and persons of conflicting rank. If the order of precedence becomes too involved, Washington hostesses consult the Chief of Protocol at the State Department. On foreign duty, the protocol officer at each embassy or legation will gladly arrange the seating for the new attaché's wife, and someone at the "Foreign Office" (the foreign State Department) will arrange seating for larger miscellaneous groups.

Let us start with table seating, which in diplomatic circles, even for the smallest luncheon, is always planned according to the rank of the guests.

At formal dinners there is usually a seating chart in either the hall or the drawing room, or both, to show the guests where they are to sit. It is not the custom for all guests to be introduced to each other at a large dinner. At formal dinners the gentlemen take the ladies in to dinner and there are "take-in" cards to tell them their ladies' names. A gentleman usually takes the lady on his right according to the chart, and if it is someone he has never met, he should ask to be presented to her before dinner.

Three are always place cards on the table, above each plate, with the writing clear and large enough to be read easily by the guests on either side. The ranking lady guest is seated on the right of the host.

Again according to protocol, the ranking lady guest is the first to leave after dinner or luncheon. There is a definite time; in many capitals the hour after dinner is eleven o'clock.

SEVEN SUGGESTIONS

An invitation from the Chief of the Mission is in the nature of a command and takes precedence, the same as an invitation to the White House. If you have accepted another invitation, inquire as to whether the Ambassador prefers that you break it or keep it. The inquiry is made through one of his secretaries, of course.

Ladies and gentlemen both rise whenever the Ambassador and his wife enter the room. This applies to groups of up to eighteen or twenty people. Sofas abroad are regarded as seats of honor in family as well as diplomatic circles. Consequently, guests should not sit on the sofas unless invited to by the hostess. The right-hand corner is the ranking seat.

The Chief of the Mission and his wife always go through doors first; their car should be allowed to pass ahead on the street. But in entering an automobile, the procedure is the same as for Navy personnel entering a boat: the junior gets in first and sits on the left of the car, the ranking person enters last, sits on the right and gets out first. If they enter from the left side of the car, the Ambassador crawls over everyone's legs, or walks around the car!

After any luncheon or dinner, some gracious gesture of thanks should be made. The most correct formal gesture is to make a dinner call or leave cards the day following the dinner. This means leaving the same number of cards, with the corners turned, as on the initial call. If a post is more casual, a note of thanks can be written or flowers sent.

Wives should watch their drinking, or better still keep clear and abstain. Often imbibing leads to undignified and improper manners such as sitting on the floor, exchanging kisses at formal parties, and various types of behavior which in themselves may not be essentially wrong but are far from a foreigner's idea of dignity.

Another American habit which is much criticized abroad is smoking during meals. Do not smoke unless cigarettes are passed to you or unless the host or hostess smokes or offers you a cigarette. Smoking is usually not done until after the salad or dessert course, and at some British formal dinners not until after the Queen is toasted.

Another point to be emphasized is the duty of all the staff to see that the Ambassador and his wife are not left talking too long with people. As for yourself, tactfully avoid getting involved in gossip about the Chief, his wife, and others of the Mission. Always remember that you are a guest in the country where your husband is serving; that everything you do or say is observed; and that the United States is judged by your behavior. This cannot be stressed too strongly with officers and their wives young in the Service since one unthinking person can do enough damage to ruin the reputation of the whole Mission.

NAVAL MISSIONS IN SOUTH AMERICA

Almost every country of South America has a United States Naval Mission stationed in its capital, in addition to its naval attachés. A detail in such a place can be wonderfully interesting, and the social round is quite formal and intense. Remember that the seasons are just reversed! July is the height of the winter season which gets under way with the celebration of their Independence Day.

Buenos Aires is as formal as Washington. There is great punctilio about leaving cards and returning cards. Argentine women dress in the French tradition of elegance, and spend most of their time at it. At Argentine parties the important thing is to see and be seen. Dinner is served at nine or later. Tea is an important meal every day at five. There is no café society, for the Embassy Club, the Charleston, the Africa, and one or two others are the only respectable night clubs. Dinners at home almost invariably demand black tie, though occasionally white ties are *de rigueur*. During the season there is opera in the old Teatro Colon, and on Sundays everyone goes to the polo games.

Rio is less formal than Buenos Aires. The winter season is the gayest time of the year. Santiago, Chile, is a popular detail. The Chileans are gentle and informal, and living in Santiago is very inexpensive. Viña del Mar on the Chilean coast, in addition to being a recreational resort, is noted for its flowers. In the autumn, Santiago has its opera season, followed by concerts and lectures. Just before Christmas everyone goes to hear the Bach chorales, beautifully sung in the dark old church of Saint Augustine.

Lima is a city of the past, rich in colonial treasures and proud of its heritage. The aristocracy keeps its Spanish titles, and the atmosphere of Spanish royalty lingers on in Peru. It is still locked in the Spanish tradition. The wives of Peruvian naval officers lead quiet lives, have large families and small pay; so you will not expect to be entertained by them. It is not at all unusual for a husband to appear at a dinner party without his wife.

The atmosphere is extremely gay for diplomats, attachés, and naval representatives of the American missions. To speak Spanish is a very valuable asset and will prove an open-sesame. The Peruvians are never critical of how poorly one speaks Spanish, but the lack of effort is deeply resented. They are a very gentle people and extremely careful of their manners and dress. It is said of them, "They will follow you to Hell if you are courteous, but not to Heaven if you are rude."

A Few Travel Tips . . . Good Any Place!

1. The more knowledge you take to a foreign land, the more you will be able to appreciate the beauties of the country and its people.

2. Know in advance what arts, shrines, and landmarks are worth seeing, and learn the stories related to them.

3. Travel with your mind. Don't transport only your body from place to place while your mind is occupied with worrying about things at home. Armed with knowledge, you will have an intelligent viewpoint, which is an unmistakable sign of a seasoned traveler.

4. An understanding of the language will open all sorts of doors to you. A foreign-phrase book with four or six languages in parallel rows is valuable.

5. Foolish spending leaves a trail of inflation.

6. Have respect for the European in whose country you are traveling. Americans have a tendency to order everyone around.
7. Watch not only your thought but your language in speaking of
your hosts. Uncomplimentary or derogatory terms are naturally
resented. Avoid calling Italians "wops" or "dagoes"; Germans
"krauts" or "Heinies"; English "limeys"; etc. Respect the dignity
of man regardless of color, creed, or nationality.

Travel with the idea of promoting a better understanding, and of
making other nations respect and like Americans. Avoid sounding
off about the superiority of everything American; making constant
comparisons is crude.

CLOSING DIPLOMATIC SUGGESTIONS

Always be exactly on time for engagements; in fact, at most American embassies the staff is supposed to arrive a few minutes ahead of
time. As in the Army, Navy, and Air Force, no one is fashionably
late.

Always speak to your host and hostess, then find your Ambassador
and his wife. Never leave before they do unless it is absolutely necessary, and then excuse yourself and say good-by.

The hostess is never served first under any circumstances. The
ranking lady guest of honor on the right of the host is the first to
be served.

The host always accompanies his guests to the door. When a high-
ranking guest such as the Ambassador leaves, he accompanies him to
his car. At most posts all the staff stay until the Minister and his wife
have left.

The wives of members of the nobility are always addressed by title
—"Lady Astor," "Countess Simploni," "Baroness Von Kimball,"
"Princess Margaret"—but the wives of men holding official titles, no
matter how exalted, are addressed as "Madame,"' or if British or
American just as "Mrs. Jones" or "Mrs. Smythe."

There is one social custom at the English table which you should
know, even though a few may find it irksome. That is the custom of
"leaving the gentlemen to their port." If there is no port then it will
be tea or cider or ginger beer. The point is not the drink but the
occasion. It is a time when the gentlemen light their cigars, pipes, and

cigarettes to indulge for a few seconds in masculine talk at the conclusion of the meal. It allows them to get the business and politics out of their systems before they rejoin the ladies; and it allows the ladies to indulge in fireside feminine chat which also would bore the gentlemen. Consequently, when the hostess rises and asks rhetorically, "Shall we leave the gentlemen to their port?" it is best not to protest, for these gentlemen will join their ladies in a short time and will usually offer more to the mixed conversation by this little respite. By being gracious guests, the American officer and his wife will quickly appreciate the generous hospitality which characterizes the Englishman's "castle-cottage."

At first, as the wife of a newcomer to an embassy you may find the strain on your memory for names and faces great, but this will soon be overcome if you like people and are socially inclined. A naval attaché, by virtue of his assignment, is usually the third- or fourth-ranking officer on the protocol list of each American embassy or legation. Consequently the social demands on his wife are exacting.

An innately well-bred Navy wife has not so very much to learn and certainly nothing to fear if she is alert, is eager to fall in with the diplomatic policy, and follows the suggestions given in the briefings arranged by the Department of State. The prerequisites for a successful Naval attaché's wife might be summed up as follows: she should be gracious, diplomatic, well-mannered, but above all *American.*

GLOSSARY OF NAVAL TERMS AND
NAUTICAL EXPRESSIONS

Abandon ship: To abandon ship is to cause all hands to leave the ship for their safety, when a ship is in danger of sinking, or threatened by destruction by fire. All personnel including passengers on every ship are assigned abandon-ship stations. For passengers on a liner or a Navy transport, the abandon-ship station designates the lifeboat in which the passenger is to leave the ship and the location on deck where the passengers for each boat are to assemble at the order, "Prepare to abandon ship." On the first day at sea there will be an abandon-ship drill, during which all passengers physically able to do so must assemble at their assigned stations, in order that there may be no misunderstanding in case of an emergency, and for instruction in adjusting life preservers.

Abeam: At right angles to the keel of the ship.

Aboard: On or within a boat or vessel. This word is seldom used by Navy personnel; the term *on board* is much preferred by seamen.

Above: This word is used in naval parlance to denote movement upward from the keel to the upper deck, or a relative position at a greater vertical distance from the keel. The term *upstairs* is never used; on board ship all means of ascending from one level to another are called *ladders*; and in place of saying *going upstairs,* one says *going above*; or *up on deck*. Altitudes higher than the upper deck, except the bridges, are *aloft* and not *above*.

Absentee: Any person in the Navy who fails to return to his ship or station by the hour of expiration of his leave or liberty is an absentee.

Accommodation ladder: A ladder suspended at the side of a ship to permit personnel in boats to ascend to the deck of a ship. In the Navy the term *gangway ladder,* or, informally, *gangway,* is the more common term. The treads of a gangway ladder are at right angles to the side of the ship, and the slope of the ladder is such as to resemble stairs. (Compare with Sea ladder.)

Action: In naval parlance this means hostile action; the use of the ship and its armament in battle. In the British Navy *battle stations* are called *action stations*.

Action, clear for: Clear for action means to make all final preparation, except going to battle stations; to prepare the ship for battle.

Aft: Toward or in the direction of the stern; opposite to forward.

Afternoon watch: The watch from noon to 4:00 P.M.

Aide: An officer assigned as a personal assistant to the President, the Secretary of the Navy, or an Assistant Secretary of the Navy, a Flag Officer, or in some cases an officer of lower rank in command of a naval unit comprising a number of ships. Not all officers assigned to staff duty are designated as aides. Those designated as such normally are Chiefs of Staff, Flag Secretaries, and Flag Lieutenants.

Aiguillettes: The insignia of an aide. Dress aiguillettes consist of a heavy braided loop of gilt cord, passing around the shoulder and attached to a button or pin in front; suspended from this loop at the point where it is attached in front are two gilt pendants. The origin of the aiguillettes is uncertain but is said to have been a coil of line carried by an aide to picket a General's horse. Undress aiguillettes consist merely of loops of cord surrounding the arm and attached at the shoulder. An aide to the President wears aiguillettes on the right shoulder; others wear them on the left shoulder.

All hands: The entire crew of a ship, officers and men, except those specifically excused by regulations covering the particular situation; i.e., "All hands up anchor"; or the call of the boatswain's mate at reveille, "Up all hands, rise and shine."

Aloft: Above the upper deck (except the bridges, which although above the upper-deck level are not considered aloft), usually applied to stations on or in the masts.

Alongside: By the side of, side by side, a boat comes alongside a ship's gangway; a ship goes alongside a dock, or alongside another ship at anchor or at a buoy. When two or more ships alongside each other are riding to one anchor, or to a mooring buoy, they are said to be *nested,* and collectively comprise a *nest.*

Anchor: A portable metal weight designed with flukes to bite into the ground, or bottom, which, secured to the ship by chains, is used for holding the ship in position when it is not underway or secured to a dock, buoy, etc.

Anchor's aweigh: The situation when the anchor is being hove in, at the instant the anchor is free of the ground. After the anchor clears the ground, the ship is free to use its engines to maintain its position or to proceed to sea.

Anchor watch: Men detailed to remain alert, during the night, when a ship is at anchor, to be immediately available to take any necessary action such as veering chain or letting go a second anchor in case the ship, due to current or wind, should drag or be in danger of dragging her anchor.

Armament: A general term comprising all weapons, guns, torpedoes, depth charges, etc.

Armor: The steel plate distributed principally on the sides and decks of a ship, to protect its hull, turrets, magazines, and engineering spaces from shells and bombs.

Astern: In a direction opposite to the course or heading of the ship; in the wake of the ship.

Attached to: This is the general form of expressing the assignment of naval personnel; i.e., attached to and serving on board the U.S.S. ———

Avast: A nautical word meaning discontinue, cease; i.e., avast heaving.

Awash: On a level with the surface of the sea.

Awning: A sheet of canvas spread over certain sections of a ship's deck for protection from the sun.

Aye, aye, sir: The traditional Navy acknowledgment of the order of a senior, indicating that the order is understood and will be executed.

Barge: A boat carried by a flagship for use of the Flag Officer; i.e., the Admiral's barge.

Battle cruiser: A large ship, approximately the tonnage of a battleship, carrying guns of more than 8″ in caliber.

Battleship: The most heavily armed and armored type of warship; the backbone of the Fleet.

Beach: A general term used frequently as a substitute for shore; i.e., *hit the beach* used for *going ashore* on leave or liberty, also said of a ship which goes aground.

Beach guard: A detail of Navy personnel to control the activities of a landing.

Beam: The extreme breadth of a ship, also one of the principal horizontal steel girders which support the decks.

Bearing: The direction of an object from the ship.

Bear a hand: Make haste, hurry.

Belay: To make fast, as a rope.

Below: In the direction of the ship's keel; the term *downstairs* is never used on board ship; the correct expression is *going below.*

Bell: Each ship has a large bell so situated that its sound when struck can be heard on the upper decks and in many portions of the lower decks; this bell is used in marking the passage of time, being struck each half-hour.

Bell buoy: A buoy located to mark a danger to navigation, or the entrance to a channel, fitted with a large bell which is rung by the movement of the buoy due to action of the waves.

Berth: The term is used principally in the Navy to designate the assigned anchorage, dock area, etc., to be used by a ship; figuratively, it is used in relation to an officer's assignment to duty; it is also used to designate a sleeping place in a stateroom, but the more common word in this sense is *bunk.*

Bilge: The bulging, lower section of a ship's hull. Water which may leak into a ship settles in the bilges. In wooden ships this leaking was such as to necessitate daily pumping, hence the word bilge has come to be used in the Navy as a verb meaning elimination due to failure, or failure to meet required standards.

Billet: On board ship, the assigned location for sleeping; hence, figuratively, in a broader sense, a good billet indicates a desirable assignment to duty.

Binnacle list: The binnacle is the stand containing the compass in the vicinity of which, at sea, the Officer of the Deck is stationed in order to watch the steering of the ship.

Bloomers: Canvas secured to the front plate of a turret and enclosing the barrel of each turret gun for a short distance from the turret face plate, for the purpose of keeping spray and other forms of dampness from entering the turret through the holes in the face plate through which the guns project.

Bluejackets: The most common term for Navy enlisted men. The word *gob* sometimes so used is not dignified, and is very distasteful to naval personnel.

Boat cradles, or skids: The supports on the deck or on overhead beams in which the boats rest when hoisted on board.

Boatswain: A Warrant Officer whose specialty is seamanship, including the handling of boats and anchor gear.

Boatswain's mate: A Petty Officer in a deck division of the ship's company whose duty is to supervise and direct the performance of the general duties of a portion of the division.

Boom: A long spar used in the handling of cargo boats, etc.

Boot: A term of comparatively recent origin used to signify a new recruit, or a recruit recently received on board a ship from a training station.

Bootlick: To flatter or cater to, with a view to one's own advancement, or other personal advantage.

Bow: The forward end of a vessel.

Boy: The general designation of an officer's mess attendant.

Bridge: The high structure in the forward part of the ship from which the ship is maneuvered and navigated. Some ships have more than one bridge, usually in the same location but at different levels.

Brig: The compartment of the ship in which prisoners are confined.

Broad command pennant: A swallow-tail pennant indicating that the ship carrying such pennant is the ship of the senior officer of an organized naval unit comprising several ships and when such officer is not of flag rank.

Brow: A large gangway provided for communication between a ship and dock.

Bulkhead: A vertical partition separating one compartment, or room, from another. There are no walls on board ship.

Bunkroom: The number of junior officers on many ships is such that from eight to twelve officers are assigned to a compartment fitted with bunks and lockers, chairs and tables. Compartments so fitted are called bunkrooms.

Buoy: A float usually moored to the bottom in such position as to mark a danger to navigation or the limits of a channel.

Buzzer: A signal for firing the guns in salvo. Guns may be fired while the buzzer is sounding.

Cabin: The quarters on board ship of a Captain or Flag Officer.

Camel: A float placed between a ship and a dock, or between two ships moored side by side, in order to prevent projections from the ship's side from fouling.

Camouflage: The use of various colors of paint in order to reduce the distance at which a ship or aircraft is visible.

Can, or tin can: A figurative term applied to destroyers, sometimes derisively but more often sentimentally by officers serving in, or who have done considerable service in, destroyers.

Captain: A rank next below Rear Admiral, but this term is used on board his own ship in addressing any officer who has been ordered to command, no matter what his actual naval rank.

Carrier: A common abbreviation for aircraft carrier.

Catapult: The mechanism installed on board battleships and cruisers for projecting seaplanes from the deck of the ship into the air.

Caulk: To drive oakum into the seams of a ship, or into the seams (spaces between planks) in the deck of a ship; hence, figuratively, to sleep on deck, and thus *caulking off* means taking a nap.

Censor: Because of the necessity for secrecy as to naval operations during war or national emergency, all communications from a ship must be examined to insure that no unauthorized information is divulged. Such examination is called censorship. Mail which has been so examined is stamped, "Passed by censor."

Charlie noble: The galley smokepipe. This name is said to come from a Captain Charlie Noble of the British Merchant Marine whose ship was noted for its highly polished brass galley smokepipe.

Charthouse: That compartment in the bridge structure of a ship designed for the workroom of the navigator and within which the charts are stored ready for use.

Chief Engineer: The senior officer attached to the engineer department of a ship.

Chief of Staff: The senior aide to a Flag Officer commanding a type, force, or fleet.

Chief Petty Officer: The highest rating of enlisted personnel.

Chit: A chit when signed, is an acknowledgment of receipt of stores, or services, the value of which is to be charged against the signer's account.

Chow: An informal name for food, or a meal.

Chronometer: An instrument resembling a clock for measuring time with extreme accuracy, for use in navigation computations.

Civil Engineer: An officer of the Civil Engineer Corps of the Navy.

Clear: To free from obstructions, to leave a dock or port, etc.

Clear ship for action: The final preparation, other than going to battle stations, to prepare a ship for battle.

Coaming: The raised wood or metal border of a hatch, or the raised doorsill in the opening between compartments. Coamings are designed primarily to prevent the flow of water on the deck down a hatch or from one compartment to another.

Colors: The national ensign. In port Navy ships in commission hoist the colors at 8:00 A.M. and haul them down at sunset; at sea colors are hoisted when and so long as they can be distinguished, in the presence of foreign shipping, or in sight of land. In time of war color must be hoisted before the firing of a gun.

Colors, strike the: To strike the colors means to haul them down as a token of surrender.

Commander: A navy rank next below Captain; in large ships when several of the heads of departments may have the actual rank of Commander, only the Executive Officer is referred to, or called, the *Commander*.

Commodore: A navy rank between Captain and Rear Admiral now obsolete except for a few officers on the retired list.

Commutation of rations: An allowance in money made to officers and to enlisted men under special circumstances in lieu of rations in kind. This allowance is usually less than the officer's mess bill.

Compass: An instrument to indicate the magnetic meridian, or in a gyroscopic compass the true meridian by means of which the ship may be steered upon a definitely determined course.

Complement: The complement of a ship is the authorized strength in officers and men.

Confidential: In time of war all information concerning vessels of the Navy is confidential, and divulging such information may result in serious legal action.

Conning tower: The armored station in the vicinity of the bridge within which the Captain controls the operation of the ship during battle.

Convoy: A group of noncombatant ships sailing under naval control and usually under escort of combatant ships; this term is also used at times in a collective sense, to include both the combatant and noncombatant ships sailing under one command.

Court-martial: A court of justice composed of officers all of whom if practicable are senior to the accused, for the trial of disciplinary offenses.

Coxswain: The lowest Petty Officer rating in the deck force; also the enlisted man who steers and is in charge of a ship's boat and its crew.

Critique: A formal presentation to officers who have taken part in it, of a detailed history of the conduct of operations during a fleet exercise, including a critical examination of decisions reached, plans made, and the manner of execution of such plans.

Cruiser, battle: A vessel of large tonnage carrying guns of 12″ caliber or larger.

Cruiser, heavy: A vessel of from 8,000 to 10,000 tons standard displacement carrying a battery of guns in excess of 6″ in caliber.

Cruiser, light: A cruiser not in excess of 10,000 standard tons and carrying no guns of greater caliber than 6″.

Davit: One of a pair of F-shaped uprights projecting over the side of a vessel for suspending a boat.

Deck: All plank or metal floorings of ships are called decks.

Demobilize: The process of returning to peacetime conditions after having been mobilized for war.

Dependent: A legal dependent is a lawful wife, a child under 21 years of age, own or legally adopted, or a mother, provided she is in fact dependent and receives the major part of her support from her son in the Navy.

Depth charge: Explosive charge carried by antisubmarine vessels for the destruction of enemy submarines so designed as to explode at a predetermined depth below the surface.

Destroyer: A comparatively small high-speed naval vessel whose armament comprises torpedoes, depth charges, and guns of 5″ caliber or less.

Disbursing Officer: The officer of the Supply Corps charged with making all cash disbursements, including the payment of officers and men.

Distress signal: The letters SOS, by radio, flashing light, or other means. Ships at sea keep guard at definite intervals on a designated distress frequency, which is used by any ship making a radio distress signal.

Division: The crew of a ship is organized in groups, each of which is called a division. Each division has a specific assignment of duties, and an assigned portion of the ship within which it bunks and messes and for the cleanliness, good order, and preservation of which it is responsible.

Division of ships: Ships of each type are also organized in groups called divisions. A division of battleships usually comprises three ships; cruisers, three to five ships; destroyers, four to six ships; submarines, four to six ships. An officer commanding such a group is a Division Commander.

Dreadnought: A modern battleship, so called after the British battleship *Dreadnought*.

Dress, full (ship) : To full-dress ship is to decorate a ship by flags in honor of a national holiday or a ruler of a country.

Dud: A shell or bomb which fails to explode.

Dungarees: Work clothes made of dark-blue denim, used on board ship by the engineer's force and by others when engaged in certain forms of work.

Duration: The period of the war.

Duty: The officers and crew of a ship are organized in two watches, and each watch in two sections. In port one section is required to remain on board. Such section is called the duty section.

Embark: To go on board a vessel.

Ensign: The national flag; also the junior commissioned rank in the Navy.

Epaulet: An ornamental gilt shoulder badge worn with dress and full-dress blue uniforms. The epaulet is said to have originated with metal shoulder pieces worn by officers to protect their shoulders from saber slashes.

Escort: To accompany merchant shipping by a warship for protection; also a ship of war so engaged.

Esprit de corps: A spirit of common devotion, honor, interest, binding together persons of the same professions, organizations, ships, etc.

Executive officer: The second in command on board a ship.

Field Day: A day for general cleaning of all parts of the ship; usually Friday.

First Lieutenant: The officer, head of department, responsible for the cleanliness, good order, efficiency, and neat and trim appearance of the ship as a whole, and of all parts thereof.

First watch: The four-hour watch from 8:00 P.M. to midnight.

Flag: The insignia of an officer above the rank of Captain carried by a ship in which such officer is officially embarked.

Flag Officer: An officer above the rank of Captain in the Navy.

Flag Lieutenant: The personal aide of a Flag Officer whose customary duties embrace supervision over all forms of visual signaling on board the flagship.

Flag Secretary: The personal aide of a Flag Officer charged with supervision of correspondence, filing, etc.

Fleet: An organized major subdivision of the Navy under command of a Commander-in-Chief.

Float: A raftlike platform used at boat landings to facilitate embarking or disembarking from boats.

Flotilla: In the United States Navy, an organized group of destroyers comprising two or more squadrons.

Flotilla leader: A ship, usually of the cruiser class, operating as flagship of a flotilla Commander.

Flourish: A series of notes on a bugle as a part of official honors.

Force: An organized major subdivision of a fleet, i.e., the battle force, the scouting force, etc.

Forecastle: That portion of the upper deck of a ship forward of the superstructure.

Forward: In the direction of the bow of a ship.

Foul: Entangled; i.e., a foul anchor is one entangled with its chain or cable.

Funnel: A smokestack of a ship.

Furlough: Leave of absence.

General quarters: The condition of a ship when all hands are at battle stations and ready for action.

Gig: A boat designated for the personal use of the Commanding Officer of a ship, or of a Chief of Staff, if below flag rank.

Guard duty: In each group of ships there is one detailed to be responsible for certain activities requiring the presence on board of certain definite personnel. At times a different ship may be required to retain on board ready for service certain personnel of the medical department; a ship so designated has the medical guard duty.

Gunnery Officer: The officer, head of department, specifically charged with the preservation and efficient operation of the ship's armament.

Hammock: A swinging bed made of canvas, suspended from hooks.

Hangar: A building, or a compartment on board ship, for stowage of aircraft.

Happy-hour: An entertainment on deck, usually by the ship's personnel for the entertainment of the crew.

Hash mark: The slang term for service stripes worn by enlisted men on the left arm below the elbow on dress uniforms; each such stripe represents one completed period of enlistment.

Hatch: A door or covering for a hatchway. Also applied to the hatchway itself.

Hatchway: A rectangular opening in the deck of a vessel for passage below.

Heave: To hoist or lift up.

Heave to: To stop a ship at sea.

High seas: Waters outside the territorial limits, i.e., more than three miles from shore.

Hold: That part of the vessel where the cargo is stored.

Home port: The officially designated operating base of a ship, to which dependents of personnel serving in such ship are entitled to government transportation.

Home yard: The Navy yard designated as the place to which a vessel will normally be sent for repairs or overhaul.

Hull: The body of a vessel.

Jack: A flag smaller than the national ensign and usually in design comprising only a portion of such ensign; i.e., in the U.S. only the blue field and stars. Hoisted on a staff at the stern of a U.S. public vessel when such vessel is not underway.

Jacob's ladder: A rope ladder with wooden or metal treads.

Jalopy: A slang term for an outmoded or broken-down automobile or airplane.

Junior Officer of the Deck: A junior officer serving as assistant to the Officer of the Deck. This is the method by which young officers obtain sufficient experience to qualify for watch duty.

Keel: The chief and lowest timber, or girder, of a vessel extending from stem to stern and supporting the whole frame.

Knot: A nautical mile—2,025 yards; a unit of speed per hour; i.e., 15 knots—15 nautical miles per hour; also, an interweaving or tying of thread, cord, or line.

Leeward: The lateral drift of a vessel to leeward of her course, caused by wind and sea.

Liberty: Permission to leave the limits of one's station for a period of 48 hours or less; this term is used only in relation to enlisted personnel; for officers such permission is called shore leave.

Lie to: To stop and drift at sea, i.e., awaiting a pilot or boarding officer.

Life lines: The lines at the edges of upper decks to prevent personnel from falling overboard.

Life raft: Warships are unable to carry many boats when cleared for action, and in action any boats carried may be put out of commission. Many rafts are carried in the hope that in case the ship is sunk, men can support themselves by holding on to the rafts until rescue vessels arrive.

Lights: The lights in various parts of the ship are required to be extinguished at definite times unless an extension of time is given by the Commanding Officer; some are eight o'clock lights, some nine o'clock, and some ten o'clock. Except when a ship is darkened for purposes of security certain definite lights are required by a ship underway, known as running lights, or by a ship at anchor, known as anchor lights.

Line: Line is the general term for what in civil life is called rope; large lines or wire lines are frequently called hawsers. The word line is also used to designate a formation of ships in which the relative bearing of the ships is 90 degrees from the course.

Lines of a ship: The form or contour of the hull of a ship.

Log: The official record of the ship's location, movement, operations, etc., in which are recorded all events which might have any bearing in relation to any officer or man of the crew.

Lucky bag: The locker or compartment in which the police Petty Officer places all personal belongings of members of the crew which are found lying about the decks or in unauthorized places. The name of the class book prepared and issued annually at the Naval Academy by the First (senior) Class.

Mail clerk: Each ship has a post office with a mail clerk in charge; the mail clerk is an enlisted man assigned to such duty at his own request.

Mess: An organization for the purpose of preparing and serving food. In flagships there are the Admiral's Mess, comprising the Admiral and such staff officers as he may select; the Captain's Mess, usually just the captain; the Wardroom Mess, comprising the Executive Officer as mess president and all other officers above the grade of Lieutenant (j.g.) and officers of such grade as assigned as watch and division officers; the Junior Officers' Mess; the Warrant Officers' Mess; the Chief Petty Officers' Mess; and the General Mess, which includes all other personnel.

Mess bill: Officers are allowed a certain sum for subsistence, but this sum is less than an officer's proportional share of the cost of running the mess, i.e., his mess bill, which must be paid in advance.

Mess, cigar: A cigar mess is an independent organization, organized to sell soft drinks, cigars, cigarettes, candy, etc.

Mess president: The Executive Officer is president of the Wardroom Mess; the senior line junior officer is president of the Junior Officers' Mess.

Mess share: The mess share is the pro rata worth of the stores and such equipment belonging to the mess as has been purchased with mess funds. An officer joining a mess must make an initial payment of the current value of the mess share in addition to his mess bill.

Mess treasurer: The Wardroom, Junior Officers', Warrant Officers', and Chief Petty Officers' messes are supervised each by a mess treasurer elected monthly from among its own members. The officer so elected performs this duty without pay, in addition to his other duties.

Mine: A heavy explosive charge in a steel container designed to float, or rest on the bottom, or to be suspended below the surface by a float or held at a fixed depth by an anchor, exploded by contact with a ship's hull, by induced magnetism, or by sound waves from propellers, with a view to injuring a ship in its most vital area below the water line.

Mine layer: A vessel designed to lay mines.

Mine sweeper: A vessel designed to remove or explode mines by means which normally insure her own safety.

Motor launch: A type of large open boat provided for transportation of enlisted personnel, stores, etc.

Motorboat: A type of boat having a canopy which is provided for the use of officers and their guests.

M.T. boat: A motor torpedo boat—a special type of high-speed motorboat designed for operation near shore bases, and carrying one or more torpedoes.

Navigator: The officer, head of department, responsible under the Commanding Officer, for the safe navigation of the ship, and care, preservation, and operation of all instruments and mechanism in connection therewith.

Navy yard: A Navy shore establishment designed and operated for the construction, repair, outfitting, and supply of Navy vessels.

Old man: A term usually applied to the senior officer on board a ship, the Captain, or, in flagships, the Admiral.

Orderly: An enlisted man, usually a Marine, assigned to attend a Flag Officer or Commanding Officer, for the purpose of carrying messages or orders. A time orderly is assigned to inform the Officer of the Deck of the time to strike the ship's bells to indicate each half-hour period, and to remind the Officer of the Deck of any required action in accordance with the daily schedule. A mail orderly is a man detailed to carry mail between the ship's post office and a shore post office.

Passageway: Spaces which on shore are called corridors or halls on board ship are called passageways.

Patrol, shore: The shore patrol comprises officers and enlisted men detailed by competent authority to assist civil authorities in maintaining order and discipline among naval personnel on liberty.

Pay: The money received as salary. The actual amount received is greater than this salary by the amount of the allowances. The allowances are greater when an officer has dependents than when he has none. The word "pay" is also used to mean the act of sealing seams in a wooden deck with hot pitch (a solid black resinous substance obtained from boiled tar). The outer plank of a deck (next to the side of the ship), because of the difficulty in keeping this seam watertight with oakum and pitch, is called "the devil." Hence the expression, "the devil to pay and no pitch hot."

Peacoat: A short overcoat of a style sometimes called a reefer worn by enlisted personnel other than Chief Petty Officers.

Pennant: A long, narrow strip of bunting carried at the masthead of each Navy ship in commission, except when it is supplanted by the flag of a flag officer or the broad command pennant of an officer below flag rank in command of a division or squadron. A broad command pennant is triangular in shape with a swallow tail, white in color with edges outlined in blue for the Commander of a division of large ships or a squadron of destroyers, and outlined in red for a division Commander of destroyers or submarines. In destroyers and submarines the official number of the squadron or division is shown by numerals of the same color as the edging superimposed on the white field.

Pilot, sky: The ship's chaplain is frequently referred to as the sky pilot.

Pipe: The boatswain's pipe is a special form of whistle capable of variation in tone by the position of the fingers in relation to the opening by which the air escapes.

Pipe down: A series of notes on the boatswain's pipe to indicate the completion of an all-hands evolution. The order to the Boatswain was "pipe down"; hence, figuratively, to stop what you are doing; generally used in the sense of "make less noise."

Pitch: The alternate rise and fall of the bow and stern of a vessel due to action of the sea.

Port hole: The round openings in the side of a ship for light and ventilation.

Pulling boat: A boat propelled by means of oars.

Quarter: A sector limited by bearings 45 degrees abaft the beam and astern, on each side. Also means mercy when used in the sense "to cry for quarter."

Quarters: Living accommodations; also, the assembly of officers and crew for muster or inspection.

Quarter-deck: That portion of the deck in the vicinity of the gangway ladder used by officers. Originally the quarter-deck included such gangway and extended to the stern of the ship; in modern ships such gangway may be forward, or in the waist. The quarter-deck is the ceremonial portion of the deck and reserved for the use of the Captain (and the Admiral in flagships).

Quartermaster: A Petty Officer rate. The quartermaster is an enlisted man, assistant to the Officer of the Deck, whose duties include at sea the supervision of the steersman and the collection of data required to be entered in the log, and in port maintaining a lookout for approaching boats or other matters of interest taking place in the harbor.

Rudder: A frame of wood or metal by which a vessel is steered.

Sabotage: Destruction or damage to property by disloyal persons or enemy sympathizers.

Sail: To leave port; usually on an extended cruise.

Sailing orders: Ships are frequently placed on sailing orders at a definite time, from two to six hours before the expected hour of departure. At the hour the ship is placed on sailing orders all personnel must be on board unless ashore on duty.

Salute: Salutes are of two classes, hand salute and gun salute. The hand salute is a mark of military respect rendered by enlisted personnel to officer personnel, and by junior to senior officers. It is acknowledged by returning a similar salute. A gun salute comprises a number of discharges of a small type of gun called a saluting gun, in honor of Flag Officers of the Navy, General Officers of the Army, Marine Corps, Air Force, and certain civil officials such as the President, Secretary of Defense, Secretary of the Navy, etc.

Salvo: A simultaneous discharge of guns, torpedoes, bombs, etc.

Scuppers: The enclosed drains from the waterways of a ship's deck to a point of discharge near the water line.

Secure: An order implying: Discontinue the exercise and return all material to its normal stowage.

Selection: The process by which officers are chosen for promotion.

Sentry: A person, usually a Marine, stationed as a guard or watchman.

Sextant: An optical instrument for measuring the altitude of heavenly bodies for purposes of navigation.

Shore duty: Officers of the U.S. Navy alternate between duty attached to ships—called sea duty—and duty attached to shore stations. In the junior grades the periods of sea duty are much longer than the periods of shore duty.

Shoulder marks: The insignia of rank worn by officers on white uniforms and overcoats.

Skipper: A term frequently used as a nickname in referring to the Captain of a ship.

Smoke screen: A dense cloud of smoke from the funnels caused by incomplete combustion of fuel oil, or from specially designed chemical tanks, to shield ships from observation.

Smoker: A form of entertainment held on board ship for the pleasure and amusement of the crew, usually consisting of boxing and wrestling matches during which free smokes are provided.

Squilgee: A hoe-shaped instrument with a rubber edge used for drying wooden decks, similar in results obtained to a windshield wiper.

Stanchions: Vertical cylindrical posts extending between decks as supports for the deck above.

Stand by: A term used as a warning to be ready.

Station: An assignment to duty; on board ship each officer and man has a definite battle station, and a station for each general drill such as fire, collision, etc.

Station, naval: Naval stations are small, usually independent or semi-independent, naval activities of the nature of a base, i.e., Naval Station Guantánamo, Samoa, etc.

Station, naval air: Each location on shore fitted and organized by the Navy for the operation of aircraft is called a naval air station.

Steady as you go: An order to the steersman to hold the ship on the heading at the instant the order was given; hence, figuratively, continue in the present direction.

Steerage: Commercially that part of the ship allotted to passengers paying the lowest fares.

Steerage way: The lowest speed at which the vessel can be accurately steered.

Strike: To lower. Hence, to strike the colors means to lower or haul down the colors in token of surrender. To strike below means to lower any object to a lower deck level.

Striker: A man assigned as a helper and apprentice with a view to qualifying for a definite position or rating.

Strip ship: The removal from a warship of material not essential for war operations.

Stripes: The insignia of rank of naval officers worn on the sleeves near the cuffs on blue uniforms and on the shoulder marks with white uniforms.

Supply officer: An officer of the Supply Corps, charged with matters pertaining to pay, general stores, and the general mess.

Taps: A bugle call indicating lights out in living quarters and quiet to be maintained about the decks.

Tarpaulin: A piece of canvas used to cover anything for protection against the weather.

Tattoo: A roll of the drum or a bugle call sounded five minutes before taps as a warning to retire to quarters and turn in. This word is from the Dutch *tattoe* which indicated the time to close all taps or taverns in a garrison town.

Topside: Slang for upper decks.

Transom: A built-in long seat in a stateroom or other living quarters.

Truck: The topmost point of a mast.

Turn to: To begin work.

Turret: The oval-shaped armored structures, capable of rotation, in which the main battery guns of large ships are emplaced.

Underway: Not anchored or made fast to any other object.

Visa: An endorsement upon a passport by a consular agent of the country one desires to visit, authorizing such visit.

Wake: The track of disturbed water astern of a ship, caused by the action of the propellers and movement of the ship.

Wardroom: The space provided on board ship as a messroom and reception room for officers junior to the Captain and senior to the junior officers.

Waterways: The gutters around the edge of the deck.

Whaleboat: A type of small boat pointed at each end, so named because it is the type most frequently used in harpooning whales.

Yardarm: The framework extending from a mast from which signal flags are hoisted.

BIBLIOGRAPHY

Knox, Dudley W., Captain, U.S. Navy (ret.), *History of the United States Navy*.

Lovette, Leland C., Rear Admiral, U.S. Navy (ret.), *Naval Customs, Traditions and Usages*.

OFFICIAL PUBLICATIONS

Personal Affairs of Naval Personnel, *NavPers 15014*, Bureau of Naval Personnel.

All Hands, Bureau of Naval Personnel Information Bulletin.

Recruiting Office pamphlets, Bureau of Naval Personnel.

The United States Navy, *Navexos P-435, A Description of Its Functional Organization*, Navy Department.

Household Goods Shipment Information, Bureau of Supplies and Accounts.

They Have to Go Out, an historical sketch of the Coast Guard, Coast Guard Information Service.

Coast Guard information pamphlets.

INDEX

Adak, Alaska, 278–80
Adams, John, 87
Aircraft carriers:
    classes, 61
    designation, 2
Air Force, grades in, 32
Air Medal, 50
Alaska, 275–80
    Adak, 278–80
    clothes for, 276–77
    housing, 276
    Kodiak, 275–76
    recreation, 277–78
All Hands, 42
Allowances:
    commissioned personnel, 46–47
    noncommissioned personnel, 46–47
    weight, 146–47
American Automobile Association, 161
American Red Cross, 242, 247
Amphibious forces, ships of, designation, 3
Annapolis, Maryland:
    clothing for, 10–11
    colors ceremony at, 14–15
    dances at, 13–14
        formal hops, 13–14
        special, 14
    drag, being, 12–13
    graduation ceremonies, 14–15
    historical background, 7–8
    June Week, 14–15
    transportation to, 9–10
Ankara, Turkey, 293–94
Announcements:
    birth, 200
    engagement, 98–100
Appointments to Naval Academy, 206–207
Arch of swords, 113
Argentia, Newfoundland, 280–82
Armed Forces, grades in, 31–33
Armed Forces Day, 29
Armed Forces Hostess Association, 145
Arnold, General Henry H., 32
Army, U.S., grades in, 32

Army-Navy football game, 14
Atlantic ports, 157–58
    Newport, R. I., 157
    Norfolk, Va., 158
Athens, Greece, 292–93
Atomic submarine crews, 74–75
Attaché duty, naval, 300–301
Authority, respect for, 22
Automobile:
    Annapolis, at, 9–10
    buying, 137–38
    children, trip with, 210–12
    emergencies when traveling by, 246–47
    insurance, 135
    records for, 126, 127
    reimbursement for travel, 149
    shipment by government transport, 155
    traveling by, 161–64
        check list for, 161–63
        trip, advice for, 163–64
Aviation, naval, *see also* Naval Air Stations
    Coast Guard, 92–93
    flight training, 52–55
    information about, 60–61
    MATS, *see* Military Air Transport Service
    morale of Navy wives, 51–52
    naval flyer's creed, 51
    preflight training, 53–55
    terms used in, 61–62
Azores, 272–74

Baggage, *see* Luggage
Balboa, Canal Zone, 263–64
Bancroft, George, 7
Barin Field, 53, 55
Battleships, designation, 2
Bayly, Vice Admiral Lewis, 18–19
Benefits, veterans', 49
Bereaved family, income for, 242–44
    gratuity pay, six months', 243
    pensions, personal, 243–44
Bermuda, 271–72

Birth certificates, 133–34
Boat etiquette, 26–27
  disembarking, 27
  embarking, 26–27
Bon Homme Richard, 17
Borrowing, 137
Bridesmaids, gifts to, 118–19
Bronze Star, 50
Buenos Aires, Argentina, 305
Buffet supper, 187–88
Burial, see also Funerals
  at sea, 235–36
  expenses, 238

Calling cards, 108–109
Calls:
  official, 25
  Submarine Service, 74
  telephone, thank-you, 190–91
  Washington, D.C., in, 218–19
Camp Lejeune, N. C., 80–81
Camp Pendleton, Calif., 79–80
Canal Zone, 262–65
  cities, 264–65
  Coco Solo, living conditions at, 263
  markets, 264
  Pacific side, living conditions on, 263–64
  recreation, 264
  shopping, 264–65
Carney, Admiral, 7
Carvel Hall, Annapolis, 9, 11–12, 13
Catlin, General A. W., 77
Cecil Field, Fla., 60
Ceremonies, see Colors ceremonies; Customs, naval
Certificates:
  birth and marriage, 133–34
  medical, 152
Change of duty, 145–68
  Atlantic ports, 157–58
  automobile, traveling by, 161–64
    checklist for, 161–63
    reimbursement for, 149
    trip, advice for, 163–64
  commercial steamer, travel by, 150
  government transport, travel by, 150–57
    automobiles, private, 155
    baggage, 153–55
    don'ts, important, 152
    mail and money, 155–56
    medical certificates, 152

passports, 152–53
  preparation for, 151
  visas, 152–53
  voyage, 156–57
home yard and home port, 157
  visit to, 159–61
Military Air Transport Service, 164–68
Pacific ports, 158
permanent change of station, 148–49
railroad travel, 149–50
weight allowances, 146–147
Change of station, permanent, 148–49
Chaplain, 97–98, 201, 241
Cherry Point, N. C., 81
Chesapeake, U.S.S., 18
Chief of Naval Operations, 3, 15, 32
Chief of Naval Personnel, 3, 32
Chief Petty Officers, 42, 44
Chief Warrant Officers, 32
Children, 199–213; see also Dependents
  air travel with, 207–10
  appointments to Naval Academy, 206–207
  behavior on naval station, 212–13
  christening, 200–202
  education insurance, 204
  expectant mothers, 199
    government hospital care, 200
    motor trip with, 210–12
  nursery, 202–204
  nursery schools, 204
  preparatory schools, 205
  scholarships, 205
Christening:
  children, 200–202
  ships, 28
Clothing:
  Alaska, for, 276–277
  Annapolis, for, 10–11
  Argentia, Newfoundland, for, 280–81
  Bermuda, for, 271
  Hawaii, for, 250–51
  Japan, for, 259
  MATS travel for, 167–68
  Midway Island, for, 256
  mourning apparel, 233
  Naples, Italy, 290
  Norway, for, 288–89
  Philippines, for, 258
  trousseau, personal, 101–103
  wedding dress, 117–18
Club parties, 193

Coast Guard, 86–95
  aviation, 92–93
  commissioned personnel, 89–90
  grades in, 32
  history, 86–88
  lifesaving service, 92
  Lighthouse Service, 93
  noncommissioned personnel, 91
  organization, 89
  peacetime duties, current, 88–89
  Reserve, 91
  weather service, 93–94
  wives, 94–95
  women in, 91–92
Coast Guard Academy, New London,
  Conn., 90
Coco Solo, Canal Zone, living conditions,
  263
Cocktail parties, 175, 177–78
Cocktail supper, 178–79
Colón, Canal Zone, 265
Colors ceremonies:
  Annapolis, 14–15
  half-masting, 20–21
  on shipboard, 21–22
Commercial steamer, travel by, 150
Commission, officer's, 31
Commissioned personnel, 31–41
  allowances, 35–37
  classifications, 33
  Coast Guard, 89–90
  commission, 31
  fitness reports, 41
  grades, 31–33
  insignia, 33–35
  material, sources, 5
  Navy Nurse Corps, 38–39, 232–33
  pay, 35–37
  postgraduate education, 40–41
  promotion, 39–40
  reserve, 6–7
  retired, in Washington, D. C., 225–26
  retirement, forced, 40
  separation from the service, forced,
    40
  service medals and ribbons, 49–50
  veterans' benefits, 49
  Wave, 37–38
Commissioned Warrant Officers, 32
Commissioning ceremony, 29
Compression chambers, 67
Condolence, letters of, 238–39
  answers to, 239

Constellation, U.S.S., 18
Constitution, U.S.S., 18, 28
Continental Navy, 17
Conversation at social gatherings, 191–
  92
Corpus Christi, Tex., 55, 57–58
Corry Field, 53, 55
Cristobal, Canal Zone, 264–65
Crossing the line ceremony, 29
Cruisers, designation, 2
Customs, naval, 19–30
  Armed Forces Day, 29
  boat etiquette, 26–27
    disembarking, 27
    embarking, 26–27
  christening ceremonies, 28
  colors on shipboard, 21–22
  commissioning ceremony, 29
  crossing the line ceremony, 29
  discipline, 25
  divine service, 20
  gun salutes, 23–24
  half-masting, colors, 20–21
  hand salute, 25
  honors, 22–23
  launching ceremony, 28
  laying the keel, 28
  manning the rail, 23
  Memorial Day, 29–30
  military funerals, origin, 236
  official calls, 25
  piping the side, 24
  saluting quarter-deck, 22
  Submarine Service, 74
  time, Navy, 27
  Veterans' Day, 30
  wives visiting the ship, 26

Dahlgren Hall, Annapolis, 10
Death:
  burial expenses, 238
  dependent, 240
  flowers and, 237
  income for bereaved family, sources,
    242–44
  letters of condolence, 238–39
  memorial services, 237
  military funerals, *see* Funerals, mili-
    tary
  mourning, 233
  serviceman, 240–41
Decatur, Stephen, 17
Deep-sea diving, 70–71

Dependents, naval:
  air transportation for, 164
    processing for overseas air travel,
      165
  emergency aid for, sources, 241–42
  illness or death, 240
  income for bereaved family, sources,
    242–44
  medical care for, 229–30
Destroyers, designation, 3
"Dilbert Dunker," escape from, 54
Dinners, entertaining at:
  formal, 179–84
    menus for, 183–84
    seating, 181
  informal, 184–85
    menus for, 185
  semiformal, 184–85
    menus for, 185
Diplomatic posts, European, 299–300
Discipline, 25
Disembarking, boat etiquette, 27
Distinguished Flying Cross, 50
Distinguished Service Medal, 50
Divine service, 20
Diving, deep-sea, 70–71
Doctors, Navy, 232
Drag, Annapolis, being an, 12–13

Education, *see* Schools
Education insurance, children, 204
Eisenhower, General Dwight D., 32
Ellsberg, Commander Edward, 70
Ellyson Field, 53, 55
El Toro, Calif., 81
Embarking, boat etiquette, 26–27
Emergencies:
  aid for dependents, sources, 241–42
  legal, 246
  preparing for, 248
  traveling by car, when, 246–47
  wartime, 247
Emergency data, records, 239–40
Emergency shelf, 144
Engagements, 96–97, 98
  announcement, 98–100
  enlisted men, 98
  premarital counseling, 97–98
  showers, 100
  trousseau:
    linens, 104–106
    luggage, 103–104
    personal, 101–103
England, service in, 297–98

Enlisted men, *see also* Noncommissioned
    personnel
  death, 240–41
  engagements and marriages, 98
  social conduct for, rules, 193–94
Ensign, national, *see* Colors ceremonies
Entertaining, 169–98
  buffet supper, 187–88
  Canal Zone, in, 264
  club parties, 193
  cocktail parties, 175, 177–78
  cocktail supper, 178–79
  conversation, 191–92
  dinners:
    formal, 179–84
    informal, 184–85
    semiformal, 184–85
  enlisted circles, in, 191–93
  enlisted men, rules of social conduct
    for, 193–94
  first guests, 174–75
  formality versus informality, 170
  Guantánamo, Cuba, in, 266–67
  house guests, 188–90
  informal tea, 187, 194
  introductions, 192–93
  invitations, 170–73
    formal, 170–72
    formal at home, 172
    informal written dinner, 172–73
    telephone, 173
  kinds, two, 194–95
  liquor, serving, 175–77
  luncheons, 186
  morning parties, 185–86
  Naples, Italy, in, 291
  Navy, in, 173–74
  Oslo, Norway, in, 289–90
  thank-you telephone calls, 190–91
  Washington, D. C., in, 220–24
Escape tank training, 68–70
Europe, service in, 283–305
  attaché duty, naval, 300–301
  complaints, 302–303
  diplomatic posts, 299–300
  England, 297–98
  France, 284–86
  Germany, 296–97
  Greece, 292–93
  languages, 302
  North Atlantic Treaty Organization
    (NATO), 283, 284
  Naples, Italy, 290–91
  Oslo, Norway, 286–90

Europe, service in (*continued*)
  obligations, 301–302
  protocol, 303–304
  responsibilities, 301–302
  suggestions, 304–305
  Supreme Headquarters, Allied Powers of Europe, 283, 284
  Turkey, 293–94
Evening colors, 22

Federal Services Finance Corporation, 137
Fire insurance, 135
First Classman (Annapolis), 13
Fitness reports, officers', 41
Flag Officers, 32
Flowers:
  funeral, 237
  hospital patients, for, 231–32
  wedding, 118
Following the ship, *see* Transportation
Food, *see also* Marketing; Menus
  cocktail parties, for, 177–78
  Oslo, Norway, in, 287–88
Forced retirement, officers, 40
Forced separation from the service, 40
  retirement, 40
Formal hops, Annapolis, 13–14
France, service in, 284–86
  household effects, 285
  medical attention, 285–86
  money, 286
  servants, 286
French Morocco, 294–96
Funerals, military, 233–34
  burial at sea, 235–36
  customs at, origin, 236
  escort, 235
  expenses of burial, 238
  flowers, 237
  letters of condolence, 238–39
  memorial services, 237
  monument or marker, 238
  procession on shore, 234–35
  taps or *nunc dimittis*, 236–37

General Officers, 32–33
Germany, service in, 296–97
Gifts, *see* Presents
Glynco, Georgia, 55
Graduation Ball, Annapolis, 14
Graduation ceremonies, Annapolis, 14–15
Gratuity pay, six months', 243

Greece, service in, 292–93
Guam, 252–54
Guantánamo, Cuba, 265–67
  marketing, 266
  recreation facilities, 266–67
Gudgeon, U.S.S., 71–73
Guests:
  entertaining your first, 174–75
  house, 188–90
Guided missiles, 75
Gun salutes, 23–24

Half-masting, colors, 20–21
Halsey, Admiral William F., Jr., 7, 32
Hamilton, Alexander, 86
Hand salute, 25
Hawaii, 251–52
Health insurance, 134–35
Hill, Virginia, 70–71
History, Naval, thumbnail, 16–19
History of the Portsmouth Navy Yard, 28
Home port, 157
Home yard, 157
  visit to, 159–61
Honors, table, 22–23
Honeymoon, 121
Hospitals, government:
  care in, 200
  general type, 227–29
  naval, 230–32
  visiting, tips on, 228–29
Household, naval, 122–44
  business log, 126–27
  closing, checklist for, 159–61
  efficiency in, 138
  emergency shelf, 144
  France, equipment for, 285
  Guantánamo, Cuba, for, 266
  Japan, equipment for, 260
  linens for, 104–106
  maid, full- or part-time, 142
  maidless, 139–41
  marketing, tips on, 143–44
  meals, planning, 143
  Naples, Italy, in, 291
  records, *see* Records
  responsibility for, 123–24
  routine:
    daily, 141
    weekly, 141–42
  silver for, 120
  system, value of, 124–25
  tropics, equipment for, 249–50

Housing:
  Alaska, 276
  Jacksonville, Fla., 59–60
  New London, Conn., 64–65
  Oslo, Norway, 287
  Hutchinson, Kansas, 55

Illness, dependent, 240
Income, bereaved family, sources, 242–44
  gratuity pay, six months', 243
  pensions, personal, 243–44
Income tax, 135
Insignia:
  commissioned personnel, 33–35
  Marine Corps, 79
  noncommissioned personnel, 48
Insurance:
  automobile, 135
  education, children, 204
  fire, 135
  health, 134–35
  life, 129–30, 132–33, 244–46
    commercial, 245–46
Introductions, making, 192–93
Investments, 136–37
Invitations, 170–72
  christening, 200
  formal, 170–72
  formal at home, 172
  informal written dinner, 172–73
  telephone, 173
  wedding, 107–108
Italy, service in, 290–91
Izmir, Turkey, 294

Jacksonville, Fla., 58–60
  city housing, 60
  climate, 59
  quarters, 59–60
Japan, service in, 258–62
Johnston Island, 252, 257
Joint Chiefs of Staff, 1–2
Jones, John Paul, 17
June Week, Annapolis, 14–15
Junior Army-Navy Guild Organization
  (Jango), 197–98

Kaneohe, Hawaii, 81–82
Keel laying ceremony, 28
King, Admiral Ernest J., 32
Kingsville, Texas, 55
Kodiak, Alaska, 275–76

Kwajalein, 252, 257

Languages, 302
Launching ceremonies, 28
Lawrence, Captain, 18
Laying the keel, 28
Leahy, Admiral William D., 32
Leases, 138
  Navy clause in, 138
Legal:
  emergencies, 246
  record, 127–28
Legion of Merit, 50
L'Enfant, Major Pierre Charles, 216
Letters of condolence, 238–39
  answers to, 239
Life insurance, 129–30, 132–33, 244–46
  commercial, 245–46
  National Service Government, 129
Lifesaving service, Coast Guard, 92
Lighthouse Service, Coast Guard, 93
Lima, Peru, 306
Linens, household, 104–106
  marking, 121
Line officers, 33
Liquor, serving, 175–77
Lockbox, 128
Log, *see* Records
London, England, 297–98
Long Beach, Calif., 158
Lovette, Rear Admiral Leland P., 76, 113, 236
Luggage, 103–104, 153–55
  motor trip with children, 210–12
Luncheons, 186

MacArthur, General Douglas, 32
Mail, change of duty, 155–56
Maine, U.S.S., 18
Manning the rail, 23
Marine Barracks, Quantico, Va., 82–83
Marine Corps:
  grades in, 32
  history, 76–77
  Marine Depot, Philadelphia, 84–85
  organization, 77–78
  posts and stations, principal, 79
    Camp Lejeune, N. C., 80–81
    Camp Pendleton, Calif., 79–80
    Cherry Point, N. C., 81
    El Toro, Calif., 81
    Kaneohe, Hawaii, 81–82

Marine Corps (*continued*)
Marine Barracks, Quantico, Va., 82–83
Miami, Fla., 81
Recruit Training Depots:
Parris Island, S. C., 83–84
San Diego, Calif., 83
uniform, 78–79
wife, 78
women in, 85
Marine Depot, Philadelphia, 84–85
Marketing:
Guantánamo, Cuba, in, 265–67
tips on, 143–44
Marriage, *see also* Weddings
certificate, 133–34
enlisted men, 98
second, 117
Marshall, General George C., 32
Maryland Inn, Annapolis, 11–12
McAfee, Captain Mildred, 37
Meals, planning, 143
Medal of Honor, 49
Medals, service, 49–50
Medical care:
dependents, for, 229–30
doctors, Navy, 232
Europe, in, 285–86
nurses, Navy, 38–39, 232–33
Medical certificates, 152
Memorial Day, 29–30
Memorial Hall, Annapolis, 10
Memorial services, 237
Menus, planning:
buffet supper, 188
formal dinner, 183–84
informal tea, 187
luncheon, 186
semiformal or informal dinners, 185
Miami, Fla., 81
Midshipmen, 7, 11, 12, 15
Midway Island, 255–56
Military Air Transport Service (MATS), 164–68, 255
children, travel by, 207–10
dependents, service for, 164
processing for overseas air travel, 165–66
dress for travel by, 167–68
facilities available in flight, 166–67
ports of embarkation, 165
Military Assistance Advisory Group (MAAG), 286–87, 288

Minecraft, designation, 3
Momsen, Rear Admiral Charles B., 67
Momsen lung, 67–68
Money:
change of duty, 155–56
France, service in, 286
Monument or marker, 238
Morale of Navy wives, 51–52
Morning colors, 21–22
Morning parties, 185–86
Mourning, 233

Naples, Italy, NATO headquarters in, 290–91
recreation and social life, 291
National Service Government Life Insurance, 129
Nautilus, U.S.S., 74
Naval Academy, *see also* Annapolis
appointments to, 206–207
source of officer material, 5, 7–8
Naval Air Stations:
Cecil Field, Fla., 60
Corpus Christi, Tex., 55, 57–58
Jacksonville, Fla., 58–60
Pensacola, Fla., 52–53, 55–57
Naval districts, 2
Naval flyer's creed, 51
Naval history, thumbnail, 16–19
Naval Reserve, 47
Naval War College, 41
Navy, U.S., grades in, 31–33
Navy and Marine Corps Medal, 50
Navy Cross, 49
Navy Deep Sea Diving School, 47
Navy Department, 1
creation, 17
serviceman and, 3–5
Navy Nurse Corps, 38–39, 232–33
Navy Postgraduate School, 40–41
Navy Relief Society, 241
Navy Reserve Officers' Training Corps:
importance, 6
reserve officer, 6–7
source of officer material, 5–6
Navy time, 27
Navy Unit Commendation, 50
Navy Wives' Club of America, Inc. (NWCA), 4, 195–97
pledge, 197
program, 195–97
"N" Dance, Annapolis, 14

New London, Conn., 63–64, 90
   living conditions in, 64–65
Newport, R. I., 157
Nimitz, Admiral Chester W., 32
Noncommissioned personnel, 42–50
   allowances, 46–47
   Chief Petty Officers, 42, 44
   Coast Guard, 91
   insignia, 48
   Naval Reserve, 47
   pay, 46–47
   promotion, 42
   requirements for, 43
   service medals and ribbons, 49–50
   shore duty, 48–49
   training, 43–44
   uniforms, 48
   veterans' benefits, 49
   Warrant Officers, 32, 44–45
   Waves, 45–46
Norfolk, Va., 158
North Atlantic Treaty Organization
   (NATO), 283, 284
   Naples, Italy, headquarters in, 290–91
   Oslo, Norway, headquarters in, 286–
      90
Norway, service in, 286–90
Nursery:
   first baby's, 202–204
   schools, 204
Nurses, Navy, 38–39, 232–33

OAO (One and Only), 12
Officer Grade Limitation Act of 1954, 39
Officers, *see* Commissioned personnel
Official calls, 25
Okinawa, 252, 254–55
Oslo, Norway, NATO headquarters in,
   286–90
   clothing, 288–89
   food, 287–88
   housing, 287
   schools, 289
   social life, 289–90
   sports, 289

Pacific ports, 158
   Long Beach, Calif., 158
   San Diego, Calif., 158
Panama, *see* Canal Zone
Panama City, Canal Zone, 264
Paris, France, 284–85
Parris Island, S. C., 83–84

Passports, 152–53
Patrol vessels, designation, 3
Pay:
   commissioned personnel, 35–37
   gratuity, six months', 243
   noncommissioned personnel, 46–47
Pearl Harbor, Hawaii, 19, 64, 65–66,
   252
Pensacola, Fla., 52–53
   life at, 55–57
Pensions, personal, 243–44
Perry, Captain O. H., 17, 18
Personal file, necessary papers for, 132–
   33
Personnel, *see* Commissioned personnel;
   Enlisted men; Noncommissioned
   personnel
Petty Officers, 42
Philadelphia, Pa., 84–85
Philippine Islands, 257–58
Photostatic copies, 134
Piping the side, 24
Plebes (Annapolis), 12, 14, 15
Porter, David, 17
Post, Emily, 189
Postgraduate education, officers', 40–41
Power of attorney, 137
Preble, Edward, 17, 28
Pre-flight training, 53–55
Premarital counseling, 97–98
Preparatory schools, 205
Presents:
   bridesmaids, to, 118–19
   hospital patients, for, 231–32
   wedding, 119–20
      acknowledgment, 119–20
Presidential Unit Citation, 50
Promotion:
   commissioned personnel, 39–40
   enlisted personnel, 42
Protocol, 224–25, 303–304
Puerto Rico, 267–70
Purple Heart, 50

Quantico, Va., 82–83
Quarter-deck, saluting, 22
Quonset huts, 253

Railroad travel, 149–50
Reception, wedding, 114–15
Records:
   automobile, 126, 127
   emergency data, 239–40

Records (*continued*)
household business log, 126–27
legal, 127–28
Recreation, *see* Entertaining
Recruit Training Depots, USMC:
Parris Island, S. C., 83–84
San Diego, Calif., 83
Renting, *see* Leases
Rescue chamber, 70
Reserve officer, 6–7
Retirement, forced, 40
Ribbons, service, 49–50
Ring Dance, Annapolis, 14
Rio de Janeiro, Brazil, 306
Roosevelt, Franklin D., 87

Same-deposit box, 128–29
Saipan, 252, 257
Salutes:
at colors, 21–22
gun, 23–24
hand, 25
to quarter-deck, 22
Sampson, Admiral William T., 18
San Diego, Calif., 83, 158
San Juan, P. R., 268, 269
Santiago, Chile, 306
Saufley Field, 53, 55
Savings, 136–37
Scholarships, 205
Schools:
Naval Academy, *see* Annapolis; Naval
Academy
Naval War College, 41
nursery, 204
Oslo, Norway, 289
postgraduate education, officers', 40–
41
preparatory, 205
scholarships, 205–207
Submarine School, 63–64
Seating arrangements, 225
Second Classman (Annapolis), 13
Secretary of Defense, 1, 15
Secretary of the Navy, 15, 17
Separation from the service, forced, 40
retirement, 40
Serapis, British frigate, 17
Serviceman, Navy and, 3–5
Sever, Captain James, 28
Shannon, English frigate, 18
Ships, types, 2–3
Shopping, *see* Marketing

Shore duty, noncommissioned personnel,
48–49
Showers, engagement, 100
Silver, 120
marking, 121
Silver Star, 50
Smoke Hall, Annapolis, 10
Social life, *see* Entertaining
Society of Sponsors of the United States
Navy, 49
Solace, U.S.S., 38
South America, naval missions in, 305–
306
Spars (Coast Guard), 91–92
Staff Corps officers, 33
Stoddert, Benjamin, 17
Stump, Admiral, 7
Submarines, designation, 3
Submarine School (New London,
Conn.), 63–64
Submarine Service, 63–75
atomic sub crews, 74–75
bases, 74
customs, 74
deep-sea diving, 70–71
description of submarine, 71–73
guided missiles, 75
names of submarines, 73
submarine base, visit to, 65–70
submarine qualifications, 64
training:
compression chamber, 67
escape tank, 68–70
first steps, 66–67
Momsen lung, 67–68
rescue chamber, 70
types of ships, 73
Supreme Headquarters, Allied Powers of
Europe (SHAPE), 283, 284, 286

Taps or *nunc dimittis*, 236–37
Taussig, Commander Joseph K., 18–19
Taxes, income, 135
Tea, informal, 187, 194
Telephone:
calls, thank-you, 190–91
invitation, 173
Terms, aviation, 61–62
Time, Navy, 27
Traditions, Naval, 16–30; *see also* Cus-
toms, Naval
Transport, government, travel by, 150–57
automobiles, private, 155

Transport (*continued*)
  baggage, 153–55
  don'ts, important, 152
  mail and money, 155–56
  medical certificates, 152
  passports, 152–53
  preparation for, 151
  visas, 152–53
  voyage, 156–57
Transportation:
  Annapolis, to, 9
  automobile, *see* Automobile
  children, air travel with, 207–10
  commercial steamer, 150
  following the ship, 161
  government transport, travel by, 150–57
    automobile, private, 155
    baggage, 153–55
    don'ts, important, 152
    mail and money, 155–56
    medical certificates, 152
    passports, 152–53
    preparation for, 151
    visas, 152–53
    voyage, 156–57
  Military Air Transport Service, 164–68
    children, travel by, 207–10
    dependents, service for, 164, 165–66
    dress for travel by, 167–68
    facilities available in flight, 166–67
    ports of embarkation, 165
  permanent change of station, 148–49
  railroad, 149–50
Travelers Aid, 247
Trinidad, 270–71
Tripoli, French Morocco, 274–75
Trousseau:
  linens, 104–106
  luggage, 103–104
  personal, 101–103
Turkey, service in, 293–94

Uniforms:
  commissioned personnel, 37
  Marine Corps, 78–79
  noncommissioned personnel, 48

Veterans' benefits, 49
Veterans' Day, 30

Victory Ball, Annapolis, 14
Visas, 152–53

Warrant Officers, 32, 44–45
Wartime emergencies, 247
Washington, D. C., 214–16
  activities, 219–20
  calling in, 218–19
  entertaining in, 220–24
  life in, 216–18
  protocol, 224–25
  retired naval officers, 225–26
  seating arrangements, 225
Washington, George, 17
Waves (Women's Naval Reserve):
  commissioned personnel, 37–38
  noncommissioned personnel, 45–46
Weather service, Coast Guard, 93–94
Weddings, naval, 106
  bridesmaids, gifts to, 118–19
  calling cards, 108–109
  dress, 117–18
  flowers, 118
  formal, 109–14
  home, 116
  honeymoon, 121
  informal, 115–16
  invitations, 107–108
  magistrate's office, at, 116
  parsonage, at, 116
  pictures, 114
  presents, 119–20
  reception, 114–15
  second marriage, 117
Weight allowances, 146–47
Whiting Field, 53, 55
Wills, 130–32
  short form, 131
Wife, Navy, *see also* Dependents
  Coast Guard, 94–95
  expectant mothers, 199
    government hospital care, 200
  Marine Corps, 78
  morale of, 51–52
  visiting ship, 26
  Washington, D. C., activities, 219–20
  working, 135–36
Winchell, Walter, 252
Women Marines, 85
Women's Naval Reserve (Waves), 37–38, 45–46

Youngsters (Annapolis), 12–13, 15